CREATING A CULTURE OF GENEROSITY

A FIELD GUIDE FOR CHURCH LEADERS

GREG GIBBS

Harpist Miner Publishing
2021

9798708162892

Published by Harpist Miner Publishing
Rochester Hills, Michigan

Dewey Decimal Classification: 332
Subject Heading: FUNDRAISING/CHURCH FINANCE/DISCIPLESHIP

Cover and book design by HillsART Studios, LLC.
Editing by Zachary Shive.
Author photo by Chris Cook.

For my Mom Mom, Dorothy Paterson, who modeled grace and generosity with meager resources but an enormous heart. I still think about the atmosphere she created in a tiny house with my Pop Pop where she raised kids, foster kids and grandkids - it remains the safest and warmest place I have ever known.

For my brother-in-law and sister-in-law Rob and Lee Unger, who have modeled the what's-mine-is-yours generosity to so many of us in their orbit. For decades now, both of them have embodied the sentiments of French philosopher Albert Camus when he wrote, "Few indeed are those who continue to be openhanded after they have acquired the means for it. Such as these are princes among men."

ACKNOWLEDGEMENTS

So many of us who write in an attempt to help the church are standing on the shoulders of those who have gone before us. I would be remiss in not acknowledging the contributions of longstanding leaders in this category. And I will take the risk of missing someone important by aiming to mention just a few—Ben Stroup, Todd McMichen, Patrick Johnson, Paul Edwards, David Thoroughman as well as former colleagues at Cargill Associates and current colleagues at Auxano—particularly the generosity guys; Kent Vincent, Mike Gammill, David Putman, and Clint Grider.

I also want to give substantial credit to my friend and colleague, Alex Calder. Together at Kensington Church in Michigan, we experimented, borrowed ideas, took risks, developed systems, faced criticism, and had lots of coffee conversations with church leaders and donors to try and create a pathway for better discipleship of generosity in the church. For his expertise, friendship, and mostly for lots of laugh-till-you-cry moments, I will be eternally grateful.

At this point in my career, I also have the vantage point of looking back over a great gift of God in my life, the supervisors and mentors over three decades who contributed so much to my leadership formation: Dave Robey, Keith Kettenring, Bill Rudd, Pat Graham, Rocky Miskelly, Kyle Nabors, Steve Andrews, Will Mancini, and Jim Randall.

My work allows me to travel around the United States with the distinct privilege of learning something virtually every day. To the pastors, elders, session members, councils, deacons, lay leaders, committee members, and men and women that make up my tribe-leaders in the church—I thank you for providing a laboratory for my learning. I only hope that I have served you as much as you have served me.

ACKNOWLEDGMENTS

CONTENTS

WAVE THREE - STRATEGY

FOLLOW A PLAN

Will We Infuse Generosity Into Our Church Life?

WAVE FOUR - COMMUNICATION

REINFORCE THE CULTURE

How Can We Teach The Importance Of Generosity?

WAVE FIVE - INTEGRATION

WALK WITH PEOPLE

How Can We Best Lead Our Congregation?

APPENDIX

FOREWORD

Most of us have a love-hate relationship with money – except in the Church, then it is all hate! Or so it seems for too many of us. We want to give generously and see our churches thrive financially, with integrity, but we need help. There are lots of books on the market and my church and friends have used some of them – usually with some level of disappointment.

I found them to be too tactical, or too philosophical, or just plug and play. Or too focused on the individual and not the overall church. Or visa-versa.

So when Greg asked me to take a look at **Creating A Culture Of Generosity,** I was skeptical. But not about Greg! I have known him for decades and trust him implicitly. I just figured this would fall into one of those predictable categories.

And there was another barrier for me. I confess that reading about money is almost as laborious as talking about money. Kind of like completing our taxes – you have to do it and you hope it turns out ok, and you even like your accountant! But deep down you despise the whole process.

So when it comes to topics like tithing, church budgets, personal finances, investing in ministry and paying for church property, it all starts to feel overwhelming. I want a workable process, led by seasoned experts, guiding me through my personal challenges, in a way that serves our church and honors God. That is what I really want…and what I desperately need.

And this resource is it! It really is! Yes, as I worked through it I was expecting to find that chink in the armor, exposing some grand weakness or oversight. I was a bit tense and critical as I approached what I thought was another guilt-trip about giving and fundraising. But as I turned each page I felt calmer and more engaged with the great questions and processes this tool addresses.

I must say that I really enjoyed it – I mean that! It is rock solid - biblically, philosophically and practically. And it is based on discipleship, not just stewardship, integrating a biblical theology with clear strategy, workable solutions, and what other resources tend to ignore - culture transformation!

Greg shows us not only a different way to address our "generosity challenge" in the local church; he offers us a different way to be the church while achieving the Kingdom financial goals we all want, and that glorify God.

Here you will wrestle with hard questions and issues; you will strive to integrate truth with life; and you will be guided through a rigorous and thorough (but joyful!) process that will reshape your personal approach to giving while also transforming the character and vision of your church.

What a gift!

Dr. Bill Donahue, Ph.D.
Associate Professor, TEDS
Leadership Coach & Consultant

INTRODUCTION

I remember as a kid playing Wiffle ball constantly in my backyard. You know what a Wiffle Ball is, right? It is a little white plastic ball (invented in California in the 1950's) with holes designed into it. I could throw a wicked curveball with it.

The ball was almost always sold with a light-weight plastic yellow bat so that baseball could be played virtually anywhere. To this day, it is still one of my favorite things to play.

And as a kid, the ball-playing venue was often my big backyard behind my house in Hatboro, Pennsylvania (a pre-revolution town known for, you guessed it, hat-making).

Whether it was Albert Wilson or Steven Mangin or any of my childhood friends, we would spend the first five or ten minutes coming up with a game plan. We had critical debates about things like:

- How many outs in an inning?
- Who's on what team?
- What constitutes a single, double, triple or home run?
- What was foul territory?

It was wildly important because we ultimately wanted to win—and how could we win if we didn't know the game plan and ground rules?

My dad had his own set of rules for success in terms of the backyard ball dynamic. It usually included making our vegetable garden not just foul territory for the ball, but something like a near-death-experience. After all, Wiffle balls tend to not be friendly to tomato plants. To dad, success was "staying out of mom's garden."

The Generosity Ground Rules

So it goes with any time church leaders are talking about money and generosity. We have to agree on what this is all about. We need to establish some ground rules.

- When we say the word "generosity," what are we talking about and why?
- Are we using terms that are commonly understood—that mean the same thing to each of us?
- What does success look like? What's a win?
- Should the church even be strategic about this or is that inappropriate or manipulative in some way?
- Is there a way to talk about generosity success? Are we simply talking about increases to the general fund of the church or is success defined differently than rising church bank balances?

And is there an equivalent to "hitting the ball in the vegetable garden"—someway that we could unintentionally run afoul?

CONTRIBUTING TO THE CONVERSATION

This is not the first or last book to address the topic of generosity. It is an attempt to add my voice to the conversation—and actually start more conversations!

Hopefully, you can be part of a big-league discussion with your team—whether it is senior-level staff, deacon board, stewardship team, council, session, leadership team, task force, elder board, or whatever it's called in your neck of the denominational woods.

This is a book that borders on being a manual of sorts. It will serve best in a group. Beyond the benefit of built-in discussion questions and suggested action steps at each chapter end, the real purpose is that together you could embrace something that may change your church for the better.

These concepts cannot define your future for you—you will decide how to apply some of these ideas. The following pages will raise questions, offer perspective, and ultimately leave you to the theological and organizational homework: *What does our church believe about this and (more importantly) what are we going to do about it?*

This is meant to start conversations with senior leaders at a church—the men and women who can actually make a difference. You will experience the excitement of doing something that could be a watershed chapter in the story of your leadership and your church! It may take time, but it will really be worth it. Guaranteed.

Is planning for increases in generosity just spiritualizing the bottom line? Is this just a book of techniques for churches that want more money?

It depends. It depends on what you are praying that your friends in the congregation will experience.

Will these principles raise more financial support for your church? Yes, that is highly likely. So, if you and your team are simply looking for bottom-line results, then you will use this book's contents accordingly.

But more than wanting a positive increase in financial fuel to support a great mission and ministry, the underlying thesis of this material is that money is actually a big spiritual growth lever. Not the lever to pull on a slot machine to see what money will pour out. But one that can pry open our white-knuckled grip on what belongs to God and cause us to find spiritual freedom.

What if the faith-factor of your congregation increased because the church leaders taught—and lived—the principles of generosity?

What if your concern for the poor ratcheted up a few notches because your church deeply drank from the biblical principles that wealth is about providing for others as much as oneself?

You may ask, "Will this really work at our church?"

Honestly, it depends.

It depends on how honest you want to be, how bad you want to change, and how willing you are to take this seriously. And, even more importantly, it requires the people who God has placed in leadership to be practitioners of generosity. Without this, you'll be pushing boulders uphill.

Here are some of the ideas I think are important to embrace before we begin:

1. Financial giving is a highly important part of both personal and organizational health.
2. Ultimately, giving is a barometer of our spiritual health, not about increasing revenue for the church.
3. The personal generosity of church leaders is critical to the outcome.
4. Talking about this without acting on it is a waste of time.

The goal is to come up with a game plan. And a game plan's objective is to win. So, once your team agrees on what a "win" is, then you can set out to pray that God will make that a reality in your congregation.

The game plan comes in the form of a written statement of beliefs and practices that will drive your behaviors and ultimately shape your culture into a generous one. That is the payoff: A plan for action called a Generosity Discipleship Plan. *(Spoiler Alert: There are some sample plans in the Appendix)*

CRITICAL REMINDER

So, let's be honest and clear: **I believe this book will increase financial giving to your church.** And I make no apologies for that.

But, it would be a very sad result if we produce financial givers that aren't motivated by an increased devotion to God. We would fail, in a way, as leaders of Christ's church if people became or remained simply charitable givers. This is not to say that charity or being charitable is wrong. It is certainly a good thing—may be a great thing—but we will talk more about that later.

But, before we go any further, let's clarify. In the world of Christian stewardship, one will often hear the idea that people need to get money in its rightful place. As the teaching goes, the best antidote for greed is giving. Again, this is good.

But there is something better.

As we go on to study givers, giving, methodologies, theologies, and practices that may increase effectiveness, we could easily get focused on looking for ways to entice giving via external motivations (primarily).

My pastoral concern is this: **Did we actually "win" if giving is increased but our people give for superficial reasons?**

We can elevate or "sell" the benefit of tax write-offs, the needs of our ministry, or that our church is a worthy recipient because of its effectiveness. And we should to some degree. But, these are supplemental reasons to why people should operate with lives of generosity.

The primary motivation for increased generous behavior has to be the reign of Christ in our lives. Giving is simply one of the chief byproducts of a life of devotion. And the charge of church leaders is to cultivate devotion. We can do this! I just know it. You and I can create climates of generosity that help and not hinder the growing disciple.

DEFINING SUCCESS

We will succeed if we constantly encourage people to consider the beauty of God's provision for us in Christ as the heart of generosity. For God so loved the world that He gave. Increased financial giving ideally is a healthy and whole response of a life centered on Christ and ordered appropriately. We were created in the image of God, in large part, to be givers.

If we were honest with ourselves about money, we would admit that the most frustration comes when we spend fruitless energy trying to keep things. And the most joy we experience with our "things" is when we have the opportunity to give them away. This angst comes from the fact that God intended money and possessions to pass through our hands for His purposes.

Author and philosopher Miroslav Volf writes that "we are givers because we were made that way, and if we don't give, we are at odds with ourselves." [1]

---

1 (Miroslav Volf, Free of Charge)

Is it possible, as Volf infers, that the condition of our soul is tied to how we manage what God has given each of us? Then there is a much bigger thing at stake here if we are avoiding generosity. Is it possible that we are at odds with what God created in us as a reflection of His image?

Remember, God so loved the world that he gave. It is at the top of his resume. And we are mirrors of his reflection.

One of the hinge points for me in understanding the spiritual power of giving in the Christian growth process was when I went through my first church capital campaign. It wasn't as a member; it was as the church's senior pastor. To make a long story short, the hearts of our people turned toward Christ in ways that I had prayed about for a long time.

As leaders of this young church, we worked hard to teach the Bible, engage the families, marry, baptize and do whatever we felt like God was calling us to do. [It was, in fact, what happened to us as disciples. The financial campaign that became a spiritual tipping point for our congregation. The giving of money because a massive spiritual attention getter—some would call it an awakening.] We listened to God, we trusted that God would continue to provide and we gave more than was predicted out of devotion to God and His church.

In watching this transformation in myself and our congregation, I became hooked on generosity. Like the Grinch toward the end of the Seuss story, my little heart "grew three sizes" almost overnight.

BAD NEWS AND GOOD NEWS

There are studies that now call Christians *"the stingiest"* of the big three religions in America.

Christians make up 70% of the U.S. populace. Data shows that the average Christian donates a little more than $817 per year, which makes them actually the stingiest of the "big three" (Jewish households donate $1442, and Muslims $1309).[2]

Many or most Christians have a sense for the idea that Scripture points toward a 10% baseline as the way to think about giving (and we will explore the nuances of this later).

In spite of this awareness, the actual giving behavior of Christians has

---

2   https://www.cheatsheet.com/money-career/average-church-religion-donation.html/

hovered between 2 and 3 percent for the last century. And as recently as 2018, it is reported that giving is going down. Down?

Clearly, discussing generosity or even teaching it with passion does not generate growth. It is highly likely that many of the people in our churches know a lot of the truth about this and it has not yet set them free.

But, I sincerely believe and purport to you that a deep diagnosis and a thoughtful prescription for creating generosity in the church can make a difference. If church leaders address just five areas with sincerity, then any church in any denomination in any economy will see giving growth. When you let these 5 Waves wash over your congregation, some amazing things will happen.

The good news is that giving goes up. The best news is that because Jesus taught us that our giving is connected with our commitment to God's Kingdom, great things happen in our hearts as well as our budgets.

HOW TO USE THIS BOOK

START HERE

The purpose of the "Start Here" or introductory chapters is to identify the challenge of creating a culture of generosity. It offers a perspective on the reality in most of our churches and what it will likely require to move in a better direction. These chapters create the urgency for change.

WAVE 1 - THEOLOGY

This section outlines a way to approach the underlying theology that provides the "why" before the "what" when it comes to generosity. It answers, "Why is generosity an important aspect of the Christian life and what does church leadership believe is the foundation for moving forward?"

WAVE 2 - DISCIPLESHIP

This section explores the ways that the church can create systems of mentoring and maturing members of the congregation in generosity.

Ultimately we need to treat the mentoring of people in this aspect of Christian life like the others—starting with a pathway of what to do first, then next, and so on.

WAVE 3 - STRATEGY

This section allows the reader to consider the various systems for the church that allow the best environment for generosity to grow. This is based primarily on the premise that an organized and scrupulous way of handling money will produce the kind of trust necessary for increased giving.

WAVE 4 - COMMUNICATION

This section challenges each church to develop a rhythm of communication that creates a culture where talking about generosity is normalized. It answers the question, "How can we teach and communicate at all levels of the church in order to encourage engagement and grow giving?"

WAVE 5 - INTEGRATION

The purpose of the following chapters is to ask questions about the best practice when it comes to weaving "generosity talk" into everyday life in the congregation. How should pastors and leaders interact with people on staff, in volunteer leadership positions, as well as members of the church when it comes to their giving?

GENEROSITY DISCIPLESHIP PLAN

The GDP is a fully articulated approach to developing generous disciples that includes statements of theology, policy, budgets and more. It will also include the first 12-month generosity calendar, the icons and descriptions related to a Generosity Pathway, and the ground rules for pastors and leaders engaging the congregation.

START HERE

UNDERSTAND THE CHALLENGE

Are we ready for something new?

CHAPTER ONE

Why I Am So Fired Up

I love to eat. And I haven't met a food I don't like. No exaggeration. I like even the things people tend to not like. I can overeat anything—including beets, Brussel sprouts, and liver. A fork is my weapon of choice in this world. I like healthy food and unhealthy food. I love all of the varieties and ethnic foods represented in the Detroit metropolitan area where I live. I like grilled food, fried food, baked treats, and more. My wife makes chocolate chip cookies that bring people to their knees. I should be 400 pounds. Though I am not that heavy, I have struggled with managing my weight almost my whole adult life.

I am the guy that clicks on the ads on my computer boasting diet tricks like "Lose 30 pounds by Friday" or "Things Middle-Aged Men Should Never Put In Their Stomachs." Yep—guilty as charged—I click on these, hoping against all hope for a magic bullet to drop the 20 or 25 pounds that I should shed. How has that worked for me? Let's just say I am doing a lot of clicking on diet stuff still.

Our two younger children both study biology. At this point, they are college pre-med students and can wear you out with their knowledge of the human body. They were both high school athletes and have a superhuman discipline in a lot of categories. Believe me, it does not come not from my loins. Their mother is the secret to anything that looks like personal discipline in our offspring.

My son, with that glint in his eye that only a son can muster, tells me "Dad. There actually is a trick to losing weight. It is burning more calories than you put in your body." Yep. Works. Every. Time. He is smiling. I am not.

It is ironic and maybe a bit frustrating that dieting in our country is a multi-billion dollar industry because people do not want to face the golden principle of managing body weight. There are lots of other factors that may play into this, but this is the cornerstone—burn more than you consume. But no one seems to want to talk about it. There must be another way!

It reminds me of what I believe to be a cornerstone of spiritual growth as a follower of Jesus Christ. It is an undeniable truth about being a Jesus person. And it has to do with generosity.

Jesus' disciples should be the most giving people in the world.

They should be the definition of generosity. The human imitation of the generous God that they claim to follow.

So, what do we see when we look at Jesus' followers? Hmmm. There is something that doesn't add up. Literally. There is smoke coming out of my calculator.

There are hundreds of thousands of churches in America, and arguably millions of Christians in this country. And Christians have this beautiful theology about money and it goes something like this: **God provides everything for us and puts things under our care so we can both enjoy creation and use resources for God's purposes in His world.**

This makes total sense. If you believe everything emanates from God and is ultimately His, then our role is to spend and invest on His behalf.

So, what do we do? We give God 2%.

Wait. Add it up again. Use your fingers and toes. Use an abacus. Try anything to make this math make sense. The wealthiest people in the history of the world are stunted in following the God they profess devotion to—a God who gave us everything including life everlasting.

Two. Percent.

Well, to be precise some research will report 2.6, 2.7, or up to a whopping 3.3 percent (during the Great Depression of almost 100 years ago). I could slip into a *great depression* just thinking about this. Instead, let's stay positive.

If the mission of the church is to nurture followers of Jesus, then the topic of money is completely underdeveloped in most churches. And it has me fired up.

Part of the fire is frustration. And part of the fire in me comes from seeing the untapped potential. Have you heard the idea that if all people who claim Christian faith in American gave a tenth of their income, world hunger could be eliminated? Is this an urban legend? Could it be true? Eliminated?! If this is even close to being true, we have some explaining to do.

People who have even done a cursory study of the teachings of Jesus know that he was consistently bringing up the topic of money—which is pretty much the opposite of what church leaders do.

You are likely a church leader reading this and I am not trying to make you mad or be accusatory—I don't know your situation. But I have met a lot of leaders in churches that are hesitant to talk about money publicly and privately.

Please understand that my motivation is to rather provide you with hope, courage, and tools for a different way forward. Stick with me. Please.

As a pastor and church leader, I have had a lifetime of exploring both personally and corporately why so few men and women who lead the church will take the time to wrestle down this question:

Why was Jesus always talking about money and why do church leaders do everything they can to avoid it?

I think there is a very powerful spiritual breakthrough beneath the layers of tradition, fear, insecurity, and discouragement.

As a pastor, I vacillated somewhere between being unwilling and being unequipped. Seminary was great. But chalk this topic up to one more thing that didn't get covered. Like the amount of times as a pastor you'd be setting up and tearing down tables and folding chairs each week in ministry. No one told us.

The occasional teaching most churches do about money and possessions in the journey of the Christian life is clearly not making a difference in the giving behavior of the Christians in the western world. Most churches, for fear of being lumped in with Christian hucksters and televangelists, just take a "hope for the best" approach because the only other solution they've heard is "talk about money more."

Whew. I'm a little fired up. Are you with me?

I have to admit—I have been frustrated for a very long time about a few statistics that have been the reality of the Christian church in America my entire lifetime (about a half-century).

Christian people disappointingly mimic the culture in terms of the use and view of money. Period. No way around it. On a statistical level, we are just like everyone else. *Groan.* That doesn't sound like the Kingdom of God to me.

And yet, a very elementary study would reveal that everything about the teachings of Jesus and the scope of Scripture seems to indicate that we should have a different (if not radically different) posture.

Instead, most of us in the church give away as little as possible. Many give away just enough to try to mitigate their feelings of shame or guilt. On top of that, we borrow more than we should. And the wealthier we get, the less likely we are to increase our generosity as a percentage of what God has provided us.

This pattern has not changed in decades in America.

But, I believe it can! What makes me think that church leaders can turn this around?

First of all, I have seen this done well in a few places. These are my glimpses of hope. And I am a big fan of senior leaders of churches—I have given my life to help them and provide tools to advance the cause of Jesus. I am in their corner. If you are a church leader, I am in your corner. I am motivated to give you the toolbox that I have seen work in other churches.

Second, I would argue that God loves us and has invited us into living the way he designed us to live. It seems to me that God's Spirit will help us along the way if we move in this direction. I'm banking on that, at least.

Third, I would argue that any concerted effort by church leaders to embrace and not avoid this topic will produce powerful results in local congregations. Particularly if the way forward involves *discipleship*.

You and I may not be able to turn the tide for the whole of Christianity in the western world with these concepts and practices. But, this can change congregations one at a time. I have seen it.

What if it changed things in your congregation? What if it changed things in you? What if we can unlock discipleship and spiritual formation breakthroughs that we have been aiming for all along?

This is why the following chapters have been arranged as a guide—a playbook for church leaders. It is meant to stir our hearts, but more importantly, stir action. We will likely need to change something about how we disciple people in this category. The book is meant to help us decide what and how.

The following chapters are a way to take a team through five major categories that need to be explored to create the kind of environment that gets the money thing right.

It is more than getting teaching right (although it never hurts to practice great teaching). It is about an environment—a greenhouse of growth—a place where generous disciples can live out their commitment to Christ by open-handed living.

When we understand our convictions about this topic and then teach and model the way of Jesus, we can lead the members of our church communities into a place of deep faith. And this, I have found in my time crisscrossing the country to hang out with church leaders, is why most of us got into this in the first place.

I believe we can learn together and make a significant change for the better. But, we have some work to do.

Here we go.

CHAPTER TWO

Why Most Churches
Need A Generosity Tune-Up

My father-in-law worked for and retired from GM (the Saturn division specifically). He really knows how to take care of cars and cares about it. I am sure I drove him crazy by marrying his daughter and then spending the last couple of decades doing a terrible job of keeping our family of six, including his grandchildren, in reliable transportation. This is not what the son-in-law of a GM retiree should model to the world.

Anyone that knows our family will tell you that I have a quirky habit of finding very inexpensive used cars and driving them until they stop. Or crash. Or require a repair bill that is higher than what I paid for the car in the first place. This paragraph serves as a public apology to my neighbors who have heard me start cars early in the morning with growling mufflers as a regular practice. I'm sorry, Fred and Tamala.

Call me an absent-minded professor or just irresponsible, but I do know that when it comes to long and full life in a car, getting it regularly "serviced" is the key. Unfortunately, I have the kind of personality that struggles to change the oil and more often than I care to admit, struggles to keep gas in the tank.

This applies to many areas of life—my physical body needs a check-up, my spiritual health requires a pastor or counselor every once in a while, and our churches need regular tune-ups when it comes to critical areas that concern our core mission: **Making Disciples.**

I am asserting in this playbook that most churches need a significant adjustment in the engine or "operating system" of discipleship. My thesis is that *a key component of making disciples is teaching and modeling generosity—* maybe THE key.

I believe that something is missing—like a spark plug—in the engine of how we disciple. The car is running but not at full power or effectiveness. And not the way it was intended to run. It is time for a tune-up.

That's why we are going to explore 5 Critical Waves for creating a generosity environment in the church. There is an action or posture that flows out of each one that is entirely based on a discipleship bias:

1. **THEOLOGY** - Renew Your Conviction
2. **DISCIPLESHIP** - Teach A Pathway
3. **STRATEGY** - Follow A Plan
4. **COMMUNICATION** - Create A Culture
5. **INTEGRATION** - Walk With People

The pages you are reading are intended to be practical—to give you something to practice. Notice the action words above: *Renew, Teach, Follow, Create and Walk.*

But first, the problem needs a bit of defining.

Until we admit there is a problem, it will be hard to be motivated to work through these things with our leadership teams. Before we get to the **"What"** (as in, "What should we do?") it is important to fully embrace the **"Why"** (as in, "Why is this so important?").

THE DE-SPIRITUALIZATION OF MONEY

Over time, we have let something slip. With the organizational behavior, leadership, and non-profit management influence on the modern American church, we have allowed money to slip into "pay the bills" and "run the business" language. It is a subtle but critical shift. And one that demands some analysis.

When we talk about money in the church as a product of our church budget it is understandable. It is a reality of modern ministry in the first world. But when we *primarily* talk about money in budget terminology or primarily bring up the topic when there is a need, crisis, or sense that we are behind budget, we unintentionally train our congregation to think of money only in financial terms.

That phrase sounds crazy, doesn't it?
Thinking of money only in financial terms.

But here is the point: **Jesus does not allow anyone to think of money in simply financial ways.**

This is a significant reason for needing a tune-up. Because most churches I have worked with have slipped into this subtle misfire when it comes to money talk. I can tell when a church has not recognized the spiritual power of money in the same way Jesus intended us to recognize it.

These churches tend to exhibit certain behaviors and characteristics:

- Money is most often brought up when talking about budgets, church finances, voting, staff salaries, etc.
- Money teaching is seen as an "eat your vegetables" obligation (church leaders do it but don't like it).
- Churches excuse their pastor from the discipleship opportunity and responsibility by saying, "He just doesn't like to talk about money— what pastor does?"
- Churches depend on committees and fundraising gimmicks to "raise money" for the ministry operation of the church (as if they were a community group or service organization with dues, members, etc.).
- Churches have a once-per-year emphasis on giving and pledging to "support the church."

Notice in many of these behaviors that money is talked about in financial ways— budgets, obligations, paying bills, etc. Don't get me wrong —this is a reality of church life and can't be avoided.

But every time we choose to talk about money financially, we are not doing what Jesus did. Jesus talked about money, possessions, and giving in a way that made it a critical temperature gauge that reveals faith in God (or lack of it).

And if we condition our congregations that the only time leadership will bring up money is when we "need more" or are "behind," then we are making money almost purely about financial stuff. And we are conditioning everyone to give based on the church's need, not based on devotion to Christ and His Kingdom.

This is a really big deal. And it is a kind of slippage to me. We don't talk like Jesus. We tend to not even choose to look more deeply into why Jesus said what he said about this topic. And if we do, it is once a year when we must.

I usually ask church leaders the question this way: **If I placed a $100M check on your desk right now, would you be tempted to <u>never talk about money</u> again in your church?**

What I am curious about is whether this would be their honest answer: **"Yes! Whew—that's a load off my back! I don't have to broach that uncomfortable topic anymore! Hallelujah for the 100 Million Bucks!"**

If we are tempted to answer this way, we have a problem. It reveals that we have missed a critical aspect of understanding how to groom disciples for following Jesus. And that is our mission.

We may have unintentionally glossed over a big part of life in the Kingdom. We may have let something critical slip: **Being an open-handed-giver and a pass-through-person for God's provision to others is a key indicator of my growing faith.**

And if my pastors and spiritual mentors do not help me understand that lack of generosity is toxic, then they will have committed a kind of malpractice.

The slippage is because members of our churches don't need to be convinced to give to the church for its programs, they need to be encouraged toward generosity because that's how God's kingdom works. Period.

When you teach me, pastor, to unburden my life and cease my constant striving for accumulation by being generous, you have led me to the way of God. You have shown me what disciples of Jesus do on this earth.

It is not about the church budget. It is about my soul. I need to give whether the church needs it or not.

So, how can we shift the discussion? How can we create this kind of approach? It is by creating a new atmosphere, a new culture, a new language—a new environment.

CREATING AN ENVIRONMENT

An environment is the surroundings or conditions in which a person, animal, or plant lives or operates. The environment we are aiming to cultivate or create is one of generosity.

And the creation of this kind of environment, where talking about money and its use is the *rule and not the exception*, is what we want to create. Because, in doing so, we will model the way of Jesus.

Jesus was on to something when he brought up money all the time. He knew it had a special kind of power that, unchecked, would *not* lead to the Kingdom of God on earth. I think we need to normalize this topic because Jesus did.

Before we get into the first section of work in creating an environment that Grows Generosity, I think it is important to take a brief time-out to explore why this may be such a difficult journey for church leaders.

It will not be condemning or shaming. It is intended to peel back some of the layers of spiritual complexity and look at why, as a group of professionals, pastors are way more uncomfortable than they are comfortable with addressing this topic and normalizing it.

I promise we will get to the nitty-gritty practical stuff soon. But, we need to do a little more diagnosis before we offer a cure. Let's talk about pastors, in particular. If you are one, I hope you will relate. If you are not one, you will understand more of why this is such a tricky part of church life and leadership. Ok—I just blew the whistle. I'm calling "Time Out!"

CHAPTER THREE

Why Pastors Tend To
Freak Out About Money

O k. Maybe "freak out" is an exaggeration. But as I read on a t-shirt one time, *I think hyperbole is the best thing ever.* I will never forget being in a natatorium 20-some years ago. We were there for swim lessons for my oldest son.

He is now grown up, married and "adulting" on the west coast with his beautiful bride. But back then he was a skinny little boy and could tend to be afraid of things here and there.

He happens to be one of the most courageous guys I know today. He played the lead role in a National Tour of a well known Broadway show and has performed all over the country to audiences of thousands at a time. But that is now. This was then.

I will never forget that day he stood on the diving board. He was six years old.

We thought it would be a great idea for our kids to learn to swim. We raised our children in Michigan—there are more lakes than you can count, and in the summertime, pool parties are the order of the day for elementary and middle school kids. So, Parenting 101 says that you either teach your kid to swim or you outsource it to the local community pool and their instructors.

What I soon learned down at the local community swimming class is that there are different schools of thought when it comes to inaugurating your child into the world of fending for oneself in the water. And one of the schools of thought, I found out when it was too late to retreat, was to put your very fragile new semi-swimmer on a diving board about 5 feet off the surface of the water so they could jump off and "figure it out," getting themselves somehow back to the side of the pool.

Forever etched in my memory was one of those "I must be the cruelest dad of all time" moments. My boy was weeping, with a look of sheer panic on his face as he looked up to the elevated seats where I and other parents sat. He raised his hand up to me as if to say, "Dad, please save me."

And I could do nothing. Absolutely nothing other than swim in my own little pool of regret, trying to muster the "you can do this" smile and thumbs-up gesture that is required.

Well, he survived. And so did I. But the look he had on his face reminds me of the panic that I see in the eyes of many senior church leaders when I say, "You really need to help your people understand the spiritual power of money and move them toward generosity. You cannot hide from it—it is too important. Let's step into it, not away from it. That is what Jesus did."

These are adult humans. They are graduate-degree professionals. They have counseled their congregants through tragedy and triumph and worked with difficult people and situations that would paralyze most of us.

But somehow, when it comes to talking to the congregation about money, I equate them to the story of my son standing on a diving board, knees knocking, tears streaming, with an outstretched hand as if to say, "God—anything. I will do anything. Just save me from this."

How does this happen? Why is this the norm? Why do people like me, who go into pastoral leadership to help people know God and find spiritual wholeness have an Achilles heel—the topic of giving, money, and generosity?

This chapter is dedicated to my tribe. Some of the finest people I know. The men and women who are leading churches—often senior pastors, but not always. The visible and vocal leaders of churches are the people I tend to hang out with. And many of us share a similar vantage point when it comes to the topic at hand.

Some of the reasons that this has remained a tough topic may sound familiar to you. How many of these could you check as something that describes your experience?

- We rarely spent time talking about money in seminary
- We rarely have an understanding of how money works because, in many ways, we swore off a life of financial success when we entered the ministry

- We feel the awkwardness of "asking for money" because ultimately it feels like asking for what will keep us employed

Ok, maybe this is just me. But, church leaders may admit that some of these things have crossed their minds.

I recently confided in a colleague and friend, who happens to be the senior pastor of a very large church. We admitted to each other that there is even a more sinister part of us that occasionally creeps in.

We pretend like we are above people who are wealthy and driven toward success. We put on the air that we are better than that—that we are too spiritual to get caught in the addiction of money-obsession. But that is play-acting. My son who lives in L.A. gets paid to do that. But when I do it —it is not pretty.

When I pretend to be something better than I am, it is deeply unhealthy. Yikes. You can probably tell already that I am still grappling with the spiritual and practical dimensions to this spiritually powerful topic. And, like any other area of the spiritual life of a disciple, it is a three steps-forward-two-steps-back kind of process.

If you are hoping to read the words of an author who has "arrived," you may want to put this book down and read a different work.

In some ways, I am still tinkering in the laboratory. Well, a few laboratories. One is the lab of the church, as we try to figure out how to lead it well. And the other is the lab of my heart as I still try to figure out how to have a healthy inner life on this issue.

So, I hope you quickly see me as a colleague and friend—a fellow sojourner. Let's go together.

Let's just say that this area of the Christian life is way more complex and nuanced than most people recognize. And you would think that complexity would demand more attention from those who are mentoring others. Instead, pastors and church leaders like you and me seem to neglect it almost wholesale. Until now.

One of the most difficult parts of any journey is simply knowing where to start. I suggest that the first step should be a bit of data collection.

We will collect it, set it on the table, and then look at it (our congregation, its behavior and attitudes, its make-up, etc.) in light of the 5 major categories of how best practice churches create generous culture. But, let's decide how to grab the information first.

The next chapter is your checklist for what to go gather. You may want to pull a few friends into the journey at this point. It will likely take a team of people to discern and decide in light of what we are about to learn about ourselves.

CHAPTER FOUR

The Data That
Describes Our Reality

A number of years ago, I had a very difficult health challenge. After having a migraine headache for 65 days straight, I learned a new term. It is called "cluster headaches." Yep. That's actually a thing. And it is not fun.

For whatever reason, when the body is not functioning properly, some humans have a bunch of terrible headaches in a row or a "cluster." I am happy to report that my health is good and back to normal. But there is more to the story.

There were other symptoms that accompanied the headaches, so I was under doctor's care and diagnosis for a number of months. I had MRIs, CAT Scans, and a battery of other tests to see what was happening with me physically—was it a neurological problem or something else?

Very early in this process—I mean VERY early—my oldest daughter sat by my hospital bedside and said, "Dad, have you considered the possibility that this is something emotional or spiritual or stress-induced?"

What was she thinking? I insisted that I was not stressed, had a great life, a full career, wonderful kids, a spectacular marriage—there was no reason for me to consider stress being the culprit. Why would she suggest this? I was virtually Superman. Surely she could see this. You probably know where my story is headed by now.

After many months, my doctor finally said, "You don't have any physical health problems to speak of—no brain or heart trouble, nor any blood pressure, sugar level or cholesterol problem. The good news is that we have run pretty much every test imaginable, so we have a good baseline study of your physical condition. There is only one thing left to surmise: Your body is dealing with stress and anxiety. You need to treat it accordingly."

There are a number of lessons learned that I could draw from this story.

And you probably are way ahead of me. We won't take the time to talk about my stunning lack of self-awareness and inability to listen to my very spiritually discerning daughter. And, we won't talk about how long it took me to throw in the towel and admit I needed significant help. We need a completely different book for the discussion of my weakness inventory. I spent months and thousands of dollars to confirm what my daughter knew from the beginning. She sized up the data and interpreted it correctly.

What we *will* talk about is how difficult it is sometimes to read the data (on anything) and interpret it. And, we all know about the propensity to be convinced of something and then use data to justify your position. That is what psychologists call **confirmation bias** (defined as the tendency to interpret new evidence as confirmation of one's existing beliefs or theories).

This applies to the difficulty of knowing what certain items of information may be telling us about our churches. Particularly when we are close to that data, and have built up a kind of insulation around what it could possibly mean.

Please consider for a second my ability, in spite of the data (symptoms) and counsel (my daughter's wisdom), to insulate myself with the notion that "I am not a guy that deals with stress."

Is it possible that the data that church leaders look at is incomplete or misinterpreted when it comes to truly helping our people on their pathway to maturity as generous disciples?

Here is where we still start to turn the corner into a new way of looking at this. Let's prime the pump by starting to talk about data in a way that is helpful to the creation of a plan. In later chapters we will explore data collection in more detail and Chapter 17 is the deep dive. For now, let's consider a new approach to reading the numbers.

A NEW WAY FORWARD

Quite frankly, most churches that I interact with have very little awareness of the data. So little that they have protected themselves (so the argument goes) from any biases about the information or the givers themselves. So, for some, what you encounter in this book may be new territory for you and your church.

One of the primary decisions each church will make is whether or not to apply a discipleship strategy to developing generosity in the life of its congregation.

I remember as a young senior pastor that I really had no clue who was giving, at what level, at what pace. I also had no sense for whether people who held leadership mantles in the church were actually leaders in this critical aspect of following Jesus. Were leaders actually leading?

I am not even suggesting (yet) that we take up the topic of whether or not I should have looked at this information. We are getting there.

The point is this: if church leaders do not have a realistic understanding of giving behavior, it may be difficult to create a discipleship pathway that leads to growth.

I am asking you to consider a new way forward. From now on, let us think about members of our congregation in a more nuanced way for what we are about to do. We are getting prepared for the naming of your generosity pathway at your church.

Generosity Pathway: Like rocks set in a pattern that enable one to cross a stream, this pathway will illustrate how each disciple in your congregation can go from step one to step two to step three and so on.

GIVING BANDS

I have been very impressed with the work coming from the men and women serving the church through the ministry of MortarStone. Their help is highly practical.

Their system allows church leaders to gather information about giving patterns and behavior in their church. The point is to understand what is happening with individual givers so that systems can be created for more effective discipleship. Each giving household is placed into one of 5 "bands" (or buckets).

I have spent a considerable amount of time with David Thoroughman, the current CEO, with whom I share a passion to coach church leaders in this category. David reminds us that we should "measure what matters and manage what you measure."

The work of Mortarstone allows senior church leaders to analyze the nature of the giving. This allows for the nuance to which I have been referring (not everyone is starting at the same point or progressing at the same pace). Here are some of the categories of analysis the software can perform:

- **Progress** - are people growing in amount and frequency to the mission?
- **Pace** - what is the frequency of giving?
- **Paralysis** - are there givers that are stuck or stagnant? Stopped giving?
- **People** - who is giving, to what degree and in what pattern?

Churches that take seriously the "pathway" approach to encouraging increased generosity will have their own version or words, but everyone has a way to talk about the 4 or 5 stages of an individual's growth. What about your church? Do you have an instinct already about the four or five stages you may identify?

Consider the simplicity of the breakdown of congregational giving behavior: Bands, Types, and Metrics.

Five Giving Bands:

- Band 1 - give less than $200/year
- Band 2 - give $200 to $999
- Band 3 - give $1,000 to $4,999
- Band 4 - give $5,000 to $9,999
- Band 5 - give $10,000 or more

Types of Givers:

- New Givers - those that have never given to the church before
- Core Givers - those that have given over an established threshold, usually frequency and amount
- Top Givers - those that give over a threshold that is considerably above average amount year over year (YOY).

Key Performance Metrics (KPMs):

- Acquisition
- Giving Increases vs. Decreases
- Retention

Thorougman offers a practical example of how giving bands are used by illustrating one of their actual breakdowns of a church they worked with (not named for the sake of anonymity):

Band	Households	Giving	Average	%Households	% Giving
1	1,108	$67,342.76	$60.78	28.66%	0.48%
2	846	$411,088.88	$485.92	21.88%	2.96%
3	1,070	$2,611,533.45	$2,440.69	27.68%	18.77%
4	471	$3,310,702.14	$7,029.09	12.18%	23.8%
5	371	$7,510,536.86	$20,244.03	9.6%	53.99%
TOTALS	**3,866**	**$13,911,204.09**	**$3,598.35**	**100.0%**	**100.0%**

Figure 4.1

To model how this data can be helpful in this church, he makes two very quick observations to show us how this works:

1. Over 50% of the total givers give less than $500/year to church
2. Out of 3,866 givers, 317 or 9.6% give over half of the total funding

David encourages the church leader with this particular palette of givers to ask themselves questions like:

- Am I ok with this? Is it satisfactory?
- What is encouraging?
- What opportunities do we have?
- How may this giving pattern reflect on a deficiency in our discipleship as a church?
- What can we do to change it?

David and his team coach churches with the belief that there is an opportunity to grow generosity if we understand the challenge more acutely.

From this analysis, you can imagine some of the common questions that can be asked in terms of Key Performance Metrics:

- Do we have more first time givers this year compared to last?
- What percentage of first time givers go on to make a second gift?
- Are core givers growing in their giving, or is there stagnation?
- How can we find out "why" things are happening the way they are and attempt a new way forward in our methodology?

Many pastors and ministry leaders will find the contents of this chapter to be a new, foreign, or even suspicious way to handle congregational giving. I am asking you to stay on board for the ride. You, of course, will take some things from this writing and leave others behind.

On the other hand, thinking and strategizing with data may be right up your alley. Maybe you love to get nerdy about the information and then translate that into action steps. You will see that one of the core premises of this book is not to tell you what to do, but what to consider. And then, it comes down to intentional action. Try something different to allow for different results.

Either way, it will be difficult for us to move ahead together if your church leadership is not willing to be more specific about the reality of your data.

NOTE:

If you are in an economically under-resourced area or run a church with a high population of college students, you may have just been frustrated by the amounts represented in each giving band. Church planters in their first few years may feel the same way. Please understand that the ranges capturing each giving band can be adjusted.

CHAPTER FIVE

The Amazing Future Ahead

I see something on the horizon. And, if I haven't painted too bleak of a picture and you are still with me, let's dig in a little further before we start to pull out the flip charts and start planning. I believe the deep dive on generosity is what so few leaders take time to do.

Something is brewing when it comes to people investing in the things that are important to God. It is partly in the next generation (my children and their peers, Christian or not) and partly in Jesus people in the church of older generations.

What I see is a posture emerging in many people that sounds something like this: **The world is a messed up place and if what I have can help correct this, I am interested in giving.**

This may seem different to you if you grew up like me. I was taught to give out of loyalty to God and the church—not a bad thing at all. But something shifted in me when I noticed how God uses generous people to restore the earth.

Many people both inside and outside the church are starting to fully embrace the idea that righting the wrongs in our world will likely require some sort of generosity. People will debate whether that generosity is from governments, businesses, or individuals. But generosity seems to be trendy. The often criticized next generation are actually very wired for generosity— it just looks very different than many understand.

> *Side note: The church proving that what they are investing in is, in fact, an effective use of this giving is increasingly the challenge. But more on that later.*

Like a lot of cultural pendulums, there seems to be one swinging back from the pursuit of wealth characteristic of the Boomers in the last part of the 20th century. The children and grandchildren of Boomers are thinking about the stewardship of the earth and its inhabitants in creative and sometimes radical ways.

Boomers have that wealth to give toward earth-as-it-is-in-heaven projects and missions. You have likely heard phrases like "the largest transfer of wealth in the history of the world" referring to what Boomers will either give away or leave behind.

Call me a cock-eyed optimist. But I'm sticking around to see how this all plays out.

Let's continue to be candid about this. For so long, the money topic has gotten a bad rap. It is the butt of jokes and considered the necessary evil—the "boring business" side of running a church or ministry. And it is true that we have slid far from any widely held understanding of the Christian ethic of giving in American culture. It used to be at least acknowledged (if not practiced).

The work ethic often attributed to the early Protestants who came to America included a charitable giving ethic to match. We are a long way from the early days of our country and its people in many ways.

Tommy Yoder, a friend from my childhood Bible church used to say in response to us asking if he'd be in church: "I'll be there after they collect the offering—it's cheaper!" Like many churchgoers, he's only half kidding.

I have discovered that church leaders that lead generous congregations affirm this key spiritual assertion:

Generosity is a key barometer of discipleship maturity.

And though we have changed many of the ways we lead churches, we still have an anemic approach in this critical category.

"We aren't in Kansas anymore, Toto." We are now living in a fully post-Christian culture. Very few people know what the Bible says about living and giving anymore. Very few care. We are realizing, like Dorothy after the twister, that our surroundings have drastically changed. The context for church ministry is like a foreign land.

The reason most people do not tithe is that they do not even know what it means anymore—it is explained less, modeled less, and believed less by each passing generation.

> **Pre-Global Pandemic, the average giving by adults who attend US Protestant churches is about $17 a week. 37% of regular church attendees and Evangelicals don't give money to church.** [3]

The bottom line for most leaders and their outlook on the future is actually connected with the *bottom line*. I have never met a church leader that does not think they need more financial resources to get the job done in a more effective way.

Many have really well-intentioned aspirations that require funding. And most pastors I have met are motivated from a very healthy place.

But the ways we feel we have been taught (or not taught) to encourage more giving seem like as much fun as a trip to the dentist. So we tend to attempt it about as often as we go for a teeth cleaning.

Some have said that if we copied the amount of times Jesus mentioned the topic and proportioned our sermon schedule accordingly, over 20 messages of our 52 per year would be on finances. *Not to chunt*

I don't know any fellow pastors who have attempted this—nor do I think this is a prescription promoted by Scripture, per se. But it is thought provoking, right?

The truth is that Jesus seemed to be buzzing around that topic in one way or another because he was teaching about how to live in a different kingdom. He knew that "the cares of this world" would threaten our allegiance to Him and that we would probably get the money thing out of whack. He said as much. And He was right.

But I think we have an opportunity to guide people toward positive and life-giving belief and behavior and there is much more to gain than just more revenue for the church.

Generous people prosper in so many ways—and they bless the earth and its inhabitants. This is about a life well-lived in accordance with God's design for us as humans. As a Jesus following person, I need to be a giver because that's my identity—that's what I was meant to do. And at a very core level, this reflects what I truly believe about myself and about God.

---

3   https://www.cheatsheet.com/money-career/average-church-religion-donation.html/

This is the most spiritual practice I can think of.

If we all began managing God's steady stream of blessing to us (money, possessions, influence, availability, mentoring, mercy, etc.) according to His kingdom values, it would put a different spin on things.

If I worked out the spiritual muscle of trusting God with my life, my spiritual health would go to a new level as well. If I did not constantly try to hoard or hold, but let resources pass through me on the way to someone else, I would be inviting a new atmosphere.

Billy Graham said, "If a person gets his attitude toward money straight, it will help straighten out almost every other area of his life." And those that have experienced this transformation will attest to how they shifted their thinking because of the inability of money to truly satisfy.

Here's the truth of the matter:

Money is powerful.

This places it squarely in competition with God for what will bring us satisfaction and peace.

In most of our lives, we act like money has won the battle.

It is time we admit that.

Princeton researcher Daniel Kahneman, PhD, shared the 2002 Nobel Prize for applying the principles of psychology to economics. When asked about his research regarding the question, "Does Money buy Happiness?" his answer was: No. It's just an illusion that wealth brings happiness.

Why does increased income have so little effect on happiness? Research shows that:

1) Relative income, rather than any certain level of income, affects well-being. If you get richer than your peers, you may feel you're better off than they are. But soon you'll make richer new friends, so your relative wealth won't be greater than it was before.
2) People quickly get used to all the new stuff their money can buy.
3) The amount of money people say they need rises along with their income.
4) When you start making more money, you spend more time making money—and have less leisure time—than you did before.

"The activities that higher-income individuals spend relatively more of their time engaged in are associated with no greater happiness, but with slightly higher tension and stress," Kahneman and colleagues note. [4]

So, as much as we may know clinically or even experientially that this is true, even good people pursuing spiritual health and wholeness still get trapped.

Malaysia leads the list with 58 percent of participants stating money to be their biggest concern, followed by China and Singapore with both 55 percent. Third one in the list is the United States with 48 percent of participants blaming the dollar for their stress. [5]

Ironically, focusing on the illusion that money makes you happy may have an unexpected side effect. It may make your life worse. In the United States, the most prosperous nation in the history of the world, we have modeled a truly messed up relationship with money. This is not coincidental.

"This focusing illusion may lead to a misallocation of time, from accepting lengthy commutes (which are among the worst moments of the day) to sacrificing time spent socializing (which are among the best moments of the day)," Kahneman and colleagues observe. "The long-term effect of income gains becomes relatively small because attention shifts to less novel aspects of daily life." [6]

Since I believe in the cosmic spiritual battle for each and every soul that ever lived, I must also conclude that there is a powerful force wanting me to not find the abundant life that God wants for me.

If the dark side would like people to live in confusion, fear, stress, anxiety, selfishness, greed, and the like—then the dark side seems to be doing quite well.

But there is another side to the story.

Money is indeed, the most important thing in the world.
- George Bernard Shaw

Perhaps Shaw was right. The economic collapse of 2008-2009 was, in

---

4   https://www.webmd.com/balance/news/20060630/study-money-wont-make-you-happy#1
5   Poll: Money worries world's greatest cause of stress www.cnn.com September 9, 2009
6   https://www.webmd.com/balance/news/20060630/study-money-wont-make-you-happy#1

fact, a spiritual issue. At the heart of it, greed ruled from the consumer to the bank to Wall Street to the federal government. When greed runs amok, it has consequences that aggravate everything in the culture—jobs, relationships, housing, and retirement to name a few.

People come to our churches with enormous stress in their lives. What we know from marriage counselors and medical doctors is that most of our trouble comes from something to do with our money.

> *The place where your treasure is, is the place you will most want to be, and end up being.*
> *- Jesus Christ. The Message*

So, Jesus knew that the condition of our hearts and trajectory of our lives is absolutely welded to the management of our money and possessions. Based on Jesus' interaction with the rich young ruler, apparently our money has eternal implications as well.

WE CAN CHANGE THE WORLD

If Christians increased their giving, it would change the world. My children keep reminding me that Jeff Bezos, Amazon's founder, has enough money to eradicate world hunger. Jeff seems to be a popular target for such a question. At the time of writing this paragraph, his net worth was approaching $200B. A moral question for millennials seems to be, "Why wouldn't a billionaire use his or her money for the betterment of the world?" I try to turn the moral question back around at my kids and ask them about whether they are doing their part with what they have, but I am not sure that is the most endearing approach.

I believe Christians have a lot to explain. Consider the following statistics tabulated just a few years ago in 2016. Though not much has changed, I remain optimistic and willing to press on. Because transformed givers transform the world. Consider this: Only 5 percent of the U.S. tithes, with 80 percent of Americans only giving 2 percent of their income.

Christians are only giving at 2.5 percent per capita, while during the Great Depression they gave at a 3.3 percent rate.

The larger point is what would happen if believers were to increase their giving to a minimum of, let's say, 10 percent. There would be an additional $165 billion for churches to use and distribute.[7] The global impact would be phenomenal. Here's just a few things the Church could do with the kind of money:

- **$25 billion** could relieve global hunger, starvation and deaths from preventable diseases in five years.
- **$12 billion** could eliminate illiteracy in five years.
- **$15 billion** could solve the world's water and sanitation issues, specifically at places in the world where 1 billion people live on less than $1 per day.
- **$1 billion** could fully fund all overseas mission work.
- **$100 – $110 billion** would still be left over for additional ministry expansion.

WE CAN EXPERIENCE ABUNDANT LIVING

Jesus invites us to abundant living. I don't know exactly what this means, but it sounds pretty awesome.

What if our neighbors and friends notice that we operate from the joy of a blessed and abundant life? When my neighbors are stressed about money and dissatisfied with never having enough, I can move in the opposite direction. I can throw a party because my money doesn't master me, I master it.

Craig Blomberg writes that Jews threw ancient "block parties" for the purpose of showing the goodness of God and thanking him for his provision. Eat up. Party. Thank God. Give a ton of things away.

When we do throw a party, is our purpose to have people view us as generous because of our gratitude for God's goodness in our lives? What if we could reclaim partying as the obvious gesture of a life connected with God? Think about how much my investment of money has to do with filling my garages and closets as opposed to blessing another person. What if I lined up the last 100 purchases I made and divided into "me vs. others" columns?

---

7   https://relevantmagazine.com/love-and-money/what-would-happen-if-church-tithed#hkeTcvPsSzbzdrlx.99

Speaking of closets, a colleague repeated a story to me about a pastor in Atlanta that had a "Generosity Closet." When he found something great, valuable or something he really liked—a bottle of wine, a ticket to a concert, a shirt, etc.—he would often buy 2 and put the other one in his generosity closet. He would then pray, watch, and excitedly try to discover who would be the person to give it to and when.

This Atlanta pastor models for me how things could get really interesting if we think differently about our future. This could get really interesting, right?

Are you willing to join me in creating a plan for your congregation (and perhaps for your own life) by organizing the 5 Waves that will lead to generous disciples in your congregation? Let's start with the right foundation for our journey. It is time for a quick trip through Scripture to set a beautiful and clear theology to give us the footing we need.

WAVE ONE

THEOLOGY

RENEW YOUR CONVICTION.

What do we believe about generosity?

CHAPTER SIX

What Do We Believe About Generosity?

I n 2002, our family started a new adventure.

An opportunity was presented to me to travel and work for Cargill Associates, one of the country's oldest and most reputable church consulting firms. When church consulting started to increase in the last half of the 20th century, the Cargill family was at the forefront.

The late Dr. Robert Cargill started his company in the 1970s. It would end up serving thousands of institutions, colleges, and churches over the last four decades. Cargill is (and always has been) headquartered in Fort Worth, TX. I did not have to move there, but I did need to move close to a major airport.

I was about to officially become a road warrior. We chose Detroit as our new home base and Kensington Church as our new home church. One of the chief highlights of our new context was this lesson: **What you believe about financial resources really affects how you live and give.**

We had been aiming to live generously but really learned it at a new level from Kensington and its leadership, particularly founding pastor Steve Andrews.

Over the nearly 20 years we have been at Kensington, we have been intimately involved in serving the mission—both my wife and I have held staff positions and have raised our children in that spiritual ecosystem. One of our primary motivations for being fully on board with Kensington was the church's value of humility and "openhandedness."

Though Kensington grew in the late 90's and early 2000's at a breakneck pace, the leadership remained humble, "off the radar," and rarely appeared in all of the superlative lists of "Top 100" and "Fastest Growing" churches though the numbers would have substantiated such accolades.

By 2010, there were regularly near 15,000 in weekend attendance at eight campuses, and the church had invested millions of dollars in 50 or 60 church plants. Baptism services were a highlight, often with hundreds being baptized at a time. It just seemed like no matter how much Kensington gave away (financially and in other ways) over those years, the buckets kept filling up.

There were many extraordinary acts of generosity based on Steve's core belief that none of the resources, buildings, people, money or anything else was his nor even belonged to our church alone. It all belonged to God's kingdom.

For instance, he would regularly bring church planters from various denominations, philosophies, and styles of ministry up on to the platform to help recruit people for the new church—from Kensington!

He would say, "This is Craig McGlassion—he is a friend of mine. He and his wife are starting a brand new church a few miles from here. He is an amazing leader and some of you need to seriously pray about joining his launch team. As a matter of fact, if you are not plugged in here at Kensington, it is time for you to go get involved in serving God somewhere. So, please meet Craig after the service, he will be in the lobby. Maybe God is calling you to leave here to go help this new church?" Regularly, people would leave: members and non-members, plugged in and not plugged in. They were off to a new adventure.

Steve's encouragement to church leaders that ask about this unlikely approach is that "You can have it all, if you are willing to give it all away." Always the provocateur, he is asking leaders to truly examine what they are shooting for. What is it that you are looking for, ultimately? What defines success for you? What does it mean to "have it all" in ministry?

The "give it all away" in Steve's statement refers to the spiritual principle that God has a tendency to refill hands that are open; open to freely receive and give in a never ending role of being a conduit or pipeline of God's mercy and grace on the world. His goodness passes through us to someone else.

Regardless of what your church context is, there is some theological and biblical homework that needs to be done. One of the reasons giving suffers in our churches is that we have a vague notion of what the church expects, what the leaders believe and what the Bible says about it.

And because preachers tend to shy away from the topic, they rarely use their training and communication skills to take up Jesus' favorite topic.

- How can we live a truly abundant life?
- What is our church's position on the tithe?
- Is it possible to be wealthy and follow Christ?
- What do we believe is our responsibility to the poor?

The point here is not that all churches agree. The point is that each church needs to decide where they stand and then teach it in a clear way.

I happen to also believe that there is a lot to learn from professionals outside the context of the church. Spiritual leaders tend to turn up their noses at "secular fundraising" as if it were an infectious disease. Which seems inconsistent to me when many of those same leaders will use "secular" bankers, architects, plumbers and painters. God has blessed many with his wisdom.

What many churches call their Stewardship Ministry (or committee) needs to be re-evaluated in light of what God has taught us through donor development practices by the major non-profits of our day. We certainly need to match our tactics and techniques against moral and biblical guidelines. And there will be nuances in each context—the things that are specific to our church or our denomination. Add all this up, and we have the beginning of a very helpful discussion.

The research seems quite clear:
Churches that are proactive and intentional in both teaching about generosity and holding the congregation to high expectations will develop a more generous culture.

What also seems to be a trend is that generous cultures are enhanced as the topic of giving is treated primarily on the spiritual or heart-level as opposed to teaching it as a sense of duty or dues, obligation and obedience or "meeting the budget."

In these best practice churches, there is preaching, teaching, classes, small groups, and even personal budget counseling for individuals and couples in crisis. They have informative websites and great printed media.

But beyond that, the people that attend these churches can catch a vibe that the leaders expect that people will be more generous. There is an aura of expectation—people that attend feel a bias toward acting out one's faith as a standard. "Wow—the people around here put their money where their mouth is."

Church leaders don't shy away from pointing out the connection between faith and financial giving. And they do a masterful job of pointing out the impact that this faith & finances combination can have in our lives and communities.

These churches know that living in a first-world economy will produce a tendency to be materialistic and unaware. Only a rare person will identify themselves as ungenerous. And Christians in America have awareness but apathy regarding income disparity or relative wealth. Many do not see money for the deeply critical spiritual category it is. Nor will they welcome the idea that giving is the primary antidote to the disease of self-dependence and greed.

Here is more of Tim Keller's conversation with his wife Kathy about Christians and their view of greed compared to other sins:

> *Why can't anyone in the grip of greed see it? The counterfeit god of money uses powerful sociological and psychological dynamics. Everyone tends to live in a particular socioeconomic bracket. Once you are able to afford to live in a particular neighborhood, send your children to its schools, and participate in its social life, you will find yourself surrounded by quite a number of people who have more money than you. You don't compare yourself to the rest of the world, you compare yourself to those in your bracket. The human heart always wants to justify itself and this is one of the easiest ways. You say, "I don't live as well as him or her or them. My means are modest compared to theirs." You can reason and think like that no matter how lavishly you are living. As a result, most Americans think of themselves as middle class, and only 2 percent call themselves "upper class." But the rest of the world is not fooled. When people visit here from other parts of the globe, they are staggered to see the level of materialistic comfort that the majority of Americans have come to view as a necessity.*
>
> *Jesus warns people far more often about greed than about sex, yet almost*

no one thinks they are guilty of it. Therefore we should all begin with a working hypothesis that "this could easily be a problem for me." If greed hides itself so deeply, no one should be confident that it is not a problem for them.

In the next few chapters, we will brush up a bit on the stance that we will take in our church. We will review what scripture says and evaluate our current practices in light of that. We will look at our current teaching and be honest about where we have shied away and what opportunities we may have to graciously step back in.

The end goal is to assert (or re-assert) what we believe to be true about this important zone of church life. And we can start with a Cliff's Notes type review of the Theology of Generosity.

The fruit of this exercise is to create or reaffirm the statements that your church will make. Just like in other important areas of theology and practice, we need to make *"We believe"* and *"Therefore, we will practice"* statements to lead our congregations into a culture of open hands.

REMINDER: If you have not brought a friend or team into this discussion yet, it is not too late. These important matters should not be deliberated in isolation.

The research and writing on giving, stewardship, generosity, and tithing is exhaustive. There are more than a handful of pastors and professors who give us plenty to wade through when it comes to collecting wisdom nuggets from mining through the Bible.

This book is not meant to be a comprehensive nor academic review of these important concepts. But it is necessary to create some lists and summaries to get our heads in the game.

I invite you to spend some time with a highlighter or notepad-checking, underlining, and noting the things that ring true for you and your church. This is an important part of the journey before we start deciding on any changes to process or practice in our church.

The theology chapters will cover the following categories:

CHAPTER SEVEN

The Language Of Generosity

T he 1987 romantic comedy *The Princess Bride* has become a cult
classic. Among the ridiculous hijinx and multi-dimensional cast of
characters in this movie is Inigo Montoya (played by Mandy Patinkin).

After hearing Sicilian boss Vizzini repeatedly describe the unfolding
events of the movie as "inconceivable," he delivers the line that has often
been repeated (at least by me and my friends who were in high school and
college in the late 80's): *"You keep using that word. I do not think it means
what you think it means."* [8]

As a result of loosely held definitions for many in the category of
Christian giving, we must define some terms before we go on to establish
our church's core convictions. Is there any consequence to regularly
interchanging words like charity, generosity, stewardship and giving? When
I hear so many people referring to their 2.7% giving as their "tithe," I must
join Mr. Montoya saying that *I do not think that word means what people
think it means.*

Many attribute Socrates with having stated almost 2,500 years ago, *"The
beginning of wisdom is the definition of terms."*

In short, sometimes one word can have multiple meanings and
sometimes multiple words have the same meaning. As obvious as this may
be, the nuance of this remains important to moving ahead.

Remember, this is an important exercise leading us to make (or reaffirm)
certain assertions about our church's belief, so that our strategy flows from
that starting point.

Let's consider some words that directly relate to the vocabulary of
generosity in the church and then turn to some less direct (but very
important) concepts that come from Christian theology and Scripture.

First, our quick vocabulary review.

---

8   https://knowyourmeme.com/memes/you-keep-using-that-word-i-do-not-think-it-means-
what-you-think-it-means

1) What is discipleship?

Some call it spiritual formation, spiritual growth, mentoring in the faith and a handful of other titles. Essentially, however, the mission of the church that Jesus established long ago is anchored in his commission to "go into all the world and make disciples" (Matthew 28).

There are many questions surrounding how to do this most effectively. But most churches with whom I have spent time are aiming at growing people in their Christian faith to know and follow the teachings of Jesus found in Scripture.

The reason we start with this definition is because the idea of growing generosity is rooted in the premise that growth or life-change is the goal of any collection of believers. If we agree that generous living is a characteristic of a follower of Jesus, the rest of your effort to create a giving culture makes sense. ***You simply cannot disciple fully if generosity is not part of the equation.***

1 John 3:16-18 — "This is how we know what love is: Jesus Christ laid down his life for us. And we ought to lay down our lives for our brothers. If anyone has material possessions and sees his brother in need but has no pity on him, how can the love of God be in him? Dear children, let us not love with words or tongue but with actions and in truth."

James 2:14-17 — "What good is it, my brothers, if a man claims to have faith but has no deeds? Can such faith save him? Suppose a brother or sister is without clothes and daily food. If one of you says to him, 'Go, I wish you well; keep warm and well fed,' but does nothing about his physical needs, what good is it? In the same way, faith by itself, if it is not accompanied by action, is dead."

2) What is generosity?

At a very simple level, generosity describes the idea of being kind in the giving away of what one holds and does not solely refer to financial giving.

For the Christian, it is rooted in our connection with a giving Heavenly Father who is our ultimate provider. The quintessential act of this generous God is the cornerstone of the Christian faith—that God loved us so much, he gave his son over to death as the act that would redeem us all.

Generosity is the outgrowth of connection with God. It is the giving away of what came from God in the first place. As God "did not spare his own Son, but gave him up for us all" (Romans 8:32), so our posture toward God and others in response to his love can be one of cheerful sacrifice and generosity.

3) What is stewardship?

For many Christians in the western world, the word stewardship has been claimed by the idea of financial giving to one's church. For denominations that hold Stewardship Sundays, Stewardship Month, or have Stewardship Committees, it has unapologetically been aligned with the idea of our efforts to remind church members of their duty to give. Yet, technically (and theologically), a steward is a person who has been entrusted with, and who manages, another's resources according to the owner's vision and values.

The New Testament calls Christians caretakers of God's truths and gifts —even God's grace (1 Corinthians 4:1; 1 Peter 4:10). So stewardship has a corporate sense (how a church manages the resources of God in line with God's priority) and a personal sense (how individual believers or families manage God's resources for His purposes on the earth).

4) What is fundraising?

Fund-raising refers to a process of asking donors for contributions to an organization. It also refers to a profession in American life, often called "development," that elicits gifts for large organizations, such as colleges, hospitals, and museums. [10]

Some would say that fundraising is focused more on the institution or organization and its financial needs than the implications of an individual's

---

9   https://www.redeemer.com/generosity/stewardship

10   Money Matters: Personal Giving in American Churches Hoge, Zech, McNamara, Donahue
Westminsters John Knox Press, 1996
Louisville, KY P143

"need to give" for spiritual health and wholeness.

Fundraising is not a dirty word or an activity that should be debased in our attempt to understand Christian giving. Many men and women are involved in this as a profession for enormously positive causes—think about humanitarian and relief organizations as well as the arts. And many Christians will choose to give to those organizations as they are led by God to do so.

The reason for distinguishing fundraising from discipleship is to help a church make decisions about how they approach financial giving with members of the congregation.

5)   What is a tithe?

The word *tithe* literally means *tenth* in Hebrew. Because the custom of tithing is part of biblical history, many Christians and Jews practice it as part of their faith. According to Leviticus 27:30 (TLB), "A tenth of the produce of the land, whether grain or fruit, is the Lord's, and is holy." And Proverbs 3:9 (NIV) says, "Honor the Lord with your wealth, with the firstfruits of all your crops."

Scripture was written in a time and context of agrarian people and economic systems, so understandably the language follows that their wealth (or paycheck, if you will) was in the form of harvested crops.

Scripture leans heavily on the concept of giving a portion, specifically a tenth, of whatever you make back to God. And *firstfruits* is just a biblical way of saying that you should give *first*—before you do anything else with your money.[11]

6)   What is an Offering?

Offering comes from the Latin word *offere* (to offer or present) and contains the meaning of a sacred action. It therefore blends with the idea of "sacrifice" from the Latin word, *sacrificium*, consisting of the two words *sacer* (holy) and *facere* (to make). A "sacrifice" or an "offering" or a "sacrificial offering" is the highest religious act conceivable. At least 14

---

11   https://www.daveramsey.com/blog/daves-advice-on-tithing-and-giving

different types of offerings can be identified in the Old Testament, the most important of which appears to have been that of animals when blood was shed symbolizing Christ's blood shed on Calvary.

A faithful Jew who practiced all of those offerings would have probably given about one third of his total income to God (Vincent, p.10-11). One could argue that if tithe was of undeniable significance, offerings were even more so when considered in the context of the cross: the Lamb of God offering Himself so our sins could be forgiven and we could be offered salvation.[12]

---

12   Vincent, John, Christ and our Stewardship, London: Epsworth Press, 1963

CHAPTER EIGHT

The Economic Roots Of God's Love

A nother aspect of understanding terminology has to do with basic but important concepts in the Christian faith that borrow economic terms to explain our relationship with God.

Our connection with God is ultimately relational. Undergirding that relationship are ideas of giving and receiving, forgiving debt, provision of needs, and so on. God is a giver. God is a provider. God has paid a price for us.

The thesis of the following review is that our faith is linked closely with the economics of life and that our belief about and use of money is more deeply spiritual than most of us give it credit for. Deeply spiritual people do not exclude money from the way they play out their faith—it is completely linked.

So, it becomes important as we are developing our approach to teaching generosity that we sit again with these beautiful concepts that we have heard before—this time with new lenses. The following review is broken into two sections: God's behavior and ours.

God's Great Favor Toward Us

- Grace (unearned favor)
- Forgiveness (forgive us our debts)
- Redemption (buying back)
- Provision (source of all things)
- Abundance (more than enough)

Our Response To God's Favor

- Sabbath (stop pursuing gain, greed)
- Contentment (enough is enough)
- Sacrifice (giving up something valuable)

- Responsibility (to manage, to serve the poor)
- Generosity (mimicking God's posture)

God's Great Favor Toward Us

GRACE

Perhaps the most foundational concept of all is grace: the favor of God upon us that we did not earn nor do we deserve.

Grace is "unmerited favor" and the doctrine that most aptly describes God's provision of Christ, whose sinless life was taken as a way to bridge the chasm between humans and God. As the sinless Christ died in our place, he got what he did not deserve and so did we. We were provided the opportunity to be in a life-giving and life-everlasting relationship with God.

The parable Jesus told of the workers in the vineyard, some who worked a few hours and others who worked all day illustrates the concept of grace. When they all got paid the same amount of money at the end of the day, it was regarded as unreasonable to the characters of that drama as it would be to you or me today.

In their frustration, they wondered, "How could someone who worked only a few hours get paid the same as someone who worked all day?" The Matthew 20 account models the goodness of God by using an economic exchange where ultimately the boss asks, "Don't I have the right to do what I want with my own money? Or are you envious because I am generous?" (Matthew 20:15).

When it comes to creating a culture of generosity in a congregation, our spiritual family heritage goes in our favor. Our heavenly Father is open-handed and indiscriminate in his love and generosity. And the parable to illustrate grace involves a transfer of money and possessions—this is something that should catch our attention and merits further study.

FORGIVENESS

A theological cousin to grace is forgiveness. And understandably and reasonably, most of us think about this as God not holding our sins against us or in an account—we are free from moral responsibility because of

Christ's work on our behalf.

Jeremiah writes about the New Covenant being a time that God will forgive His people's iniquity and "remember their sin no more." (Jeremiah 31:34) In this passage we capture one of the most wonderful aspects of God: his forgetfulness of our sin.

In the disciples' prayer, we pray, "Forgive us our debts as we forgive our debtors." I was primarily taught by parents and pastors that this was best interpreted (as some traditions will recite) as "trespasses" (sins) and those who "trespass against us" (people who have wronged us in some way). And that our commitment through a prayer like this was to treat people's wrongs as God treats ours—by not holding it against them in any way. And this notion certainly still stands.

Even a cursory survey of commentators, however, reveals that this prayer was written against the backdrop of biblical seventh-year laws (Deuteronomy 15) where actual monetary debts were forgiven as a practice of God's people. The tie to the financial facet of indebtedness is clear. Yet, likely most of us do not attribute the undertone of actual financial debt relief in this prayer to the way we interpret it.

REDEMPTION

Redemption refers to the deliverance from sin and also links to the idea of being "bought back." In culture, where slavery was a part of the social and economic structure, the concept of paying a price to free a person from bondage to another was not unfamiliar.

In Christian theology, redemption is a metaphor for what is achieved through the Atonement; therefore, there is a metaphorical sense in which the death of Jesus pays the price of a ransom, releasing Christians from bondage to sin and death.[13]

Peter writes reminding believers that "it was not with perishable things such as silver or gold that you were redeemed from the empty way of life handed down to you from your ancestors, but with the precious blood of Christ, a lamb without blemish or defect." (1 Peter 1:18-19) So, redemption here clearly shows that something was paid (the blood of the perfect Christ) for our release from an empty way of life.

13   https://en.wikipedia.org/wiki/Redemption_(theology)

Again, another block in the foundation of our theology has a tie to economy, further forging the idea that money and its use is a reflection of the give and take of the spiritual dimension.

PROVISION

Years ago, someone pointed out to me the link between Psalm 24 (everything belongs to God) and Psalm 23 (we shall never be in want).

The concept of God's provision is a peculiar one because there is so much disparity between what some people have compared to others. Some believers in this world will have more than just their "daily bread" and have much to spare. Arguably, others may not even have daily bread. My first visit to Kenya revealed the difference between the reality of those in third world settings and my experience in the suburban United States. We eat two or three meals a day, and many of the people I spent time with eat a meal every two or three days.

Still, the Scripture seems to remind us that God is a God of provision. He is Jehovah Jireh which means "the Lord will provide," the name for God used in the narrative of his provision of a sacrifice to replace Issac on the altar. My suspicion is that we are more likely to misinterpret or mismanage God's provision than the possibility that God missed his promise to take care of us.

When Jesus is teaching about the lure of serving money instead of God because we cannot serve two masters, he asks, "Look at the birds of the air, that they do not sow, neither do they reap, nor gather into barns, and yet your heavenly Father feeds them. Are you not worth much more than they?" (Matthew 6:26).

So we need to be reminded of our Heavenly Father's love and provision for us and perhaps offer the prayer captured in Proverbs that says, "Give me neither poverty nor riches; feed me with the food that is my portion, lest I be full and deny Thee and say, 'Who is the Lord?' Or lest I be in want and steal, and profane the name of my God" (Proverbs 30:8-9).

ABUNDANCE

Abundance, as illuminated by the Old and New Testaments and the words of Christ who desires that we would have "life to the full" (John 10:10) is about God's provision regularly and constantly available to meet our needs. Some have taken it to an extreme to justify opulence or surplus as a sign of God's favor.

The theology of Abundance is a fairly straightforward aspect of the Christian faith in particular; it says that you shouldn't hoard your resources out of fear, but that you should give freely as God has given to you.

The opposite is the glass-half-empty of a *scarcity mindset*—that there is a limited or scarce amount of resources so we should act like misers even while calling it frugality. The inner dialogue of this person or group is, *"Don't let anything slip away—you may never get it back."*

> *A theology of scarcity*
> *causes us to clench our fingers*
> *around God's gifts.*
> *We'd better hang on to that one*
> *because it might be the last one*
> *We know that we've done wrong*
> *and must trick God into thinking*
> *we're deserving of these gifts.*
> *A theology of abundance*
> *keeps our fingers splayed open*
> *and allows us to give our gifts away*
> *because we know there's an infinite amount more*
> *where that came from*
> *deservedly so or not.*
>
> *- Jonas Ellison* [14]

I asked my friend Pastor Wendell Hutchins about the idea of prosperity and abundance in the network of charismatic churches of which he is a part. He wrote, "Some of us unknowingly allowed the conversation about abundance to be hijacked by television preachers with all the hocus-pocus prosperity teaching. Many of us are now lumped in with the buy-a-new-jet preachers. But at a very basic and childlike level, we have a theology that says we believe God is inclined to bless his children and has a history of doing that. There are not guarantees, and people with wealth are not better nor more favored than those without it."

---

[14]   https://medium.com/tabletalk/a-theology-of-abundance-6917e21d1d31

Our Response To God's Favor

SABBATH

It may come as no surprise at this point in our review that when God established the Ten Commandments, so many of them were centered on being satisfied with what God has provided. Ultimately, this is an outgrowth of our money or economic life—at least in part, right?

Walter Bruggeman, in his work Money and Possessions, recognizes the socio-economic nuance of the Ten Commandments as a sign of how we are to understand the power of money and insatiable desire.

The last five commands (no murder, adultery, stealing, lying, and coveting the neighbor's wife, land and belongings) are about not taking or desiring to take something that doesn't belong to you. And to top it all, he writes that Sabbath, a quintessential concept in all of the Bible and spiritual life, is "counter-cultural because it is counter-economic." [15]

At some level, the 10 Commandments point out the fact that our behavior can quickly slip into what equates to saying to God: "What you gave me is not enough; I will take what I want whether it belongs to me or not."

Sabbath is not only about rest, it is about restraint. As it says in Proverbs, "Do not wear yourself out to get rich; have the wisdom to show restraint." (Proverbs 23:4) And in Deuteronomy 8:17-18, Moses reminds the people that when they have settled down on the other side of the wanderings in the wilderness and begin to enjoy the modern lifestyle:

"You may say to yourself, My power and the strength of my hands have produced this wealth for me. But remember the Lord your God, for it is he who gives you the ability to produce wealth..."

Our relationship with God should be characterized by stopping our economic energies regularly to show gratitude to the one who allows us the opportunity to have resources in the first place. Once again, economic behavior is a barometer of spiritual loyalties.

---

15   Money and Possessions, Walter Bruggeman, p196

CONTENTMENT

One dictionary defines *contentment* as "the state of being mentally or emotionally satisfied with things as they are."[16]

The Bible presents a vision for economic life that doesn't depend on ever-increasing consumption to prevent us from feeling disappointed. In this vision, it is possible to have enough and to cease longing for more.[17]

In the teaching of Jesus, Paul, Timothy, and in many places in the Old and New Testaments, the theme of contentment seems to be critical. I am convinced that God knew we would need multiple reminders from a mosaic of teaching voices over a thousand years because it is a deep struggle for most. Consider just a few excerpts from Scripture:

Jesus said, "Therefore I tell you, do not worry about your life, what you will eat or drink; or about your body, what you will wear. Is not life more important than food, and the body more important than clothes?" (Matthew 6:25).

Paul indicated he knew the secret of contentment: "I know what it is to be in need, and I know what it is to have plenty. I have learned the secret of being content in any and every situation, whether well fed or hungry, whether living in plenty or in want. I can do everything through Him who gives me strength" (Philippians 4:12-13).

Paul wrote to Timothy: "Godliness is a means of great gain, when accompanied by contentment. For we have brought nothing into the world, so we cannot take anything out of it either. And if we have food and covering, with these we shall be content. But those who want to get rich fall into temptation and a snare and many foolish and harmful desires which plunge men into ruin and destruction. For the love of money is a root of all sorts of evil, and some by longing for it have wandered away from the faith, and pierced themselves with many a pang. But flee from these things, you man of God; and pursue righteousness, godliness, faith, love, perseverance and gentleness. Fight the good fight of faith; take hold of the eternal life to which you were called..." (I Tim. 6:6-12)

Solomon reminds us that "whoever loves money never has enough," (Ecclesiastes 5:10) and the writer of Hebrews encourages us to be

---

16   https://www.dictionary.com/browse/contentment

17   https://www.theologyofwork.org/key-topics/provision-wealth/redeeming-the-economic-sphere/we-are-to-develop- and-model-right-attitudes-to-provision-and-wealth/from-an-attitude-of-discontentment-to-contentment

free from the love of money "being content with what you have" (Hebrews 13:4).

SACRIFICE

A word that may have distorted meaning or connotation in the modern context is sacrifice: a critical theme of scripture. Those less aware of the arc of Scripture may tend to think of animal sacrifice—and this is not entirely off the mark. Or with little knowledge of scripture, sacrifices of all kinds (including human) are part of exotic religious practices or B-level horror films.

But, in a precursor to the arrival of Jesus Christ, various sacrifices were made as faithful foreshadowing of a time to come when the ultimate sacrifice, Jesus, would abolish the practice forever.

The reason this theme is important is because of what it compels us to do. Because of God's great sacrifice on our behalf, we make sacrifices to honor God. "For God so loved the world that he gave his one and only Son, that whoever believes in him shall not perish but have eternal life" (John 3:16).

We are no longer in a tribal and pre-modern context. And regardless, the need for animal sacrifice was obliterated by the death, burial, and resurrection of Jesus Christ.

But what stands of the concept are a few important things:

1) God is willing to give up something he cherishes (His son) for a greater mission (our salvation).
2) We can mimic that part of God's image in each of us—that is, we can "give up" things of value for a higher purpose.

STEWARDSHIP

Stewardship is a common word in the church, but may need a "brush up" on its definition. It has been perhaps worn out and overused to the point that many members of the congregation may associate the word with the annual fund drive. Yet, it holds more significance to the Christian than an annual pledge.

Stewardship is a theological belief that humans are responsible for taking care of the world. People who believe in stewardship are usually people who believe in one God that created the universe and all within it—that they must take care of creation forever.

A biblical worldview of stewardship can be consciously defined as: "Utilizing and managing all resources God provides for the glory of God and the betterment of His creation." The central essence of biblical worldview stewardship is managing everything God brings into the believer's life in a manner that honors God and impacts eternity.[18]

Stewardship connotes the idea of responsibility and opportunity. We are responsible to use God's gifts to us for God's purposes and we have the opportunity to make a big difference in the world. It definitely covers more than the management of financial resources, but is often utilized to remind people of the fact that God is the owner of all things (Colossians 1:16) and we are to manage His resources with His values as preeminent in our decisions.

We get the sense that any resources we have may be passing through our hands on the way to someone else. Paul reminded the Corinthian Christians that, "you will be made rich in every way so that you can be generous on every occasion" (2 Corinthians 9:11).

GENEROSITY

This is where the rubber meets the road. The whole idea of this book is to declare what we believe about generosity and its importance in the Christian life, and then integrate it into the way we lead our congregations.

According to the Cambridge English Dictionary, generosity is a willingness to give help or support, especially more than is usual or expected.[19]

There are a number of words in Scripture that have meanings that hover around generosity (good, noble, ready to impart, abundance, etc) and the word *eumetádotos* ("giving over what is good") refers to spontaneous, willing giving and emphasizes being ready for outreach.

According to Strong's, eumetadotos describes someone who "open-handedly" and willingly shares and stands "ready to impart."[20]

---

18   Charles Bugg, "Stewardship" in Holman Bible Dictionary (Holman: Tennessee, 1991), 1303-1304
19   https://dictionary.cambridge.org/us/dictionary/english/generosity
20   https://biblehub.com/greek/2130.htm

It is this greek word that is used by Paul when giving instructions to Timothy regarding people with wealth. He reminds Timothy with one of the most often quoted (and perhaps misquoted) lines in all of Scripture: "The love of money is a root of all kinds of evil" (1 Timothy 6:10).

But his primary encouragement is to "Command them to do good, to be rich in good deeds, and to be generous and willing to share" (1 Timothy 6:18). And, in one of my favorite declarations in all of the Bible about what generosity results in, we read the idea that "they may take hold of life that is truly life." (6:19)

The power of this phrase is that true life (eternal life beginning now and stretching into forever) is the kind of life that is linked with generosity.

By no means am I implying that generosity alone earns someone an eternity in the presence of God. But Paul tells Timothy to pastor his people in such a way that their willingness to open their hands is a chief sign of a life transformed by Christ. It is as if Paul is saying, "If your people do the generosity thing well, they will be exhibiting the kind of life that only Christ can produce in a human."

So we are beginning to build a case for generosity being a critical part of Christian theology and practice. At the very least, we have a way to use language with our team starting with a common definition. It can be eye-opening to see how much giving, receiving, spending, redeeming, and managing are common themes in the spiritual realm and in the teachings of the Bible. Now, let's turn more specifically to how they apply practically to how we can live out what we find in both the Old and New Testaments.

CHAPTER NINE

The Major Themes And Theologies

Along with colleagues, I had the opportunity to meet Leonard Sweet, professor, theologian, and author of over fifty books.

Twenty years ago, when I was a young pastor, I first encountered his writing and would read it in a bagel shop near the church office. Little did I know back then in Kalamazoo, Michigan I would one day visit with him in his home on an ocean island near Seattle.

There were a handful of mind-blowing aspects of being with him. He is an art collector, book collector, and has set up his home and grounds for spiritual retreat—pathways for prayer and contemplation and multiple buildings to host guests, doctoral students in his care, and more.

As we sat on his sprawling deck on Orcas Island that overlooks the ocean waters north of Seattle, we wondered if the whales that he occasionally saw from that vantage point would swim by during our morning coffee. We did see the bald eagles in the trees above us.

He is a semiotician (an expert in signs and symbols and their meaning) and gave us repeated lessons on word meanings as well as the significance of the furniture we sat in and food that was served—all of it offered because of its deep significance. The word that none of us will forget is Ostranenie.

Ostranenie (pr. Ah-stra-nen-ee) is the concept of defamiliarization—looking at common things in an uncommon or strange way in order to more deeply appreciate or understand. Sweet helped us see this as a spiritual practice of high significance—that we tend to get in ruts about our view of Scripture, God, people and the creation around us and need fresh perspective. We may be missing something God is trying to tell us.

A fresh perspective came for me through the writing of professor and author Craig Blomberg. I am indebted to him as he has wrestled with this topic with doctoral level precision, but boiled the concepts down for the rest of us.

My book is a far cry from an academic treatment of the topic of generosity. It is meant to be a practical reference, a playbook for creating a congregation characterized by generous living. But minds like Blomberg can do some of the heavy lifting for us and we can benefit from his work. [21]

In Blomberg's seminal work on giving and generosity for the Christian called <u>Heart, Soul, and Money: A Christian View of Possessions</u>, he curates and interprets Scripture and distills themes from the Old and New Testaments as well as the teachings of Jesus.

The ones that bubble to the top include wisdom related to wealth, sabbath, justice, debt, giving, generosity, the poor, and prosperity.

In a massive oversimplification of both Scripture and Blomberg's work, I will cite some key thoughts without comment from each of these sections.

Again, this is a quick reference for church leaders, aiming to provide an Ostranenie experience—a deeper appreciation for something that we have perhaps seen before.

Themes from the Old Testament:

- Humans were fashioned in God's image and called to be his stewards.
- Early in the Bible we learn that it is possible to be both rich and obedient to God.
- As best we can tell, the only loans granted in ancient Israel were to help poor people.
- The Sabbath, sabbatical year, and Jubilee prevented the uninterrupted accumulation of wealth.
- In addition to taxes Jews paid to foreign empires, they were under the "triple tithe of Leviticus and Deuteronomy as requiring them to pay back temple authorities twenty-three-and-one-third percent of their annual income.
- The laws of gleaning taught farmers to leave on the ground what was not collected on the first try at any harvest for poor people to pick up.

21 Heart, Soul, and Money: A Christian View Of Possessions
Craig L. Blomberg College Press Publishing, Joplin, MO 2000

- In many texts the foreigner was grouped with the widow, the orphan, and the poor in classic examples of the marginalized whom God's people should help.
- To the extent that the people of Israel, especially their leaders, were obedient to his commandments, God would reward them with peace and prosperity.

Themes From The New Testament:

- There need to be no fixed percentages on how much we spend and how much we give away when we are passionately consumed by the commitment to be good stewards of 100% of our material possessions.
- Luke includes the episode with Simon the Magician to warn his readers against any attempt to manipulate God for personal gain.
- The new religious movement (Christianity) was made up of people from all socioeconomic strata almost immediately from its inception.
- Material riches count for nothing in God's eyes and will not outlive life in this world.
- The affluent are tempted to think that their material possessions can replace God.
- If a person claims to be a Christian, is aware of the acute physical needs of desperately poor believers at home or abroad, is in any position to help, but never does a single thing except wish them well, that person's inaction disproves his or her profession of faith.
- God's people should peacefully be at the forefront of movements in every day and age that work for justice for all in this life as well as preparing people spiritually for the next life.
- Paul makes clear that giving is the voluntary outgrowth of the larger Christian process of sanctification.
- The implementation of Paul's principles should call on Christians who earn more than others to give a higher percentage of their income to the Lord's work, including caring for the poor.
- Material possessions are a good gift from God meant for his people to enjoy.

The Teachings Of Jesus:

- No Christian is promised material prosperity as the result of adequate obedience to Christ.
- God wants to answer prayer for assistance at both the spiritual and material levels.
- Faithfulness with material possessions has a direct bearing on the amount of trust God will give us with spiritual treasure.
- The one who refuses to do anything with what he or she has been given is condemned outright as no true disciple. The true disciple will care for the needs of hurting people in our world today.
- Believers should not give with the hopes of receiving public acclaim.
- Jesus calls his followers to give generously and sacrificially.
- The widow's mite counted for more because it was a higher percentage of what she owned.

I suggest you pause for a moment (or longer) and consider the thick-with-importance bullet lists above with your team. If you haven't already, you may want to grab a highlighter and mark the bullet points above that are particularly relevant to you and your church.

I grew up in church, went to Christian college and seminary, pastored churches, and have been around Christian leaders for arguably my whole life. Yet, I have never heard a teacher or preacher illuminate the topic to this extent, so I have a lot of ground to make up. Perhaps you do, too?

How can these above concepts pulled from Blomberg (and Scripture) inform the way we lead, teach, and act when it comes to the very important and deeply spiritual topics of justice, the poor, wealthy, the foreigner, the widow and more?

Remember that we are on our way to articulating (actually writing out) what we believe about generosity and giving. So mark up the phrases and concepts that you think may make the final cut for your church's statement.

One of the most appealing parts of our Christian faith is this thread of deep generosity urged by Scripture that, if lived well, could truly bring God's heart to earth as it is in heaven. While we are at it, let's take one more pass through parts of Scripture that may help us as we curate some of this beautifully rich teaching as we develop our statements of belief.

CHAPTER TEN

Proverbs, Parables, And Paul

I f you are anywhere near as old as me, you will remember a book that captured the hearts of many in 1990. Robert Fulghum's <u>All I Really Need To Know I Learned In Kindergarten</u> not only became a *New York Times* best-selling book, but the title itself became a euphemism for getting back to the basics.

The book was a smash hit because it represented a pursuit of the simple and (literally) elementary approach to how life works well. Consider a few of the book's reminders:

- Share everything
- Play fair
- Don't hit people
- Put things back where you found them
- Clean up your own mess
- Don't take things that aren't yours
- Say you're sorry when you hurt somebody
- Wash your hands before you eat
- Flush
- Warm cookies and cold milk are good for you [22]

When it comes to the basic themes of Scripture in regard to creating a culture of generosity, it is not hard to identify the core principles.

You could ask a non-Christian person on the street and they would probably guess mostly correctly: be giving, help poor people, don't let wealth make you a jerk, and so on.

At the same time, the references to giving and the life of a faithful disciple feel as numerous as the stars—thousands of little flashes of light scattered throughout the pages of the Bible. And this can actually cause

---

22   Robert Fulghum, 1990. All I Really Need To Know I Learned In Kindergarten. Villard Books: New York, 1990. page 6-7

some level of confusion. How do we collect them all and which should inform how we write out our theology of generosity?

That is why, as you can tell by now, I have attempted to summarize and list out concepts for us to consider as we are developing our theology of generosity. So as much as this chapter could be a whole book (and those books have been written), it is meant to be a brief download of some of the "hot spots" in Scripture. Let's turn to Proverbs, the Parables of Jesus, and the instructions from Paul.

Proverbs

Author and theologian Kevin DeYoung provides a healthy approach to what he describes as an overabundance of Scripture on the topic of money and possessions.

The Bible says so much on the topic, some create what looks like a patchwork quilt of sewn together Bible verses as opposed to a healthy sense of what God would have us live out.

For instance, he says it is easy to see where someone could either create a theology of prosperity (God wants us to be rich) or austerity (God prefers us to be poor) depending on how they want to pull proof from the text.

He believes (and I agree) that Proverbs is a good place to start in developing a biblical theology of possessions. If you started with Genesis, you might conclude God always prospers his people. If you started with Amos, you might think all rich people are oppressors.

But Proverbs looks at wealth and poverty from several angles. And because Proverbs is a book of general maxims, the principles in Proverbs are more easily transferable to God's people at different times and places.

DeYoung's Ten Principles on Money and Possessions from Proverbs

1. There are extremes of wealth and poverty that provide unique temptations to those who live in them (Prov. 30:7-9).
2. Don't worry about keeping up with the Joneses (Prov. 12:9; 13:7).
3. The rich and poor are more alike than they think (Prov. 22:2; 29:13).
4. You can't out-give God (Prov. 3:9-10; 11:24; 22:9).

5. Poverty is not pretty (Prov. 10:15; 14:20; 19:4).
6. Money cannot give you ultimate security (Prov. 11:7; 11:28; 13:8).
7. The Lord hates those who get rich by injustice (Prov. 21:6; 22:16, 22-23).
8. The Lord loves those who are generous to the poor (Prov. 14:21, 31; 19:7; 28:21).
9. Hard work and good decision-making usually lead to increased prosperity (Prov. 6:6-11; 10:4; 13:11; 14:24; 21:17, 20; 22:4, 13; 27:23-27; 28:20).
10. Money isn't everything. It does not satisfy (Prov. 23:4-5). It is inferior to wisdom (Prov. 8:10-11, 18-19; 24:3-4). It is inferior to righteousness (10:2; 11:4; 13:25; 16:8; 19:22; 20:17; 28:6). It is inferior to the fear of the Lord (Prov. 15:16). It is inferior to humility (Prov. 16:19). It is inferior to good relationships (Prov. 15:17; 17:1). [23]

The Parables and Teaching of Jesus

Many of us who are pastors or in church leadership will often lean on the truth that Jesus was often talking about money. I will exaggerate for effect when presenting and say things like, "Jesus seemed to be as obsessed with money as I am."

Ironically, though we regularly note Jesus' emphasis on money in his teaching and conversations with both rich and poor alike, he rarely asked someone to give. And at that point in history, there wasn't an organized form of the church that we would understand today. So we certainly cannot cite his words to compel people to become a recurring digital giver to their church.

I am convinced, however, that Jesus was cleverly showing how his hearers were missing the point about the deeply spiritual nature of possessions. As mentioned earlier, Jesus could recognize a rival and knew that in the first century as well as today, money creates a false hope that needs to be ruptured.

Jesus regularly pointed out the power of money via illustration or parable. Volumes have been written about the meaning and importance of the parables of Jesus that broach the topic of money.

"Jesus talked about money all the time. Look closely at the parables of Jesus and count the ones that refer to money," says stewardship expert and author Dan Conway. "If you didn't know better, you'd say that all Jesus cared about was drachmas, denarii, and the coins that belonged to Caesar." [24]

Not everyone agrees on how many parables are in the Gospels—since parables can be defined many ways as stories, pithy quotes, or proverbs— but most Scripture experts agree on roughly 40 recorded parables of Jesus. Of those, nearly half speak directly about money—for example, the pearl of great price, the lost coin, the silver talents.

Of the other parables, many also touch on material wealth: the Prodigal Son squandering his inheritance (Lk 15:11-32), Lazarus and the rich man (Lk 16:19- 31), or the day laborers in the vineyard (Mt 20:1-16).

The use of money also occasioned many of Jesus' teachings: the widow's two coins (Mk 12:41-44); Caesar's taxes (Mt 22:15-22); the rich young man (Mt 19:16-24); and Zaccheus the tax collector (Lk 191-10).

Then there are the famous quotes: "Where your treasure is, there also your heart will be" (Mt 6:21); "Take nothing for the journey, neither walking stick, nor sack, not food, nor money" (Lk 9:3); and, most famous of all: "You cannot serve both God and Mammon" (Lk 16 and Mt 6:24).

Understanding all of the implications of Jesus' teaching here for both the first hearers as well as the modern context is not always simple. Suffice it to say, however, that the topic was critically important to our Savior. [25]

For instance, an excerpt from Dr. Klaus Issler's book <u>Living into the Life of Jesus</u> can give us a super-summary of Jesus' view:

1. **Stop letting obsessive worry about material needs overwhelm us.** Doing so demonstrates lack of trust in God ("little faiths," Matt. 6:30; Luke 12:28). Through such paralyzing anxiety we become enslaved to money (Matt. 6:24–25) and act like those outside God's family.

2. **Grow our trust in God's provision for material needs. Nature offers a daily reminder:** if God provides food for birds and beauty

24   https://www.thecompassnews.org/compass/2003-10-24/foundations.shtml
25   Living into the Life of Jesus, by Dr. Klaus Issler (ThM, 1977), published by IVP Books https:// voice.dts.edu/article/christs-teaching-on-money-issler/

for flowers, God can provide for his children, who are more valuable to him (Matt. 6:26; Luke 12:26). Trusting in God frees us to pursue God's kingdom as a number one priority (Matt. 6:33; Luke 12:31).

3. **Be thankful to God for past provision of material needs.**
   God already knows and cares about our material needs (Matt. 6:32; Luke 12:30).

4. **Manage wisely the finances God entrusts to our care, with an eye on the future.**
   Jesus commands, "But store up for yourselves treasures in heaven" (Matt. 6:20), giving our uppermost attention and ambitions to what lasts for eternity. Jesus commands us to become "faithful and wise manager[s]" (Luke 12:42, 16:10–12). At death, we'll give an account for our use of God's material resources on loan to us, as illustrated in two parables (Matt. 25:14–30; Luke 19:11–27; cf. Matt. 12:36–37). To give a good account requires wise planning.

5. **Give generously to the needy from the material resources on loan from God.**
   "Sell your possessions and give to the poor" (Luke 12:33; Matt. 6:2–4). Jesus provides a basis for our giving now: "'Do not be afraid, little flock, for your Father has been pleased to give you the kingdom'" (Luke 12:32). With such a grand inheritance guaranteed—the new heavens and new earth involving both immaterial and material benefits—we can grow trust in God now for our own material needs and increase our generous sharing with the needy.

The primary takeaway for church leaders from even a drive-by study of Jesus' teaching is that we can gain courage. If our Lord knew that the spiritual life would be highly influenced by one's belief and practice around money, then we can leverage the topic to challenge and grow disciples. Said more directly: The topic of money should not be conspicuous in its absence from our teaching, since we claim to be grooming people to know and follow Jesus.

Paul's Teaching on How to Give

As the early church developed, the instructions and warnings about money became more tactical. The teachings of the Apostle Paul are likely the most familiar to church leaders as they seem to be more direct (less conceptual) and helpful when it comes to helping congregations know how and why to be generous.

The early church, with all of its stops, starts, and stumbles as it grew in its understanding of itself, had more than a handful of instances where money needed to be addressed.

Taylor Martin Wise provides a helpful listing of Paul's instructions to the church on <u>how</u> to give:

Generously	2 Corinthians 8:2-4; 9:6
Regularly/Systematically	1 Corinthians 16:2
Proportionately	1 Corinthians 16:2; 2 Corinthians 8:11-12
Sacrificially	2 Corinthians 8:3-5
Willingly	2 Corinthians 8:11-12
Voluntarily	2 Corinthians 9:7
Cheerfully	2 Corinthians 9:7
Eagerly	2 Corinthians 8:10-11; 9:2
Enthusiastically	2 Corinthians 9:2
Excellently	2 Corinthians 8:7
Strategically	2 Corinthians 9:12-15
Scrupulously	1 Corinthians 16:3-4; 2 Corinthians 8:18-21 [26]

26   The Biblical Purpose Of Money: A Balanced View
A Thesis By Taylor Martin Wise, Reformed Theological Seminary, 2005 p200

So, we have created a reference guide in this chapter and the previous one—looking at Old and New Testament concepts, as well as the teaching that emerges from "hot spots" like Proverbs, Parables, and Paul.

One more stop-off before we start penning our theology of generosity: the most frequent questions we tend to hear from members of our congregation when we broach the topic of giving.

CHAPTER ELEVEN

The Most Frequently Asked Giving Questions

My grandfather was a fascinating man. I knew him but was young when he passed. Most of what I know about him, I learned from my father.

Travis Pearson Gibbs (Pop Pop to me) was the son of a coal miner. He took up the harp like his father and became proficient enough to sit in on occasion with the Philadelphia Orchestra in the 1950s. He also sold sheet music for Wurlitzer in Baltimore for a while. He did interior design. One of his hobbies was building H.O. scale trains, along with hand-crafting the dramatic scenes and figurines that would adorn the train platforms. I would love to sit and chat with him again, but I will have to wait to pass to the next life so we can hang out for a while.

But his primary job for the years he raised my father was that he was a "super"—a handyman and superintendent for apartment complexes in downtown Philly.

Therefore, when he passed away, my father inherited hundreds and hundreds of tools of every size and shape. There were racks and racks of tools so specialized that my father kept them only for sentimental reasons, and moved them from house to house until one day when he retired, he was able to finally retire from toting tools.

And here's the fact. Most of us in modern life only need a handful of essential tools—not hundreds. Brett McKay, founder of the Art Of Manliness website says there are a dozen tools everyone needs.

See if you agree with him:

1) Claw hammer
2) Flathead screwdriver
3) Phillips screwdriver

4)   Tape Measure

5)   Crescent Wrench

6)   Socket Wrench

7)   Vise Grip

8)   Needle Nose Pliers

9)   Cordless Drill

10) Crosscut Saw

11) Level

12) Utility Knife [27]

The point is, if you have these 12 tools, you have the answer to most average-guy-in-average-home problems and challenges. Not only do I agree with the above list (although I do really like my battery-powered stud finder), but I see that a lot of life and leadership boils down to having some basic stuff in order.

In the case of being in senior leadership of a church, the good news is that if you wrestle down the answers to nine or ten frequently asked questions about giving and stewardship, you will likely have the "tools" you need.

I have compiled a list of the frequent flyers—the questions leaders will most often be ased. I will order them from the most often asked to the least, from my perspective:

1) Are Christians required to tithe?

The tithe is a concept that is fairly understood as a tenth of one's increase or income. What is less understood is the level of intensity with which followers of Christ should adhere to this kind of giving. Is it an Old Testament concept or rule that got upended by Christ's insistence on being free from any burden of the law?

Another confusion lies in what each church expects of the faithful, and whether or not that has any consequence. Meaning, there is a significant difference between churches that see tithing as an act of obedience versus a target to shoot at and possibly hit someday.

In the former case, does not tithing mean one is living in disobedience

---

27   https://www.artofmanliness.com/articles/12-essential-tools-for-a-toolbox/

to God (and therefore sinning)? And in the case of the "tithe as the ideal target," what level of accountability or challenge is built into this less clear instruction? A church moving even farther away from the tithe concept will have a "give whatever you feel led to give" paradigm.

Said another way: "There are those who uphold tithing as an integral part of the Christian life, believing it is required of everyone. At the other extreme, there are those who reject tithing as a practice along with circumcision, foot washing, and the observance of the dietary laws. Between these two extremes are many variations of interpretations and opinions." [28]

As you reaffirm (or re-consider) your church's position on the biblical concept of the tithe, consider the following continuum:

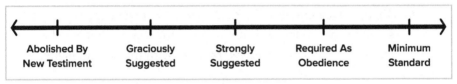

| Abolished By New Testament | Graciously Suggested | Strongly Suggested | Required As Obedience | Minimum Standard |

Figure 11.1

The way pastors and leaders decide to assert a position on the tithe will become part of the generosity culture of that church.

For over 15 years, since I met him at Branch Creek Community Church in Pennsylvania, I have referred to Pastor Dave Detweiler's easy-to-digest breakdown of the tithe in scripture:

Here is what the Bible says—and doesn't say—about tithing. This summary doesn't address all of the issues, but it keeps the conversation going in a biblical direction.

1. Many ancient cultures practiced tithing in some form (perhaps because most people counted in tens, based on ten fingers. Good thing we don't have 30 fingers, huh?!).

2. Genesis 14:17-20 is the earliest biblical reference to "tithing," and it is prior to the old covenant law being given to Moses. However, it appears to be a one-shot deal that was voluntary.

28   Powell, E.A., and Rushdoony, R.J, Tithing and Dominion, CA: Ross House Books, 1979 p213

3. Same goes for the only other reference prior to the law, Genesis 28:20-22. That is, there is no indication there either that such an act was commanded or repeated.

✓

4. Leviticus 27:30-33 is the first reference under the old covenant law, where tithing is required of God's people as an act of worship (note also Deuteronomy 14:23).

5. In Numbers 18:21-32, we find that such tithing went to support the Levites (one of the 12 tribes of Israel), who served in the Tent of Meeting (tabernacle), and later the Temple. They had no other source of income, as per God's instruction, and they were in turn to tithe to the priests.

6. Then, in Deuteronomy 14:22-27, we read of what appears to be a second tithe—one that is not to go to the Levites, but is to be enjoyed in a kind of *"national potluck"* (with the Levites invited)!

7. What's more, in Deuteronomy 14:28-29 we read of yet another tithe, given every three years, that is directed to the poor and marginalized of society. This is perhaps related to the second tithe.

8. So how many tithes were commanded under the old covenant? There remains some debate, but by the time of Jesus most Jews understood there to be three, adding up to a 23.3% *"tithe"* (prorated annually: two annual tithes, and one every three years).

9. Toward the end of the old covenant era, in Malachi 3:6-12, we learn that God's people were not obeying God as it related to tithing (and other obligations under the old covenant), and they suffered for it—just as God said they would in the stipulations of the covenant (see, for example, Deuteronomy 28).

10. Jesus mentions tithing only twice, and both references still have the old covenant era in view (Matthew 23:23 = Luke 11:42, and

18:12). He never connects tithing with the new covenant.

11.   Similarly, and quite significantly, no other New Testament text explicitly commands tithing (even where we might have expected it), although much is revealed about being radically generous. The standard is, in a sense, much higher: The more we have, the more we are able to give—and should give!

12.   All this being said, "tithing," or giving 10%, can be a great initial goal on the path of radical generosity. But Christians are not *required* to tithe. Nor should we stop at 10%! Our question, as committed followers of Christ, should be, "How can I manage my affairs so that I can give more?" [29]

2)   Should the whole tithe come to the church?

When I was a Senior Pastor, I would have preferred that people in the congregation gave 10% (which most did not do) and all of it to the church as well (which most did not do). Most pastors that I interact with are fully aware of this reality. Though neither happened, I was mentored by a theological tribe that would have used Malachi 3:10 and the phrase "bring the whole tithe to the storehouse" to undergird the idea that in fact the tithe should be given to the church (their interpretation allowed for storehouse to be synonymous with the current local church body).

Since then, I can think of more practical reasons than biblical justification for such a position. I still think it is a great idea for church people to give 10% to their church and then even more to other groups and individuals as well. What a blast that would be!

The point of this book, however, is for your church not to agree or disagree with me, but to use the thoughts within these pages to catalyze a discussion—then you decide as a church how you will respond to this question.

It may be helpful to get a sense for the landscape of what Christians actually think about this question through the result of a research project

29   Used with permission by Dave Detweiler

conducted by Lifeway. Here are some of the raw findings:

- 98% say money from tithes can go to their church
- 48% say funds can go to a Christian ministry
- 35% say tithes can go to another church
- 34% say tithes can go to an individual in need

Some churchgoers (18 percent) say their donations to a secular charity can be part of their tithe:

- Lutherans (44 percent)
- Methodists (33 percent)
- Baptists (12 percent)

Fewer than half of churchgoers (47 percent) say only giving to the church counts for tithing. [30]

In a practical sense, I have seen churches that promote tithing to the church suggest (even strongly) that the tithe comes to the church and offerings (over and above the tithe) can be spread around to works of God through charities and other organizations. In more recent years, I have seen more church leaders loosen their laces a bit more around the insistence that it come only to the church and simply encourage generosity toward the work of God.

Side-note about the wealthy giver: I have also found this "tithing only to the church" to be impractical for very wealthy people, for whom regular income is not what most of us can relate to. Sometimes they don't even take a paycheck in a regular pattern. Sometimes they do not need to. And tithing from people with way-above-average wealth (or primarily asset-based wealth) could actually hurt their church.

In my experience, they tend to spread their giving around to multiple organizations (including the church), but giving 10% to any one group would make them too large of a percentage of that group's income—it creates a vulnerability at a church, for instance, when one family's tithe would account for 20-30% (or more) of the church's annual revenue. More on this later in the book.

---

30   https://lifewayresearch.com/2018/05/10/churchgoers-say-they-tithe-but-not-always-to-the-church/

3) Should I tithe before or after taxes?

This has always been an interesting question to me. I have to admit at the outset a bit of cynicism about it—please forgive me.

In my frustration, sometimes when asked this question in a live audience I blurt out something like, "Well, just pick one—because most of you in the room give 2 or 3% of your income, so if you are actually choosing between 10% of gross or 10% of net, we are headed in the right direction." It is rather uncharitable of me to shift into my "grumpy old pastor" routine at that point, but it certainly gets everyone's attention.

But my frustration is rooted in a real belief. Let's imagine Christ himself showed up and handed me my paycheck every two weeks. And, imagine the one who is fully God and Creator as well as suffering Savior for the whole world said, "Hey, Greg—the best way for this to work is for you and everyone else to at least put 10% of this into my work in the world." I just can't imagine my reply to Him being, "Thank you, my Lord. One quick question before you leave—should that be on gross or net income?"

Because in my view, if you are asking this question, you have already missed the point.

Ok—that's out of my system. Now some help from the much more gracious Matt Carter of Austin Stone Community Church:

> *In Matthew 22:27, scripture affirms that out of our income we should pay our government what is theirs, and this is in addition to giving God what is His. While giving 10% of our net (after-tax) income may address the issues of the tithe, I'm not sure it addresses the issue of giving the first portion to God.*
>
> *God has granted that we each reap certain income. When we tithe off of the net, we are giving the very first portion of our income to the government. Thus, I personally tithe from my gross (before-tax) pay. By giving Him, not the government, the first portion of my income, I'm practically expressing my trust in God.* [31]

---

31   http://rh-firstfruits.s3.amazonaws.com/firstfruits/files/2014/02/Austin-Stone-on-Giving.pdf

4) Should pastors look at the giving records?

The reticence on the part of so many pastors to look at giving records, in my experience, either comes from the history and culture of the church or a personal commitment rooted in humility. In the first case, there is an awareness that "our pastor does not look at any of the giving records." This is how the church has always operated.

In the second case, pastors will often say to me, "I don't want to be burdened with knowing who gives what." Or they say, "I don't trust what my heart would do if I had this information."

The often-taboo topic of money is evident when examining clergy's access to financial and donor records. According to a study done by Church Law and Tax, only 55 percent of congregations claimed that their clergy had access to giving records, and among that group, only 58 percent of clergy actually looked at that information. However, these congregations were much more likely to be growing in their revenue. [32]

Malphurs and Stroope offer an alternative viewpoint by contending that "If a pastor needs to know who his mature people are, the acid test is likely their giving. Not only is this important information for raising funds but also for raising up leaders, such as board members, staff, and other critical positions." [33]

They go on to write, "We believe that just as a pastor should know those who have the gift of teaching, gift of faith, or the gift of leadership, they should know those who have the gift of giving." [34]

Thom Rainer gives churches options to consider with the caveat that it always has been a difficult decision for churches. Here are his options for who should be looking at giving records:

The lead pastor and one layperson. This perspective argues that financial stewardship is a spiritual discipline, and the pastor should have access to individual giving to be able to see how the members are doing in this regard. The layperson, of course, is the person who actually keeps the records.

One layperson who guides the pastor. The layperson again is the

---

32   https://www.churchlawandtax.com/web/2019/october/reliable-help-for-building-financially-healthy-congregation.html?start=5

33   Money Matters In The Church: A Practical Guide For Church Leaders Aubrey Malphurs, Steve Stroope Baker Books, Grand Rapids, MI 2007 p40

34   ibid, p41

member keeping financial records. He or she is the only one who has access to giving records. But that person is able to share information with the pastor or other leaders as needed. For example, the financial secretary can inform the pastor or elders about potential future elders according to their giving patterns. I took this approach as a pastor. I did not have access to individual giving patterns, but our financial secretary would let me and other leaders know if a person should be eligible for a leadership role according to their stewardship in the church.

One layperson only. In this example, only the financial secretary (or equivalent) has access to individual giving records. He or she does not provide any input that would reflect this information.

A key group in the church. In some churches, this group is the elders. In some other churches, it is the nominating committee.

A staff person other than the pastor and a layperson. The pastor is specifically precluded from individual giving visibility. Instead, another staff person, such as an associate or executive pastor, has access to the records along with the financial secretary.

No church members. No church member can see the records. Instead, a non-member is recruited or hired to keep the records, but that person does not share the information with any church members. [35]

5) Should giving always be done in secret?

I have a deep respect for many of my mentors from Cargill Associates, with whom I worked from 2001 to 2006. My former boss, Pat Graham, long time president of Cargill Associates had a number of phrases, questions, and teachings that still remain in my heart and my teaching. For instance, he used to wonder out loud, "People are always talking about what they spend. Why can't they talk every once in a while about how or what they give?"

He taught that people talk about their spending by what cars they drive, what vacations they go on, what house they buy or what group they pay dues to. For whatever reason, Christian people have no problem with "spending talk" but insist on silence about their giving. "Giving is between me and God." So they are not silent about money—they are silent about giving.

My experience has led me to conclude that one of the problems with generosity in the church is the silence <u>around specifics</u> when it comes to discipling people with regard to giving. One may hear phrases like, "God loves a cheerful giver" or "Give whatever you feel led to give." And these are not bad, unless that is all people hear.

In my case, my father was very specific with me (as we are with our children) about what we give, how much, and why. But many in the church may have not had that kind of specific mentoring. When we look to places in Scripture like David who specifically enumerated how much of his wealth he would give to the building of the temple, we can see how leaders using specifics (whether public or private) are desperately needed in the church.

Randy Alcorn in his notable work, <u>Money Possessions & Eternity</u> treats this issue at length with a helpful view of the Matthew 6 passage most often cited, "do not let your right hand know what your left hand is doing."

1) The passage is about seeking man's approval instead of God's
2) The phrase is hyperbole—it is to emphasize that we should not give in a spirit of self-congratulation—not that we shouldn't be aware of our own giving or someone else's.
3) Christians were often aware of people's giving—when they (Acts) sold their goods and gave to others, the gift was public.
4) The body of Christ can benefit from seeing open models of generosity like Barnabas's.
5) Christ affirmed the public act of the widow when she gave her two coins.
6) Our congregations need models of every spiritual discipline.

Alcorn goes on: "Though confidentiality in the giving record makes sense, it creates another temptation. Many believers take advantage of the veil of privacy by using it as a cloak for their disobedience in not giving."

It is peculiar to me that if one was consistent with the right-hand-left-hand quotation as being an injunction to "never talk about your giving,"[36] then we should also never pray in public but always in private, and never

---

36   Money, Possessions, and Eternity, Randy Alcorn

talk about fasting or give any indication that we are doing so, since these are all contained in the same passage (Matthew 6:1-18).

6) Should leaders in the church be expected to be generous?

Linked to the question regarding who can see the individual giving data is the question of what is expected of someone in leadership.

John Piper offers a characteristically pointed charge in reference to the example leaders are setting in the church:

"My take on tithing in America is that it's a middle-class way of robbing God. Tithing to the church and spending the rest on your family is not a Christian goal. It's a diversion. The real issue is: How shall we use God's trust fund—namely, all we have—for His glory? In a world with so much misery, what lifestyle should we call our people to live? What example are we setting?" [37]

The research demonstrates that, ultimately, generous churches are led by generous pastors and leaders. It probably should not require any research to understand a basic leadership principle that many of us learned from John Maxwell and others like him: **Everything rises and falls on leadership.**

Another leadership principle that is paramount in my counsel to churches is that leaders need to be able to say, "I am not asking you to do something I am not willing to do myself."

Because I believe that leaders (at all levels) have influence on the church's culture, I ask churches to strongly consider the implications of trying to increase generosity culture if this is not an expectation of leadership.

And as you have already read, I believe this is a deeply spiritual topic (one of the most critical ones for discipleship in the way of Jesus). Therefore, I do not know how we would allow non-givers to lead children, adults, classes, small groups (or anything else for that matter) if they are the primary disciplers, mentors, and teachers of people.

The question of leaders giving needs to be approached carefully at first—especially if it is a shift in philosophy. And, one of the acid tests of accountability is whether or not a board member or senior leader is willing to sit down with a staff member or volunteer leader and talk with them

---

37   https://www.azquotes.com/quote/1317442

directly about the topic.

7) Can I talk to wealthy people about their resources?

Because a majority of money tends to be held by a minority of any population, the concern about how we treat wealthy people versus poor people ought to be a significant concern for the church. This was the case in the early church as much as it is today.

The go-to passage regarding the special treatment of the wealthy is James 2:1-4:

> *My brothers and sisters, believers in our glorious Lord Jesus Christ must not show favoritism. Suppose a man comes into your meeting wearing a gold ring and fine clothes, and a poor man in filthy old clothes also comes in. If you show special attention to the man wearing fine clothes and say, "Here's a good seat for you," but say to the poor man, "You stand there" or "Sit on the floor by my feet," have you not discriminated among yourselves and become judges with evil thoughts?*

It is important to understand that one of the major battles of the early church was to demolish social and economic structures in light of the level playing field that Jesus Christ created. He modeled a new kingdom, a kingdom where everyone has value no matter what. This is the beauty of the gospel.

At the same time, a stern warning to the early church about giving the rich a preferential seat at worship (reinforcing class distinction—the opposite of Jesus' message) and talking to a modern wealthy family about their unique ability to fund the mission of the church are two different things.

It is worth considering the possibility that wealthy people in our churches could benefit from a spiritual conversation about the use of their gifts to make, invest, and give money. We equip and encourage the use of other gifts (teaching, serving, etc.); shouldn't we consider how this would apply to a unique group of people with great opportunity and responsibility in our churches?

If this is viewed in light of the spiritual mentoring (discipleship) of the wealthy, it has great potential for good and healthy discussion. If it is not seen in the light of discipleship but rather as a platform for extra or undue influence of big givers over the church, it is a totally different and unacceptable posture. In this case it edges more closely to the violations James warned about. The wealthy, if anything, often feel more of the weight of responsibility for managing well what God has given them. And pastors and church leaders can be helpful with this.

8) What is the proper view and use of borrowing and debt?

Once again it seems as though church leaders need to decide where they stand on a continuum. To some leaders, and some denominations in particular, debt is seen as very negative and no-debt is a non-negotiable value. To others, it is hardly a discussion point—if the church has borrowing capability and the debt service payments are reasonably "handled" by the church cash flow, it can be used for capital needs. Very few churches will use a line of credit or lending to pay operational costs—this seems to be on the outside edge of the continuum. So borrowing is almost always a question related to building projects.

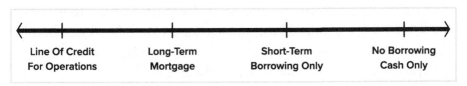

Figure 11.2

Again, Malphurs and Stroope offer a helpful paradigm in deciding your church's approach, as you make a written assertion about your position. Consider these concepts and a short explanation by the authors of what each implies:

Be Careful - Proverbs 22:7 says, "The rich rule over the poor, and the borrower is slave to the lender." Though this is not an outright condemnation of debt, it is a severe warning to avoid it whenever possible. Debt automatically implies vulnerability of some kind.

No Prohibition - The Bible does not seem to prohibit debt. It does warn against it. But someone who claims that the church should not borrow because "debt is sin" has stepped over a line that is not substantiated by the Scripture. It would, at a practical level, be condemnation of anyone who has borrowed money to buy a house.

Reasonable Debt - This is a popular term employed by many churches to talk about the boundaries around debt. These churches will not use debt for operational expenses, for example, and would not borrow more than two times the church's income (even if the bank allowed it).

Opposition to Any Debt - Often connected with the age of a person, their personal view of financial best practice. Some churches still hold declared positions about no debt under any circumstance. The point here is that it is not bad, per se, for a person (or a church) to hold a no-debt stance. Yet, a member of the congregation may be overstepping if they insist their church hold the same stance.

Good Debt vs Bad Debt - Here again, the authors urge thoughtfulness about the reasons and the nature of the debt. Church leaders need to be aware of appreciating vs depreciating assets for which debt may be incurred. As well, there are times when borrowing to build may be better stewardship than waiting for a cash-only build when the costs of construction (because of inflation) will cost the church more in the long run. [38]

My friend and colleague Todd McMichen offers some very practical advice regarding buildings in particular:

The average church which maintains a manageable debt load usually expends 25% or less of its income on a facility. If a church has recently engaged in a significant building project or has over-built in the past, that portion can be up to 30-35%.

The following is a summary explanation of what McMichen recommends as a pathway to avoid putting a church in a position where the size of their debt puts a lid on agility into the future:

38   Money Matters In The Church: A Practical Guide For Church Leaders Aubrey Malphurs, Steve Stroope
Baker Books, Grand Rapids, MI 2007 p137-139

1) Build the right facility at the right time in the right location and it almost always causes growth.
2) Under-build (allowing for future phases) and keep your debt load as low as possible.
3) Develop more leaders and more cash flow—this sets the church up for a stronger ability to address future phases. [39]

9) What About Giving With Strings Attached?

Undoubtedly at some point, each pastor or church leader will be faced with an offer to give from a member of the congregation that is considered *directive giving*.

Whether veield or unveiled, someone will say, "Pastor I will give x amount if you do_____." The directive might be to invest in a particular aspect of ministry, hire a certain person, or any number of other projects.

Sometimes this directive comes from a person seeking undue influence. Often it is a person that has a passion for one area of ministry and wants to avoid the possibility of their gift getting diluted in the general fund. Whatever the motivation of the giver, church leadership needs to decide how they will handle both directive and designated giving.

Directive Giving - when the giver wants an action taken that was not already part of the plans of leadership and for which there is no designated fund into which the money can be invested.

Designated Giving - when the giver has a particular passion that is in line with a special account or designated "bucket" that church leadership has decided should be outside the general fund. For instance a Missions Fund or Building Fund.

The point here should be simple. For instance, you cannot spend the building fund money on the youth mission trip. Or at least you can't without a lengthy process, approvals, and aggravation. But it seems to be a constant tension in the day-to-day decisions of church spending.

---

39   Leading a Generous Church, Todd McMichen, p71-72, Rainer Publishing, 2015

Particularly when one budget line or fund is depleted and another is not.

Thom Rainer writes about how designated funds are not an intrinsic problem themselves—because a designated fund is a bucket that church leadership established for a certain reason. Yet, even these (especially if there are too many of them) can create a problem: they allow givers to circumvent the will and the plan of the church as a whole (which is why I would join Thom in recommending that churches do not create too many of these).

Designated givers are basically saying they don't like the unified budget of the church, so they are going rogue and dictating their preferences over the church as a whole. A church with numerous designated funds can find it has a budget with no teeth. Rainer offers other potential problems designated funds may stir up for churches:

- They create division in the church. Each designated giver is doing things his way or her way.
- They create an environment where advocates of a particular ministry or need of the church might solicit designated funds.
- They often come with stipulations that are difficult or impossible to comply with.
- They often hurt the budget giving of the church.[40]

After looking at these nine questions, perhaps you and your leadership team could add a few that seem to pop up in your context regularly. Again, the point of exploring these questions in the Theology section is that ultimately the day-to-day choices you make are a reflection of what you believe about generosity and its integration into the life of your church.

It may be a fascinating journey to take a leadership team one by one through each of the questions. It will likely give you a better understanding of where people stand with the goal of coming to an assertion by the church (in writing) about a view on debt, designated giving, who can look at the giving records, and more.

By now, I hope you have a page or two of scribbled notes or have dog-eared a few sections of the previous chapters that will help you as you build your plan for the congregation.

---

40   https://thomrainer.com/2018/02/five-dangers-church-designated-funds/

No matter how sound our doctrine is, we know that Jesus ultimately calls us to the life-by-life guidance of discipleship. The most difficult and intimate issues of our spiritual lives are best worked out in friendship and fellowship. That is why the next wave is all about discipleship.

WAVE TWO

DISCIPLESHIP

CREATE A PATHWAY.

Can we disciple people toward generous living?

CHAPTER TWELVE

Our Church's Giving Type

When I was in high school and college trying to figure out my identity, personality, and place in the world, there were fewer official tests and tools than there are today. Most of our discovery came from chatting with friends and mentors. And when I was really on the ball, I would ask God for guidance.

Today, the personality sciences are bigger than ever. Take it from a 3-wing-2 who is an ENFP with a propensity to look at life with the themes of Futurist, Strategic, Achiever, with some Ideation and WOO tossed in.

I can get lost with how much information I have about myself.

Tests like Myers Briggs, DISC, Strengthsfinder, and Enneagram are often met with a common critique: **I don't want to be stereotyped by a test result.**

At the same time, like our parents told us, *"stereotypes exist for a reason."* And though we have realized that this can lead to unfair behavior when it comes to things like race and gender, when it comes to understanding our own personality wiring, it can be very helpful. Personality science helps us with self-awareness as well as appreciation for people different from us. It is also valuable when we are considering moving in a different direction. *Who am I? How do I tend to look at the world? In what context will I thrive?*

My friend and mentor, Will Mancini, has developed a helpful grid for allowing churches to self-identify in answering an essential question: **What is our church's personality type?**

He does not use those exact words, per se. In his book *God Dreams*, he writes about twelve "templates" for churches. Some tend to *prioritize leadership multiplication* or *spiritual formation* or *crisis mobilization*. Other churches can lean toward *geographic saturation* or *need adoption*. Still others are about *institutional renovation* or *anointed amplification*. These may not make sense if you have not read the book (which I highly recommend), but suffice it to say, churches have a certain vibe that impacts their primary mission. [41]

One of the reasons I am writing about developing generosity culture through the framework of the 5 Waves (theology, discipleship, strategy, communication, and integration) is that being prescriptive about a certain tactic or technique will not serve every church *"personality."* A framework like the 5 Waves provides questions and constructs for discussion and self-discovery. Ultimately, each church will have to decide *who are we? and how will we move forward?*

YOUR CHURCH'S GIVING TYPE

Churches need to accurately assess the generosity culture they are creating—either intentionally or unintentionally. There are a few ways I've found to coach church leaders to have a self-discovery conversation with their teams. It all centers around intentionality.

Some churches have a plan—either evolving out of tradition, created by a team or committee, or some combination of both. It may not be as effective as the church would like, but it is certainly proactive. And this is a step in the right direction.

Perhaps your church has a personality that reflects a family resemblance; perhaps you have simply inherited a likeness to your denominational kin. I have been in more than a few half-joking conversations about how Lutherans view debt, or how Baptists teach the tithe. The fact is, *there are repeated patterns of language and expectations that become part of an organizational DNA.* And like all families, there is a mix of functional and dysfunctional.

Churches that do little or nothing proactive about discipling people to be generous also create a kind of culture. It is the "wing and a prayer" approach—a laissez faire attitude toward stepping into giving conversations. Other leaders have struck out on their own and established unique patterns and processes.

None of these options are inherently problematic in one way. For instance, the hands off approach may have worked for a church in terms of

---

41   God Dreams, Will Mancini

its ability to meet budget. I have heard church leaders nearly boast, "We do not talk about money and God just provides."

But all of this should be evaluated in light of its effectiveness in growing hearts and growing generosity. Remember that the mission of the church is discipleship, and the handling of money is only part of that—albeit an essential one.

The importance of this chapter is self-awareness (or church-self-awareness). Consider where your church may land in the following four frameworks when it comes to Giving Type:

1) Tithing, Pledging, or Offering
2) High Expectation vs Voluntary Association
3) Live-The-Vision or Pay-The-Bills
4) Mueller, Taylor, Moody

TITHING, PLEDGING, or OFFERING

At a very basic level, churches tend to reflect one of three principal types in terms of the way they encourage generosity: Tithing, Pledging, or Offering.

This thesis, from the authors of *Money Matters*, is worth considering as we move ahead. The research this team curated led them to the conclusion that "giving is high in tithing churches, medium in pledging churches and low in offering churches. In reality, not all churches fit into one of the three types. Some fall between the types or contain elements of two different types."[42]

In summary, here is the way they describe each type:

Tithing Churches - The defining characteristic of tithing churches is that they see their financial support as coming mainly from members who tithe. All leadership energy is given to ministering to the people and strengthening their commitment to tithing as a part of a life devoted to God. These churches have no annual stewardship program, no pledging, no annual appeal, etc.

42   Money Matters: Personal Giving in American Churches
Hoge, Zech, McNamara, Donahue Westminsters John Knox Press, 1996 Louisville, KY, p98

Pledging Churches - Pledging churches favor tithing, but believe it is unrealistic to expect most members to tithe. The crucial characteristic of these churches is that they have annual stewardship programs asking for pledges, normally in the fall of the year. They usually strive to have all members pledge, and they ask members to think in terms of a percentage of household income when considering what to pledge.

Offering Churches - Offering churches believe in tithing and pledging, but they do not stress either. Their pastors usually wish that the people would tithe or pledge, but they are not forceful in talking about it, and the congregation has no overall sense that tithing and pledging are needed to be in good standing with God and the congregation. These churches have little teaching about the theology of stewardship and the spiritual meaning of gifts to the church. Efforts to increase the giving tend to stress the quality of the program, the cost of maintaining the building and property, and the future vision of the leadership. [43]

One way of evaluating your church in light of these types is to place them on a continuum. Tithing Churches, in this view, represent the churches that teach the expectation is that members give 10% or more of their income. This is the expectation—whether or not it is realized is a separate question.

On the other side of the continuum would be the churches that are—to use the words of the *Money Matters* authors—less "forceful" in talking about it, and have little teaching about the theology of stewardship.

Tithing ———— Pledging ———— Offering

Figure 12.1

In addition to their macro-level description of church types, the specific research Malphurs and Stroope conducted revealed:

1) Having lay leaders manage the finances and lead the stewardship programs helps reduce any suspicions that the clergy are promoting giving solely out of self-interest.

2) Having broad lay participation in the congregation's budgeting and priority setting contributes to the sense of ownership.

43   Money Matters, p99

3) Locally developed mission projects, more than denominational or national mission projects, tend to excite interest and financial support.

4) Congregations must avoid any perception that small cliques of laity run the place and exclude others from having any part in leadership.

5) Full financial accountability and reporting allays suspicions that clergy or a few lay leaders are doing anything in secret.

6) Stewardship teaching about the joy of giving should be coupled with concrete mission efforts that add to the laity's sense of ownership and bring about joy in doing participation and giving. [44]

HIGH EXPECTATION vs VOLUNTARY ASSOCIATION

A small Mennonite congregation in Indiana sets the ultimate example of high expectations and sharing with God. Each year in the late spring, church members gather and share their federal 1040 income-tax forms with one another, so that all will know they have returned the appropriate portion to God. [45]

You may not be reaching for your 1040 right now to hand over. You may even be outraged by the thought. But it does prompt a powerful discussion about what expectations we have, whether they are high or low, how they are communicated, and to whom and how often.

Lyle Schaller makes a basic distinction between two types of Protestant churches, *"high expectation"* churches and *"voluntary associations."* They are two ends of a spectrum with variations between.

High Expectation – require strict adherence to certain doctrinal statements, agreement on criteria to be used in interpreting the Holy Scriptures, regular attendance at corporate worship, a commitment to tithing, and an additional commitment that the whole tithe will come to the specific congregation rather than to other ministries or organizations.

Voluntary Association – have members who maintain great autonomy in belief, participation, the right to withdrawal, and financial support. The

---

44   Money Matters, p172
45   High Expectation Churches Creating Congregations of Generous People, Michaell Durall

members resist demands for adherence to rules.

The closer a church is to a voluntary association, the greater the percentage of the members' giving that will go to causes other than to the church itself.

Also, the higher the income of a family in a voluntary association church, the greater percentage of the family's income that will go to causes outside the church.[46]

In addition to the work referenced above, the discipleship tools and teaching that has come out of the discipleship movement 3DM has crisscrossed the country in the last decade. Some of its early leaders are friends of mine—and though they have re-invented themselves into a different form—remnants of the wave of the original work spear-headed by Mike Breen and taught by a band of coaches can be found all over the world.

Among many of the helpful diagrams that came from this movement, the Invitation-Challenge matrix is the most utilized in my experience.

It is a way to describe the delicate but doable balance between truth and grace as we mentor someone in the faith. We need to "invite" people into a loving relationship but at the same time "challenge" them to operate in harmony with the truth about themselves and God's call on their life. In this matrix, without both invitation and challenge, people can gravitate toward being stressed, bored or lazy in their Christian lives. But the goal is for them to be spiritually empowered.[47]

Figure 12.2

An Alban Institute Publication, 1999 Bethesda, MA p35

46   Money Matters, p172

47   Building A Discipling Culture, Second Edition, 2011, Mike Breen p.19

The reason 3DM felt permission to talk about discipleship this way is because of the model of Jesus Christ himself. He was simultaneously the most loving and challenging person to ever walk the earth. In a sense, the upper right quadrant of the matrix is a goal for all human relationships—think about healthy marriages, parenting, and friendships. We all want to feel loved and accepted, and we all need to be challenged to growth.

If you buy into the thesis of this book, that growing generosity is an essential outgrowth of spiritual maturity, then *making budget* remains important, but not as important as *making disciples*.

PAY THE BILLS vs LIVE THE VISION

PAY THE BILLS

This describes the approach that allows for money to remain a functional dynamic of the church but not necessarily a component of the spiritual formation dialogue. Said another way, church's pastors tend to leave talk about money to the finance team or finance office.

In *Passing the Plate*, the authors explain that pastors have a tendency to see talking about money and giving as "unspiritual" and thereby beyond the realm of their true vocational calling. "That's not what I was ordained for."

"Our training is much more about celebrating the sacraments, about preaching, about pastoral calling. So it's funny how much of our time and consciousness money can take up." [48]

Despite apparent struggles and frequent uncomfortable-to-negative experiences, the Pay-the-Bills approach is not entirely unsuccessful for some churches. As much as this is not my preference (for reasons you have read), it follows the giving pattern that I see in a lot of nonprofit organizations. That is, when the money gets tight, there is an appeal and people come through—often a few families will make up a bulk of the gap.

Many pastors described their positive experiences with people "coming through" when there was a need. Another success for some pastors was defined by the fact that this approach allowed them to separate themselves from the financial matters of the church. [49]

---

48   Passing the Plate: Why American Christians Don't Give Away More Money Smith, Emerson, Snell Oxford University Press, Inc. New York 2008 p 130
49   Ibid, p131

LIVE THE VISION

Pastors in this approach view talking about financial giving as merely another one of the many aspects of Christian life that they are called to address. "Obviously money is something that we are dealing with all day long. We are constantly thinking about it when we buy things. It is part of us, of our lives. Therefore, money has power. And it is something we really need to deal with."

"It's a big deal in people's lives. Jesus talked about it in various ways, recognizing it would be a big deal to people. And to avoid talking about it just because it makes people uncomfortable sends the message that, "Well, this part of your life really isn't spiritual. We can talk about prayer, and we can talk about good works, but money is off limits. And that's not helpful spiritually." [50]

Instead of talking about money out of a sense of obligation, because the building needs heat and the mortgage is due, talking about giving is conceptualized as *providing people with an opportunity to be part of something larger and more important than themselves.*

One pastor stated: "When you give people a chance to step up to the highest purpose under heaven, and you invite them to join you in the most important purpose of the universe, it's a moment of joy, and you bring meaning." Live the Vision culture tries to sacralize money for believers. [51]

The difference in approach seems to be fundamentally about what is driving the discussion. Rather than being need-based, giving is described as a means of showing gratitude.

Years ago, a congregational giving study revealed that the amount of dollars and the percentage of income given to churches were significantly influenced by the degree of proactivity regarding congregational giving. In other words, when leaders were clear about the future and what it would take to get there, there was an increase in amounts committed and given to that vision.

The difference between giving "what one thinks one can afford each week" and deciding on an annual dollar amount to give doubles the proportion of income given. *When a household decides annually on a percentage of income to give, the percentage given increases even more.*

---

50   ibid, p132
51   ibid, p134

Multiple studies (by Dean Hoge, the Gallup Organization and others) point to a similar paradigm. Random, *"what I can muster"*-type giving is the lowest amount. Intentional, pre-planned, and percentage-style choices demonstrated much more generosity.

Often the difference (on a continuum of highly random to highly intentional) to is up to <u>four times more.</u> [52]

What the study concluded about reasons for lack of generosity:
1) People have not seriously grappled with the theological and moral teachings of their traditions to give generously.
2) Churches settle for low expectations in the domain of financial giving.
3) People lack complete confidence in the trustworthiness of the churches or organizations to which they do or would give money.
4) There are not real costs to being stingy or intermittent with giving or not giving at all.
5) Most people practice giving on an occasional or situational basis. [53]

Possible solutions to increase generosity:
1) Maintain high expectations of and collectively honor generosity.
2) Confidently teach the normative instructions of the faith tradition regarding generosity and giving.
3) Strongly encourage believers to make theologically informed, principled decisions about commitments to generous financial giving.
4) Create multiple means through which Christians can follow through on their principled decisions in ways that are structured and routine.
5) Establish better procedures, systems, and practices of transparency, communication, and accountability that systematically increase trust.

We believe there is good evidence to think that low expectations in Christian churches for financial giving is a large contributor toward the unimpressive giving of American Christians. [54]

---

52   ibid, p138
53   ibid, p97
54   ibid, p98

MUELLER, TAYLOR, MOODY

Perhaps another way to self-evaluate our church and its posture is to look at three different approaches of noteworthy Christian missionaries in terms of their posture toward money and fundraising.

Men and women who have been exposed to philosophies of missionary support will be familiar with this continuum. Likely, it is an oversimplification of these amazing men (Mueller, Taylor, and Moody) and their approach but it is rooted in enough history that it has stood the test of time.

George Mueller was a lawyer turned prolific preacher. He began numerous orphanages in London and trusted God alone for finances. His claim was that he never asked anyone for a single penny and yet the money poured in—often just in time and sometimes beyond what was needed. The final forty years of his life were spent telling the same story every night to overflow crowds in cities all over the world.

Hudson Taylor, a young missionary who struck out on his own, began the influential China Inland Mission Society in 1865. Taylor was another extraordinary man of faith; reading his prayer journals alone is a lesson in utter dependence on God. He was a friend of Mueller, and told Mueller of his needs. Accounts chronicle the fact that a substantial amount of support actually came from excess donations that Mueller passed on to him.

D. L. Moody, a barely educated mountain of a man, went from selling shoes in Boston to the world's leading evangelist. He wrote and personally asked scores of people to invest big dollars in the Kingdom. He was criticized for being too brazen, but he kept on asking—and it worked.

The point of this quick history lesson is to look at three approaches which could be summarized this way:

Mueller only prayed.
(no information, no solicitation)

Taylor prayed and shared needs.
(full information, no solicitation)

Moody prayed, shared needs, and asked.
(full information, full solicitation) [55]

---

55   https://supportraisingsolutions.org/muller-taylor-or-moody-whose-approach-is-best/

This quick reference is meant to be another discussion starter for your church leadership. For instance, if I described these three approaches to members of your congregation and asked them to describe the leaders of their church as either Mueller, Taylor or Moody, what would they say?

Second, there are some nuances to the historical accounts that should be noted. For instance, both Mueller and Taylor distributed monthly reports that enumerated money received and spent. And, as far as we can tell, neither of them prescribed their approach as the only biblical way. Mueller was explicit in describing his as a special call on his life. [56]

SUMMARY AND SELF-EVALUATION

You have likely already noted which construct or continuum will serve your church the best. You may have quickly ascertained where you stand on that continuum. And that is the point.

If we are moving from a certain approach or posture to another, it will be helpful to understand where we are starting.

So look back through these descriptions and then make a mark indicating where your church may land on the line or even circle the title that best characterizes the current state of your church's approach:

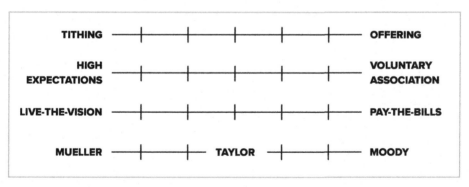

Figure 12.3

The beginning of our discipleship wave asks each church the question, "What is your style or approach to talking about giving and generosity?" Or like my kids would ask, "How do you roll?" And perhaps more importantly,

56   https://www.desiringgod.org/interviews/should-missionaries-fundraise

now that you have seen the options listed above, is there something you aspire to that will require you to "roll" differently in the future?

The next stop in this process is to start assembling the component parts of how you will disciple people more intentionally. Our discussion starts with the inner working of people's view of giving: their motivations and what causes them to think and act the way they do.

CHAPTER THIRTEEN

Generosity As A Mark Of Discipleship

I grew up in a home with a worn out welcome mat.
What I mean by that is that our house was not only frequented by my friends and my sibling's friends, but Mom and Dad regularly hosted people —be it one at a time or 20 at a time.

It was normal for us to invite missionaries on furlough to live with us. My parents would regularly feed friends from church and school or host neighbors and family. My folks would often remind people that "the garage door is always unlocked," and that anyone could stop in and use the house or bathroom whether we were there or not.

My parents also hosted the "Grads," which was the name given to a couple dozen post-high school young adults at our church. They would eat pizza and "Sloppy Joes" and play ping-pong well into the night. Legend has it that on winter evenings, they would pray that it would snow so much that they would "have to stay at the Gibbs." As a young boy I was awestruck with the college-age kids in my home. My parents would often find me asleep at the top of the stairs, having snuck out of my bed to listen to the fun that was happening in the living room below.

We invited people disconnected from nearby family or friends to every holiday meal. I played high school soccer, and one year Kennedy Torrez joined our team. He came in from Brazil that year and, not surprisingly, was the best player by far (and went on to play in college at the top level). My parents reached out to Kennedy and his brother—the only two from their family in the States—and invited them to Christmas dinner in our home. Their English was still a bit rough around the edges, but it didn't seem to bother anyone. This is just one example of strangers who became friends at our table.

I remember eating my first curried chicken one summer. Friends from India who stayed in our home prepared the simmering pot that would expose me to a decidedly different taste. My palate was accustomed to cheesesteaks and Tastycakes (those who grew up in or near Philadelphia will understand) and either Mom or Mom Mom's wonderful, yet mild, cooking. I was not ready for the spice-level that would cause smoke to emit from my ears. But I loved it. I don't ever remember resenting the constant and diverse traffic through our home.

As a young man I had no idea that what I believed about generosity and giving was born out of my family context. Ultimately, much of how we live is tied to or rooted in what was formed in us as "normal" in our younger years. For some people, the environment of their home during childhood was deeply damaging and has to be undone. Others were set on a positive course from the moment they took their first breath. I was in the more fortunate of these two groups.

At some deep place, all of this "garage is unlocked" living was rooted in a belief system, a theology. If you believe that ultimately anything you have is not solely for you, but for the good of a larger group, then you tend to be less attached to your things.

My parents never sat me down and said, "Greg, we have a theological conviction that ultimately everything comes from God and is to be used for God's purpose on the earth." I would have rolled my eyes. But, by their behavior and actions, the value of generosity and the conviction that we were just caretakers of God's belongings was crystal clear to me.

I want to remind you that we have a problem. And the problem is: *teaching and preaching alone will not increase someone's practice of generosity.*

So what will? Discipleship.

The reason we defined this term in Chapter 7 was to make sure that we have a common understanding of what I mean by discipleship. You may have a different association with the word. But what is more important is to recognize that what Jesus set into motion still works to this day. It is the process whereby one person shares his or her life activities with another person in order that the disciple can learn.

This is why I often hear people saying things like, "I think our pastor had been talking about giving for a while but I never really *heard* it. Or I wasn't ready to deal with it. But in my small group, we all talked about how hard and emotional this topic is and I started to change my behavior because I was challenged by my peers and my small group leader."

There are a few strikes against most modern churches in this category:

1) Churches tend to use programs and classes that are more education and information-delivery formats than a mentoring paradigm.
2) Church people tend to get their spiritual hunger fed by public speaking (preaching), which is the least effective form of personal change motivation.
3) Church leaders tend to relegate the discussion of money to a "making the budget" functionality of church life instead of seeing money as a lever for spiritual growth.
4) Until people have a life-on-life discussion (or even debate) about this topic, they will stick with their inner narrative or what they were taught (or not taught) when they were growing up.

One of the ways I describe the difference between budget talk and generosity discipleship is this:

We need to see generosity, giving, money and spending as something that should be addressed by the discipleship ministry, not by the finance ministry. I say, **"Take it out of the finance department and put it in the discipleship department."**

The nuance is not just to be clever. It is an important distinction. Part of the thesis of this book is that it is difficult, if not impossible, to create a generosity culture if the "talk" remains about pledges, P & L's, and pie charts.

If the role of the church is to honor God by making disciples, then what would Jesus have us do or say to those disciples about money? Do we really believe that increased faith is marked by increased generosity? These are the questions that should hang over whatever plans we choose to employ at a tactical level.

UNDERSTANDING THE INDICATORS

Another reminder is that the diagnosis of a church's generosity is often limited to certain indicators that may or may not help with the spiritual formation of individual givers. We often look at things like the **amount** of a gift, the **pace** at which people give, and the **mediums** by which the gift is given.

In other words, we tend to capture and study the *transactional* aspect of giving. And this is for obvious reasons. First, it is definitely something that should be accurately recorded. And second, it is very difficult to evaluate a congregant's motivation or inner life regarding giving. Very simply, the transactional is easier to measure.

Pause for a moment and see if you agree with my viewpoint so far.

- Teaching and preaching have limits in catalyzing change
- Measuring giving transactionally is important but has its limits
- Discipleship is the way to create a culture of generosity

One of the ways to start to reshape the discussion is to figure out how to nurture the heart of the disciple and his or her inner life, not just convince them by using external motivations or angles.

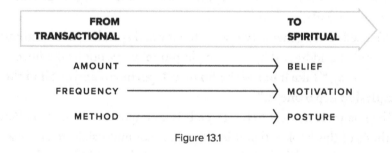

Figure 13.1

How can we change the conversation without people feeling like they are being manipulated or badgered for more money? How can we avoid people being skeptical that our concern is truly for spiritual growth and not just about the bottom line?

I want to be clear here that this is not an either-or proposition. The transactional *is* important. I still encourage applying stewardship principles like charitable giving deductions and charitable giving vehicles (non-cash assets, family foundations, etc.) because this is good management of money. But this is fairly matter-of-fact stuff.

But there is more. The mission of the church is to invite people, with God's help, to increase their understanding and practice of the teachings of Jesus. Jesus, like other Jewish rabbis, had followers in the first century who modeled their lives after him. Unlike other rabbis, people have been giving their devotion to Jesus ever since.

One thing we can know is that using one's resources for those in need and supporting the center of religious life are not new ideas. It has been the model of the church for millennia.

Discipleship is the process of inviting people, through mentoring, to live a life that is characterized by increasing maturity across many categories. The category of Christian Generosity is no exception.

My colleagues at Auxano have kept the generosity conversation alive in discipleship-oriented ways for many years. The team asks the right questions of each church:

1) What do you believe about the importance of generosity in discipleship?
2) How should we talk about steps of maturity in each individual context and congregation?
3) What is the best way to integrate a new kind of speech and a generosity pathway to move people from one level to the next?

WHAT ARE COMMON MOTIVATIONS FOR GIVING?

In the following descriptions, I have taken the four motivations that are offered by the authors of *Money Matters* and added my own experience and language.

I agree with the aforementioned authors that these motivations are phenomena not directly observable and measurable, and are alloys of motives, never pure ones.[57]

Every one of these categories is a mixture of both positive and negative and should be viewed with a spirit of grace as not everyone is in the same

---

57   Money Matters: Personal Giving in American Churches
Hoge, Zech, McNamara, Donahue Westminsters John Knox Press, 1996 Louisville, KY p130

place in their journey of generosity. As much as it may seem critical, it is meant to be descriptive.

Giving As A Quid Pro Quo With God - In this case, givers are motivated because of a sense of respect or even fear that not exhibiting generosity to God may not bode well for their own lives. This is a kind of self-interested giving cloaked spiritual generosity activity. Give to God and God will repay you in some way—both now and in eternity.

Giving As A Financial Donor to the Church - There are givers who are motivated by "fair share" thinking. The motivation here is that everyone needs to do his or her part to keep the church going. This is a charitable donation in the purest sense. The idea is that an organization that is doing good should be supported by those who have the resources to fuel that activity.

Giving As A Beneficiary Of Church Ministries - In a "pay to play" mindset, people in this category are motivated by the fact that the church is providing great benefit to themselves or their family. Akin to the previous category, the urgency here comes from the idea that "if we don't keep this church going, I won't be able to hear the preacher I like or my kids won't benefit from the youth group."

Giving As An Act Of Gratitude - Givers of this type have a sense of God's blessing in their lives. They know that they are fortunate and as a way to show their awareness of that fortune, they share it. The motivation here is recognition of God and an awareness that blessing can be taken for granted. The antidote to presuming upon God is to continue to return thanks by being a giver.

Giving As Obedience - Though the word obedience may have a prickly edge to it in some theological environments, there are still many Christians who are motivated to give because they see it in Scripture as an obligation of a follower of Jesus. When Jesus encouraged, "If you love me, you will obey what I command," he did so in a loving way. At the same time, giving may be motivated by a desire to do everything expected of a person of faith.[58]

58   Money Matters: Personal Giving in American Churches
Hoge, Zech, McNamara, Donahue Westminsters John Knox Press, 1996 Louisville, KY p131-132

AUXANO'S UPPER ROOM AND LOWER ROOM

A tool the Auxano team regularly uses is the Upper Room and Lower Room diagram. This picture was originally created by Will Mancini in his book Church Unique. It helps church leaders see the difference between church members connecting with a clear vision (an Upper Room way of thinking and living) and those who are connecting with something else.

The Lower Room describes where most church people "live." It describes the idea that most are linked with their church because of the *programs* it offers, the *people* that attend, the *pastor,* and the *place* itself. This is not all negative; clearly those things are important.

Upper Room disciples, on the other hand, are connected to the mission of the church. Because of their deep commitment to the ultimate goal of making disciples, they will weather challenges and change to the 4 P's (programs, people, pastors, and place).

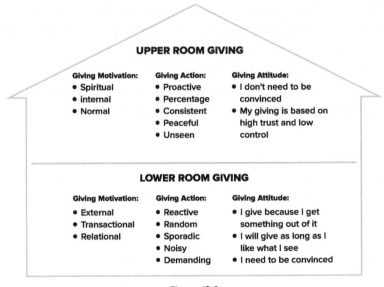

Figure 13.2

In short, Lower Room giving is less intentional and more self-oriented giving. Upper Room giving is proactive and more mission-of-God focused. Lower Room givers tend to have less trust and more skepticism about the church and its leadership and Upper Room givers tend to have higher trust in leadership and be more open-handed in terms of not demanding what happens with the money once they give it.

This is not meant to disparage people who are in the Lower Room. It is meant to be descriptive of the journey toward maturity in Christian generosity. And to the point of this book, it is meant to illuminate church leaders about where people often "live," so we can design the discipleship process to move them into a different kind of living.

The reason we are painting this realistic (and possibly painful) picture of where giving in the church stands is to motivate church leaders to ask the hard questions.

If there is a lack of maturity, even in long-time Christians, in regard to the spirit of generosity in our church, what must we change or do differently going forward? You know by now that the "meat and potatoes" of this book is the Generosity Pathway that each church will develop, rooted in their theology, context, and culture. And we are getting so close!

Let's make one more quick stop to increase our understanding of what motivates people to engage in generosity. No two people are alike. No two givers are alike. Understanding that nuance will help us when we name the various steps we may need to highlight for people. Again, it is not a light switch that we flip on and not a one-size-fits-all approach. So what else do we need to know about what motivates giving and generosity?

CHAPTER FOURTEEN

Beginning To Understand The Complexity

My wife and I have two sons and two daughters. We are blessed, for sure. And as any parent of multiple children will attest, the differences between them are astounding sometimes.

We are not the only parents who have asked ourselves, "How can four humans—who were raised by the same two people in the same house with the same values and went to the same church and same schools—turn out to be such different people?"

We learned this in sometimes funny and sometimes painful ways, as the signs of their uniqueness show up in each different stage of development.

Consider these differences:

- Ones who needed constant attention versus ones that needed quiet or alone time
- Ones who liked to perform in front of anyone versus ones who would rather have a root canal than be in the spotlight
- Ones who thrived with complex science and math problems and ones who would rather explore the nuance of a game like charades
- Ones who were gunning for scholarships and had dreams of post-graduate education from as early as middle school and ones who had little interest in long hours in the classroom

Now, as they navigate early adulthood, the differences are becoming more pronounced as they have opinions and biases toward certain political, religious, recreational, and relational styles. It is absolutely fascinating, sometimes frustrating, but always a study in the complexity of what it means to be human. My wife Andrea and I are having a blast watching them evolve before our very eyes.

I have also found that in my church leadership, whether I'm working with a congregation thousands strong or a church plant of a few dozen, we tend to overlook the stunning levels of diversity represented in our congregations. This is understandable—what senior-level leader can get to know scores of people on a deep level?

And yet each individual's money "personality" and posture is shaped by a number of things that are deeply intimate and certainly complex. Is there a way to understand people to be able to engage with them on this topic?

There is definitely a lot to learn about people and their motivations as well as hesitations about giving. Some of the pertinent factors are spiritual and some are practical. Some are connected with socioeconomics and some are not.

The point here is that churches need to decide if they have the capacity to do anything other than a "one size fits all" approach to engaging with the array of donors in their midst. It is not a question to be taken lightly. *How motivated are we to act differently to develop a culture of generosity?*

One thing is sure. Maybe only one.

Members who are actually involved in congregational life give more.

This has been proven repeatedly through research. Church attendance and hours spent volunteering for church work are highly predictive of giving. Virtually all church research studies agree. My suspicion is that your personal experience affirms this as well.

To a great extent, generosity trails engagement. And as many have repeated, the wallet is the last thing to be baptized in a person's life.

Volunteerism and involvement in spiritual formation activities do not guarantee that a person's heart for generosity will grow. Yet, with very rare exceptions, low involvement equates to low generosity. Beyond the positive influence of involvement in terms of generosity, the rest of the picture gets a bit complex.

COMPLEXITY IN THE PEWS

One thing that seems to be common across any age or circumstance is that members of congregations who are involved in the mission of the church give more. Just one step beyond that broad generalization, things get a little murky.

When church leaders view people in oversimplified ways, we can unintentionally exclude people from opportunities for spiritual growth.

For example, when pastors make general statements or even challenges to "be generous," this does not recognize the diversity of perspectives on what this word means.

For some, generosity may entail emptying their wallet on a Sunday morning. That forty-five dollars may be the most generous gesture they have made all year and more than they have ever given to a church. Others will regard generosity as only applying to money and not time, attitude, skills, influence, spirit, and more. And still others believe that tithing is the baseline and generosity only kicks in once one is giving beyond the tithe.

The point is that we as church leaders should make no assumptions.

Think about how each person has their own "view" of their money and how it relates to the church.

- Can we presume that high-net worth people view this the same as the unemployed?
- Do we think that the "offering moment" strikes the long-time Christian the same as the first time visitor?
- What about fixed-income friends? College students?

The main question here is—What is our leadership role in the lives of people to whom we minister regarding their financial lives? To whom are we preaching? In one way, it is a diverse and complex group. In another way, there are some assumptions that can be made based on the reality of modern church giving.

For instance, approximately 80% of the people you are talking to have lives that are characterized by keeping for themselves 98% of what God has given them to manage, spending more than that 98%, and then complaining that money stress is ruining their relationships and quality of life. These are the same people that complain when the church talks about money.

Pastors will recognize that this response is shockingly similar to that of an alcoholic when confronted with his out-of-control life.

Preachers need to recognize the somewhat discouraging reality that 80% of the people that listen to them will never, ever tithe. A life of generosity is, unfortunately, not the norm. When Jesus walked the earth and even performed miracles—most people did not follow him.

This does not, however, mean that we reduce our expectations or teaching to the lowest common denominator. Christ has called us to lift people's eyes "to the hills from whence cometh their help." [59]

"I cannot afford to give" though a common pushback, is true and not true in most of our lives. In one sense, it is true because most of us have mismanaged our money or not arranged it in a way that allows for generosity. On the other hand, it is a cover up for many—we afford what we want to afford.

Only 60% of people who attend any church in any denomination in America will give a gift that can be recorded. As I have tested this axiom over a few decades, it has held up. Some churches may be 58% and others 63%—but every church seems to hover around that rule of 60 percent. How can we encourage such a group?

START BY THINKING IN 5 GENERAL CATEGORIES

By now you know that my assertion (perhaps soap box) is to remember that this is not two groups of people—those who are generous and people who are not. Generosity is nuanced and every church contains a multitude of motivations and individual journeys.

Soon we will get very specific about the people (and givers) in your congregation. But for now, let's think in a few general categories.

To start thinking about this in terms of the ways to disciple the various groups in your church, I invite you to close your eyes and imagine your sanctuary or auditorium filled with its typical Sunday attendees.

Now imagine them divided into five categories, each with a different color of shirt. I will provide a starting point for this discussion but I encourage you to bounce the idea off a few people you trust—see if there is agreement or if you would change the descriptions or percentages.

59   Psalm 121:1 KJV

Let's start very simply so we can break down the complex nature of the humans in our midst:

Group 1: Committed to Tithe and Beyond *(5-10% of the congregation)* – This group bases their decision on a deeply held belief about giving 10% or more of their income to the church. Their giving is not dependent on income, economic circumstances, or even church budget needs.

Group 2: Committed to Give Regularly *(15-20% of the congregation)* – This group gives as a portion of their income regularly (often 5-8%) but is not unflagging in their commitment to ten percent. They care spiritually and consider themselves generous, but will change amounts or pace depending on feelings, fears, or economic factors.

Group 3: Willing to Give Charitably *(20-25% of the congregation)* – This group is motivated by feelings of generosity and charitable giving. They may give 1-3% of their income—the typical American Christian giving pace —but treat the church like the Red Cross or the United Way, as a good place that deserves some support.

Group 4: Willing to Give Sporadically *(20-25% of congregation)* – For this group, giving is a nice add-on to life and is approached as tipping or token giving. This is "what's in my wallet right now?" giving. This group often ends up giving a few hundred dollars to the church each year.

Group 5: Not Giving Yet *(30-35% of the congregation)* – this group may be giving elsewhere but have not registered a gift with the church. In other words, they may be giving cash in a way that is not associated with their name in the church database.

Several research groups including The Barna Group have reported that church giving and tithing in recent years have been decreasing. The other trend emerging in recent years is that the number of households giving a majority of the funds continues to shrink. Even in the model above, about half the congregation gives most of the money.

There seems to be at least two major differences. One of them is givers versus non-givers. The other is people committed to giving versus people willing to give. The difference in posture is significant.

There are a number of writers and teachers that aim to diagnose the softening commitment in giving to churches.

In a 2005 update on "Why People Do Not Give More," The Barna Group's director, George Barna, said this trend is influenced by the five factors. In my experience, these reasons still ring true over a decade later:

1) Some people lack the motivation to give away their hard-earned money because the church has failed to provide a compelling vision for how the money will make a difference in the world.

2) Some see their giving as leverage on the future. They withhold money from the church because they do not see a sufficient return on their investment.

3) Some people do not realize the church needs their money to be effective. Their church has done an inadequate job of asking for money, so people remain oblivious to the church's expectations and potential.

4) Others are ignorant of what the Bible teaches about our responsibility to apply God's resources in ways that affect lives.

5) Still some are just selfish. They figure they worked hard for their money and it's theirs to use as they please. Their priorities revolve around their personal needs and desires.

How about at your church? Is this an accurate description of what you suspect about the current state of giving in the church? If not, how would you amend the above list?

STAGES OF MATURING FAITH

In *Creating a Revolution in Generosity*, Wesley Willmer adapts James Fowler's research on stages of faith and applies it to maturing in generosity. Decades ago, Fowler articulated stages of transformation in the Christian life. It has become a seminal work for those who are committed to discipleship in the church.

Insofar as we continue to link faith maturity with giving maturity, it seems right to consider the Wilmer's breakdown of givers into six groups:

- **Imitator**
  Is able to mimic the examples of others in giving when shown or instructed.

- **Modeler**
  Gives sporadically when given an example to follow.

- **Conformer**
  Gives because it is the thing to do. Likes recognition, tax benefits, and other personal gain from giving.

- **Individual**
  Starts to give in proportion to what God has given. Danger of becoming prideful regarding giving or of giving for the wrong motives. Wonders why others do not give more.

- **Generous Giver**
  Recognizes that all one owns is from God. Begins to give of one's own initiative rather than obligation or routine. Derives joy from giving.

- **Mature Steward**
  Recognizes the role of a faithful steward of God's possessions. More concerned with treasures in heaven than on earth. Content with daily provision.

PREPARING TO NAME YOUR CHURCH'S PATHWAY

I turn again to my friends at *Mortarstone* who have committed a great deal of their organizational energy to help with the great wealth transfer of our day. Though planned giving (mentioned below) is a part of what we will discuss in a later chapter, the focus of this chapter is to help you declare the steps of your pathway. What they have developed for their planned giving approach may be helpful to you.

My hope is that you see that they have created their own understanding of a pathway. Planned Giving refers to the giving that involves non-cash assets and vehicles that allow the giver to make a big impact, reduce taxes, and see a lot of this happen while they are still alive. This may not be on your radar right now, which is ok. It is not the reason I am showing you their pathway.

Though this is slightly different than what a church may devise, it allows for a very practical look at a generosity journey. *It primes the pump perfectly for what you are about to experience in the next chapter.*

It begins with a person who is not a giver and illuminates the trail all the way through to a high level of commitment and maturity. The top level they describe is a person or family who is not only tithing but will consider a planned gift of some kind to their church. While your church probably won't need seven levels or names, I find it helpful as a way to process the step-by-step nature of discipling people toward maturity.

1) **Awareness** - Aware of the need to give and how to give.
   a. Giving is available online, during service, in worship areas, on app, and in classrooms.
   b. Giving is spoken about at every service as a form of worship.
   c. Specific causes are offered and giving can be designated.

2) **First Time** - Believe in the cause and have given for the first time.
   a. Very vulnerable stage that requires nurturing.
   b. Connect with phone, email, text, and handwritten notes.
   c. Will become intentional givers and more if they are connected with your church and the cause.

3) **Occasional** - Give randomly throughout the year.
   a. Emotion-led giving. Will tend to give at special events, holidays, or during a specific ask.
   b. Should be contacted to encourage a recurring gift. Target the communication to the cause they have given towards.

4) **Intentional** - Give regularly but less than 10% per year.
   a. Demographic information on these givers is needed to determine their potential giving.
   b. Disciple these givers in generosity and in stewarding all of their finances for God. These givers would benefit from a Financial Freedom course.

5) **Tithing** - Give regularly at 10%.
   a. These givers are your biggest supporters because they believe in the vision of your church.
   b. Regularly thank and celebrate these givers.
   c. They will be more likely to give above their tithe for a cause.

6) **Abundance** - Give regularly above 10%.
   a. These not only believe in the vision of your church but want to see it grow.
   b. These givers are typically age 45-60 and have potential for asset based, non-cash giving.

7) **Planned** - Give regularly above 10% (are often at the very top of the church's giving households and would consider a planned gift)
   a. These givers are 50+ years old and are financially ready to give in ways that benefit the church and save in taxes.
   b. These givers should be educated in gift planning options.

The purpose of this chapter was to get your creative juices flowing. Are you starting to sketch out (in your mind or on paper) what you think the divisions or segments may be for your congregation?

What is the make-up of your congregation? What do you presume about the mature stewards in your church? What percentage of the congregation do you suppose give 10% of their income or more to the church? Does your church match national averages or is the giving higher or lower?

No matter which of the above breakdowns or titles seem to resonate with you, the point is that you are beginning to think in a segmented way for the sake of discipleship in your congregation.

So, bring your pages of notes and ideas to the next chapter. It is time to create a customized Generosity Pathway for your church.

CHAPTER FIFTEEN

Naming and Creating A Pathway

remember waking up on Saturday mornings with a pit in my stomach. Back then, Saturdays were game day for my local soccer team. I was the goalie. Dad was my coach. And every Saturday, a battle of great consequence would ensue. I was six.

I didn't lose my passion for soccer until about my second year of college; I'd played at every level in between. I started back when soccer still was the stepchild to America's darling, football. Soccer wasn't even on most people's radar unless they were recent immigrants. In the late 70s when I moved to a new town and told my friends I played soccer, they looked at me like I announced I was into witchcraft.

Nevertheless, I was mentored and discipled by my dad and other great coaches and grew into a pretty decent player. Good enough to make the college team, even though I rode the bench most of the time.

But the point is this: to become a mature soccer player, for whom good sense on the field turned into effective decisions and behaviors off the field, I needed a lot of time. I needed years in fact.

I started with being taught which way to face so that I wasn't going the wrong direction as well as what the white line on the side of the field meant. "Don't let the ball go over that line!"

And over practices, camps, and lots of mistakes and yelling coaches, I matured. The pathway I traveled had me advancing gradually over time. Elementary, middle and high school teams, travel teams, and eventually a college team.

But one of my fondest memories to this day happened years after I'd stopped playing. I had the opportunity to coach a Christian high school men's soccer team for half a season when their head coach had to step down.

In one fall in Muskegon, Michigan, all of the years of practices in the heat and bruised shins had turned into the knowledge I needed to help these young men get all the way into the playoffs. I had been discipled over time to grow in my soccer "maturity." It was evidence that I had gained a high level of understanding of the game. When I realized this, it was enormously gratifying. I loved it.

Anything we have become proficient in likely took a road of gradual steps. There are some overnight success stories, but those are not the norm.

In categories of spiritual transformation in particular, we likely started at an elementary level and through time, experience, and the hand of God, grew to a new level of maturity.

In <u>Outliers</u>, Malcolm Gladwell references the writing of neurologist Daniel Levition: "The emerging picture is that ten thousand hours of practice is required to achieve the level of mastery associated with being a *world-class* expert—in anything." [60]

Though we are not talking about world-class mastery of the violin or golf, we are talking about a critical aspect of spiritual wholeness, faith, and following Jesus Christ with everything we are and have.

That point is in many ways the apex of this book. We are about to center the discussion into a discipleship framework. More specifically, it is time to consider what our generosity pathway is.

What are the steps that we will design for a disciple who desires to grow in this category?

Discipleship is about growth and maturity. It is about seeing someone go on a pathway toward being a more generous version of themselves. It takes coaching, encouragement, skill development, and time. Yes, it will also produce more funding for the church. But, that is not the primary objective —it is just a wonderful aftereffect.

Todd McMichen, Director of Generosity at Lifeway, reminds church leaders that the pursuit of money is not the same as producing a generous disciple. [61]

There are many places in Scripture that are pictures of the process of growth that we all can experience over time. Take for example Paul's

---

60   Outliers, Gladwell p.40
61   Leading a Generous Church: Making Disciples without Chasing Money Todd McMichen
Rainer Publishing, 2015 p15

reference to growing believers no longer desiring spiritual milk but spiritual meat—which presumes we are all in a maturation process.

In other places it talks about growing in wisdom, turning away from old habits and creating new ones, and more. Likely if you are reading this book, you are quite familiar with spiritual formation and its roots in Scripture.

2nd Peter is one of the places in Scripture that seems to encourage us to be on a pathway: *For this very reason, make every effort to add to your faith goodness; and to goodness, knowledge; and to knowledge, self-control; and to self-control, perseverance; and to perseverance, godliness; and to godliness, mutual affection; and to mutual affection, love. For if you possess these qualities in increasing measure, they will keep you from being ineffective and unproductive in your knowledge of our Lord Jesus Christ.* (**2 Peter 1:5-8**)

Do these character traits sound like they build on each other in a kind of spiritual sequence?

1) Faith
2) Goodness
3) Knowledge
4) Self-Control
5) Perseverance
6) Godliness
7) Mutual Affection
8) Love

Whether this is meant to be as sequential as it sounds is not as important as the idea that we are all on a journey. And God adds things to our spiritual character as we grow. And as we grow there is always a new level of commitment to experience and spiritual fruit that it will produce.

I am indebted to Alex Calder (and again, the Auxano team), with whom I developed the 5 Levels of Giving Maturity approach which serves as the prototype I use to lead churches into the discussion about discipleship toward generosity.

Churches will then use their own words, approach, and culture to reword and rename things. But, the foundation for this came in a conference room white board in 2019.

We are not the first to do something like this, nor will we be the last. In fact, Alex and I were probably a bit late to the party; the many wonderful stewardship pastors in America right now are likely ahead of us.

Hearing about the Generosity & Giving office we developed at Kensington over a decade, many churches ask Alex and me for help in the category of donor development, nurturing the congregation, and the discipleship process that moves people toward generous living. So we have developed a prototype that expedites the conversation:

1. **Pre-Giver**
2. **Periodic Giver**
3. **Proactive Giver**
4. **Percentage Giver**
5. **Partner Giver**

These levels are meant to be a framework from which any church can start. Many churches will adapt and re-create the wording and the actual steps of the pathway. Some may choose four levels instead of five. But if this model allows for healthy conversation about this topic, we will have done our job.

Consider some friends of ours who have developed a way to talk about these growth steps in their own way:

242 Church	Brookwood Church	Harvest Church
Rookie	Occasional	Emerging
Recurring	Consistent	Tithing
Relational	Obedient	Expanding
Radical	Generous	Extravagant

Idlewild Church	PushPay	Crossroads
Emerging	Non-Giver	Emerging
Engaged	Occasional	Engaged
Entrusted	Mobile	Established
Expanding	Recurring	Elevated
Extravagant	Above and Beyond	Extravagant

The goal of the *5 Levels* is that church leadership would begin with questions and convictions about giving and generosity and then move toward creating clear pathways so that any person in any church knows how to take the next step.

Often churches during the Launch Phase of their new Generosity Pathway (described in the next chapter) will graciously ask members of the congregation, **"What is your Next Move?"**

It is about knowing what the next step is. It is always about that in discipleship. *Help me know what to do next.*

So many churches and church leaders have a light switch approach presuming that people at some point will just flip the switch. The belief is that people are either generous or they aren't. Or a person is a tither or not. This zero to 100 miles per hour generosity plan is unrealistic when every other aspect of discipleship seems to have a maturation pathway.

For instance, when my parents and Sunday School teachers taught me about the importance of diving into the Bible, it was with short books with thick pages and lots of pictures and few words.

Mrs. Steever gave me root beer candy when I learned a verse, and Mrs. Kaufmann used flannel graph figures (anyone know what flannel graph is?) to make the stories come alive!

But as I matured in my ability to read and discern, I found myself in fascinating and nuanced discussions about the Bible, its veracity, and its application to my life as early as junior high and high school.

And, then in a Christian college and eventually in seminary, the discipleship practice of diving into Scripture took on new and deeper levels and required growing faith, skills, and to some degree, sophistication. There were a lot of steps in between root beer candy and Systematic Theology. The same happens with our journey toward generosity. It is not a switch to flip. It is a pathway to follow.

The following can serve as the discussion guide—pick a few potential names or titles and then ask these questions to flesh them out. This is another one of those grab-some-coffee moments. It may take a little while:

Title:	Can we give a name to describe this disciple?
Place:	What describes the state or stage of their giving?
Narrative:	What could this person be thinking? What's their inner narrative?
Posture:	Describe them more fully—how do they feel? What do they believe? What is their struggle?
Relationship:	Is there a formal donor stage or name?
Our Action:	What is our strategy to connect with this person? What could the church or church leadership do?
Opportunity:	What is the best/most appropriate giving opportunity to present to this person?
Next Move:	What is the next step we are asking this person to take?

Perhaps you will do what Alex and I did? We started with a blank white board and had an old-fashioned brainstorming session. It was based on our understanding of the givers we had gotten to know at Kensington—which means the words, phrases, ideas, and actions that you use for your church context may be very different than what you see listed below. Because, of course, the ideas will match your context.

Here are the edited contents from that brainstorming session. The extent to which we tried to describe each person may be a little overkill for you or your setting. If you sense that is the case, please skip to a more basic version of this contained later in the chapter.

But at least you get to see how we were thinking back then:

LEVEL 1

Title:	**Pre-Giver**
Pathway Place:	Before first recorded gift
Narrative:	"I am not sure and I am not ready"
Posture:	Little buy-in
	Uncertain and Skeptical
	Maybe cash in plate/box but not registered giving.

	Lack of Understanding Sometimes in a spiritual "stuck" position or stronghold
Relationship:	*Uninitiated Prospect*
Our Action:	Talk about community impact Demonstrate integrity with money Show worthiness of cause Use web/social, Offering Moment
Giving Opportunity:	One time gifts—crisis/disaster relief, backpack for under-resourced child, special Christmas offering, Year End gift
Next Move:	Making their first registered gift

Figure 15.1

LEVEL 2

Title:	**Periodic Giver**
Pathway Place:	Beginner, Inconsistent but giving and registered as giver
Narrative:	"I like giving to good causes and this seems like a good one"
Posture:	Initial buy-in Willing to give occasionally Likes the "feel good" of generosity, Positive about the church
Relationship:	*Transactional Donor*
Our Action:	Thanking & Encouraging Teach Basic Bible Principles Challenge To Be Consistent Inviting them to Personal Budgeting Classes

Giving Opportunity:	From Cash to Checks, from Checks to Digital Digital Giving—Text, ACH, EFT, Credit, Debit Envelope Giving Taking the steps to give intentionally and proactively (and recurring)

Figure 15.2

LEVEL 3

Title:	Proactive Giver
Narrative:	"I regularly give out of gratitude for what I have been given"
Posture:	Love the church View themselves as "all in" and part of the team Made a family decision to start regularly giving, Giving is planned not random
Relationship:	Charitable Friend
Action:	Contact with pastoral leadership (in person), Weekend teaching about percentage giving/tithing "Do the Math" - calculate percentage of income given 5-minute Testimonials in Worship Small Group or Mission Team involvement
Giving Opportunity:	Tithe Challenge Summer Giving Challenge Electronic Recurring Giving Campaign
Next Move:	The step of committing to give a percentage of income

Figure 15.3

LEVEL 4

Title:	Percentage Giver (Proportional)
Narrative:	"I calculate a percentage of my income and give it consistently to the church because of faith and gratitude"
Posture:	Trust in church leadership, Personal discipline/ obedience Less connected with "feel good" motivators, Needs little convincing or coddling. Regularly operates in a counter-culture way with money
Relationship:	*Good Steward and Sustainer*
Our Action:	Regular Reports of Impact Low-key relational expressions of gratitude, 1-on-1 conversations with ambassadors/leaders/pastors Vision Trip with senior leadership [Recurring Tithe/Percentage to General Fund]
Giving Opportunity:	Over and above giving beyond regular/recurring (Capital Campaigns, Year End, etc.) Local and Global Missions Support
Next Move:	Indicate to leadership openness to be asked regularly

Figure 15.4

LEVEL 5

Title:	Partner Giver
Narrative:	"I want to be invited and asked to fund more mission impact"
Posture:	Thinks about long-term impact and legacy of both their family and the church. Interested in leveraging their giving to inspire others

	Enjoy being "tapped" by leadership for special projects. Proactively modeling for children and grandchildren. Open-handed attitude about God's provision in their lives.
Relationship:	*Joyful and Generous Disciple*
Our Action:	Thanking, Pastoring, Nurturing Collegiality and collaboration in the ministry, Retreat/ Seminar/Conference for Generous Disciples (J.O.G.) Training and treating them as ambassadors of the mission
Giving Opportunity:	Charitable Remainder Trust Business Proceeds, Stock Transfers, Family Foundations, Estate Planning Designated Gifts toward Legacy Projects
Next Move:	Becoming an ambassador for generosity for the church

Figure 15.5

NAMING THE PLACES ON THE PATHWAY

This is an important step and I think the most exciting part of this journey. It is critical to take the time to come up with names based on what you know both instinctively and behaviorally about your congregation.

This is also the reason we started with asking about your theology and commitment to discipleship. This is where the one-size-fits-all approach is not helpful. You have a particular church in a particular place with a particular set of people. Spend some time thinking about what challenges they may face when it comes to the journey toward generosity.

STEP 1
Brainstorm Characteristics Of Generosity

Again, McMichen prompts each church to create a list of at least 10 personal life priorities or habits you would expect to find in a generous disciple. These should be tangible expressions of a personal faith that you should be able to disciple toward. [62]

Generosity goes beyond financial giving, so be sure to widen the lens of your discussion to include generosity of time, influence, skills, presence, listening, neighboring, and more—be as creative as possible and as customized as possible (to your specific church and context).

might not be to the church

STEP 2
Draft Some Titles For Levels

Make an exhaustive list of the different types of givers you believe you have in your church. You can think in terms of dollar amount, gift frequency, personal motivations, spiritual growth, involvement levels, etc.

Without overcomplicating this step (because you will likely come back later and modify it anyway), use your white board or flipchart and a group of trusted leaders to ask the questions modeled above in the 5-levels exercise Alex and I did together.

Keep in mind the list of the generous characteristics of a disciple and be constantly asking the question, "What is our dream for each disciple in terms of their most generous life?" In other words, remember that financial benefit to the church is a positive consequence of the maturing of disciples in your midst, not the main goal.

STEP 3
Consider a Simplified Version

To simplify this process, you may want to use what we often share with clients of Auxano when doing a consultation about developing Generosity Culture:

- **Name** - what could you call this level of generosity?
- **Posture** - what might the person be thinking or saying?
- **Scripture** - what Scripture seems to characterize this stage?
- **Application** - what are some possible "next steps" for this disciple?

Example 1: In the case of Harvest Church, one of their pathway steps or places is called an Expanding giver. So the name they chose was Expanding and the explanation is as follows:

Expanding

"I am growing in my faith by expanding my tithe to God through Harvest. (I am learning to be generous.)"

"But since you excel in everything—in faith, in speech, in knowledge, in complete earnestness and in the love we have kindled in you[a]—see that you also excel in this grace." 2 Corinthians 8:7

Individual Application

- Periodically review my "giving increase" --the amount I am giving to God through Harvest.
- Increase my percentage on an annual basis or as the Lord leads. (A good rule of thumb is to increase my percentage giving to my tithe by 1/2-1% each year.)

Figure 15.6

Example 2: This church used a picture of four places on the pathway and an arrow to model the steps of the journey from Occasional Givers to Generous Givers:

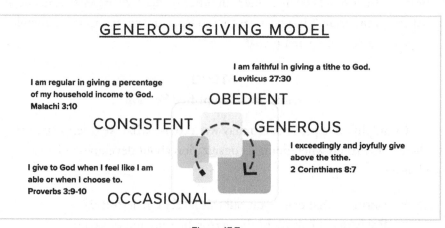

Figure 15.7

You may even come up with more than five personas or types of givers in your congregation when you brainstorm. Next, if you take your list and gather them into 3-5 buckets, what would your buckets look like? Remember, from this list we will develop a repeatable discipleship process, and an easily discernible measure of success. [63]

If you are like me, you already looked at some of the examples from other churches and may have said, "We would never use that!" or "Wow— are we allowed to just steal these great words from this other church?" All of this is part of the discovery. You discover what seems to fit with your culture, and what does not. And by the way, the answer is "Yes." You can use any names you find in this chapter if that fits your church and its context.

Now it is time to strategize how to let this approach soak into the culture of your church. When you launch a clear picture and pathway of generosity into the congregation over a series of weekends, it will have a long lasting effect. And it probably should start with a bang. Or at least it should be a big enough start that no one can miss it. Let's turn to the practical steps of getting pathway language into the water at your church.

---

63   Auxano Generosity Culture Training Manual 2015 p28

CHAPTER SIXTEEN
Launching Your Generosity Pathway

In Philadelphia, I grew up hearing about the Quaker movement; I saw signs, literature, and buildings referring to the Society of Friends. I never gave it much thought. It was part of the landscape of my youth that I knew had something to do with our Founding Fathers. Recently I have been motivated to study and understand more about their approach to the Christian faith.

One thing that struck me in reading one of their leading voices, Elton Trueblood (former chaplain to both Harvard and Stanford Universities), was his writing regarding *pledge cards and signatures*. Though I was taught by the Cargill company to help churches facilitate financial pledge campaigns with these cards, I have always found it a bit old-fashioned. Are they necessary? Do they really work?

Trueblood asserts that signatures have a value and even a kind of power that aids "persistence." It helps the vagueness of commitments that are so often part of our religious context, and in Trueblood's words, "does not mean that the signer has arrived, but does mean that he is *definite in intention*."[64]

The thesis of this chapter is that enhancing the culture of generosity at your church will be accelerated by a public campaign as well as private discipleship. And the culmination of the campaign should call for a commitment.

Conducting a campaign (or generosity initiative) will allow for 3 critical steps:

1) Teaching or revealing what the church has decided are the steps of their generosity pathway

64   Alternative to Futility, Elton Trueblood, Harper and Brothers Publishers, New York, 1948 p116

2) Allowing for people to decide what station or "place on the pathway" they find themselves

3) Graciously challenging individuals and families to take the next step on the pathway

Remember the idea (from Chapter 12) that churches with more intentionality see more development of generosity? Launching a Generosity Pathway is where we have the opportunity to take a significant step forward in the category of intentionality.

Take courage and remember that the congregation will be more receptive than you imagine to an approach like this. It is helpful and clarifying; it gives people language to discuss something that for most churches is hardly discussed.

This campaign (or call it an *initiative*, if you prefer) is not intended to be heavy-handed nor back people into a corner. Instead, many find it extremely helpful because they can quickly identify their place on the pathway and then know what the next step is for their family to consider. Whether or not they are ready to take the next step is not the point yet. Knowing that steps exist is the key. This will go a long way to creating growth in generosity over the long run in the congregation.

Because even if a family is not ready to do something different in their practice of generosity now, when God's spirit moves them, their next action or step will not be vague or mysterious.

This is our golden opportunity to put discipleship, growth, maturity, and positive momentum language on what is normally discussed primarily in financial terms.

The following explanation of the Generosity Pathway is in a question and answer format. It is my favorite method for succinctly explaining virtually anything, and may be helpful to use as you explain this new idea to your staff, an elder board, session, etc.

What is a generosity pathway?

A generosity pathway creates language that allows each person to know where he or she stands in terms of their journey toward becoming a generous person of faith. It explains the steps that one could take to get from one place on the maturity path to the next.

Why is it important?

The importance of the pathway is for the church leadership to know that they have a developmental process about a God-honoring form of generosity. We cannot expect people to go somewhere that we cannot show them. And if we show them, we can encourage them to grow in a gradual way that seems to fit with other aspects of discipleship.

What features need to be present?

The pathway needs to be undergirded by the church's core convictions and theology about money and possessions in the life of a Christian. It needs to have accessible and easy-to-understand language that will hopefully become a common way to talk about this topic in your church.

How can each church customize these levels of giving maturity to its setting?

The key is to think through a few categories for each of the levels that are chosen. So if a church has four or five levels (or some other number of levels), they will want to intentionally entitle each level and then discern what characterizes the person at each one of those levels.

PLANNING FOR A GENEROSITY CAMPAIGN

In many ways, a campaign is a campaign. Which means that if you have ever conducted an Annual Stewardship Campaign or a Capital Campaign, you are halfway to knowing what you need to know already.

And if you have not led a congregation through something like this, understand that the word "campaign" has stuck for most congregations in spite of it triggering the distaste many have for political campaigns. This is partly out of tradition and partly because the technical definition is still helpful: *work in an organized and active way toward a particular goal.*

In this case, the goal is to elevate the importance of generosity for the individual, family, church, community and world in a way that links it with following Jesus Christ and Christian teaching. The goal also includes the challenge to take action and provides a clear pathway to do so—both in terms of spiritual and practical commitment.

What are the steps to prepare?

1) Finalize Your Pathway - We have spent a lot of time highlighting the importance of a customized pathway for your church. At some point, the 4 or 5 titles or levels of generosity need to be vetted by senior leadership or a trusted group so that they can be finalized. This requires some wordsmithing as well as a "cultural check" of asking, "Does this seem like it will work for our people?" Once the names and descriptions are complete, the graphics, icons, and style of the campaign can be created by a media team or person. This is a reminder of the elements of the simple format, but you can add or edit your description as much as you want if you think it will be helpful to the campaign:

- **Name**
- **Posture**
- **Scripture**
- **Application**

2) Create A Calendar - Ultimately, our commitment to developing a Generous Culture is proven by its place and priority on our church calendar. First, are we willing to give it a place in the life of our church as an important initiative? And second, can we clear the calendar enough that the campaign doesn't get lost in the shuffle, or seem like one option to engage with the church among a hundred? A solid campaign is not rushed, but requires a preparation phase to be ready for a public phase. Consider the following ideas as well as a sample calendar:

- **Planning Phase (4-6 weeks)** - look at your current giving data, decide on and design the pathway, create support media including digital and print assets.

- **Develop Teaching Series (4-6 weeks)** - based on both your theology articulation and the explanation of each of the levels on the pathway, create a teaching or sermon series, if not a small group study as well.

- **Anonymous Survey** - issue an anonymous self-evaluation survey or check-the-box type study in your congregation. With this study, we will get a snapshot of how many members are at each of the levels we described.

- **Report Back To Congregation** - generate excitement and conversation by talking about the potential for spiritual and organizational growth by reporting the results of the anonymous survey.

- **Vision Casting** - describe to people a vision for their lives as they take a new step in generosity as well as a vision for the church as it sees generosity increase.

- **Commitment/Pledge Sunday or Weekend** - give each household an opportunity to take a "next step" in their generosity and register it with a commitment to God and the church.

- **Report and Celebrate Results** - use the report of Commitments to express gratitude and offer words of encouragement and support.

Example Of Fall Generosity Campaign Calendar:

May 1	Get GC on church calendar
May 15	Finalize Icons/Names/Pathway
Jun 1	Draft Version of Teaching Series
Jun 15	Draft Version of Anonymous Survey
Jul 1	Communicate with Staff & Volunteer Leaders
Aug 15	Finalize Media/Collateral
Sep 7	Launch GC Initiative - Week 1
Sep 14	Teach the Pathway & Take Survey - Week 2
Sep 21	Results of Survey & Vision Cast - Week 3
Sep 2	Commitment/Pledge - Week 4
Oct 4	Celebration & Next Steps - Week 5

3) Create Campaign Media - It is important that there is clarity and synergy between the preaching, teaching, printed materials, website, and any other way that the church chooses to communicate. Each person will need to know *What we are doing, Why we are doing it, and What is being asked of them.* Often churches will create a brand or "look" for their Generosity Campaign so that people recognize the various elements as linked together.

TITLES/ICONS - a name for each step and perhaps some graphic representation of each of the steps
PATHWAY - everything put together in a generosity pathway visual (including next steps, scripture, etc.)
WEB - create a place on the church website for the generosity pathway teaching and visuals to stay "evergreen"
CURRICULUM - consider small group or Sunday school curriculum to supplement the sermon series
SURVEY - create physical and digital survey to allow congregants to self-assess their place on the pathway
PLEDGE CARD/PROCESS - pledge card or digital pledge process

4) Conduct Commitment/Next Step Process - These elements are in regard to the engagement church leaders have with the members of the congregation. Initially, the action involves having someone understand your theology of generosity and pathway in order that they can self-assess (asking themselves, "Where am I on the pathway?").

Finally, it has to do with asking for a commitment ("Will you take the next step in your commitment to generosity?") and then responding with gratitude and encouragement when a person or household makes that commitment (often using a digital or physical commitment card or pledge card).

Create multiple responses that match each "next step" category. For example, create a letter for all of the households that chose Recurring Giving as their next step in generosity. Thank them specifically for this step and point them to a person who can help them with questions they may have about the process. So, if there are five kinds of "next steps," then there should be five distinct letters.

GETTING THINGS ROLLING

Some congregations will want to finish up the process suggested in this book and make a plan that involves all five of the waves before they engage the congregation with a campaign to embed the pathway. I suggest that you do not need to wait for the final version of your Generosity Discipleship Plan to do so, but I fully respect why you would want to do so. In part, I believe you can work on your plan while you are gradually incorporating aspects of it. This will give you even more understanding of the discipleship challenges ahead. The next wave will enable your church to *dig in* and *structure up* to create the best environment for discipleship.

See media samples on the next page.

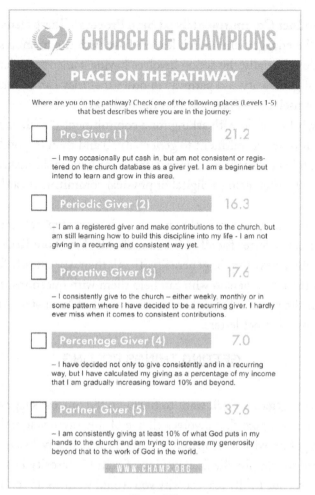

Figure 16.1

Figure 16.2

WAVE THREE

STRATEGY

FOLLOW A PLAN.

How can we infuse generosity into our church life?

CHAPTER SEVENTEEN
Collecting the Data

D ata is a funny thing. We have known for a long time that people can manipulate data to communicate virtually anything. At this point, we know it depends on "how you slice it."

How about the "fact" that smokers are less likely to die of age-related illnesses? Or the worn joke that goes something like this: 70% of all statistics are made up on the spot by 64% of people that produce false statistics 54% of the time they produce them.

The point is this: I have not met any church leader who misrepresents data or stats intentionally. But I have met a lot of them who do not know what to do with the data they have—or have to make educated guesses about the data they do not possess.

This seems to be a vulnerability in our leadership that sometimes can be mitigated by the skill set of executive pastors (a relatively recent addition to the staff roster in American churches). Yet, this position usually exists only in the larger congregations that can afford it.

The generosity conversation in churches could use a better handle on data. Though national research groups tell us that Christians give less than 3% of their income, we really don't know this for sure about people in our churches— we can only surmise it. We must make educated guesses about where people stand in terms of their personal generosity since members of our congregation don't tell us what they actually make (in salary) or own (in assets).

The great conundrum we are in is that when it comes to diagnosis, we can only look at the size of a gift. And of course, the challenge with looking at merely the amount of a financial gift is that a very *large gift* may be a *small sacrifice* for the giver. And vice versa.

Understandably, this is the primary critique leveled against looking at the giving records. And it is an appropriate critique from a biblical perspective.

The widow who gave 2 coins (arguably 100% of her income) would have not been considered an advanced or mature giver via a computer software program that *buckets* givers on giving amounts alone. There is a part of me that wishes there was a way to find "the widow" and learn from her—that level of devotion to Christ and loyalty to the church would be something to behold.

As much as the imperfection of our analysis breaks my heart in the likelihood that we overlook the kind of giver like the widow, I have become more comfortable over the years with the soft science of looking at the giving list.

Here is why I am comfortable with this imperfect approach:

Because the alternative (which most churches choose) is to do very little —or nothing. In the minds of many churches, the possibility of dishonoring "the widow" and her sacrificial gift is not worth an imperfect attempt at creating a discipleship pathway.

If discipleship is our main concern in the church, and if how we handle money and possessions is one of the top growth barometers for a maturing believer, *we must try something*. We must strive to uncover more ways to look at this.

Please understand that the motivation is not to be judgmental or even place "big givers" in some elevated status—I have never bumped into a theological system that says to do this.

Hopefully, our teaching (sermons, small group curriculum, etc.) will make it very clear that it is not the size of the gift that indicates the fruit of spiritual maturity, but the level of sacrifice. And more importantly, the purity of the giver's heart in terms of posture and motivation is what Jesus seemed to be searching out.

You likely have a giving report of some kind at your church—whatever it is, we can start from that. Maybe your church even has a sophisticated software platform that can give you very detailed reports. Again, please get those now, print them out, or find a way to have them "on the table" as we move ahead. That is what this chapter is about—what data needs to be on the table and how are we going to understand it and move from data to decisions to discipleship.

In my experience, however, there are only a few ways we tend to look at financial information in the church. They seem very limiting to me lately. Especially in the world of big data, where a social media conglomerate probably knows more about my inner life than my spiritual mentors and pastors.

Let me explain. You may want to pour a cup of coffee and settle into your comfortable reading chair if you haven't already—this gets a little nerdy. Consider the four ways we can look at information or data concerning the church and its generosity environment:

1) **Transactional**
2) **Organizational**
3) **Spiritual**
4) **Environmental**

As senior leaders, we tend to look mostly at data or information that is either **Transactional** (what people give) or **Organizational** (how we manage or spend that giving).

Remember we referred earlier to talking about money only in financial ways? We also tend to collect (and try to interpret) data that is primarily quantitative.

What we rarely look at is the subject of this book:

How does a church (with God's help) *move* someone from one state of maturity in his or her generosity to the next? **How can we grow generosity?**

So it is not so much about how much a person gives, but why they give and what might cause them to consider a different level of generosity— what would change in either their outer or inner lives to cause them to give more?

This is the missing information in most congregations. There must be more to the story. Something still doesn't add up.

There are two other critical pieces of the puzzle to growing generosity that are the neglected ones.

SPIRITUAL

We need to figure out what cultivates a heart of openhandedness. There is a deeply spiritual dimension to generosity. But under the notion of protecting confidential information (which is a good thing), we have made giving to the church such a private affair that we virtually cannot talk about this dimension of the inner life (and that is *not* a good thing).

Add to that our propensity to stay quiet about money topics for unhealthy reasons and we are in a real pickle. Now, we are honing in even further on defining our problem.

Tim Keller tells this story:

> *Some years ago I was doing a seven-part series of talks on the Seven Deadly Sins at a men's breakfast. My wife, Kathy, told me, "I'll bet that the week you deal with greed you will have your lowest attendance." She was right. People packed it out for "Lust" and "Wrath" and even for "Pride." But nobody thinks they are greedy. As a pastor I've had people come to me to confess that they struggle with almost every kind of sin. Almost. I cannot recall anyone ever coming to me and saying, "I spend too much money on myself. I think my greedy lust for money is harming my family, my soul, and people around me." Greed hides itself from the victim. The money god's modus operandi includes blindness to your own heart.* [65]

With rare exceptions, if church leaders do any "looking into" this area of congregational life, they tend to look at people's giving in the transaction sphere—the amount, the frequency, etc. Very rarely do they have a way to explore people's motivations, postures, hesitations, and spiritual-emotional approach to giving.

In other words, we look at the outward appearance of generosity and not the heart of it. It is easier, for sure.

---

65   Counterfeit Gods, Tim Keller.

But discipleship is about figuring out ways to get to the heart of the matter. That's what Jesus *always* did. On any subject—including financial giving.

Remember when he said to the Pharisees that they would get an A+ on their tithing but were really screwing up some other issues that revealed their true motivations? Clearly Jesus looked beyond the *amount of the gift* to the *heart of the giver*.

This question for us is primarily addressed in chapter 13 of this book. Is there a way to study the heart aspect or spiritual dimension of giving and generosity in the church? Because Jesus seemed to be always looking past the amount and straight at the motivation.

ENVIRONMENTAL

Beyond organizational money talk (budgets, voting, annual meetings, being behind or ahead of projections, paying bills, etc.) we need to think about the pathways and opportunities we create for members of our congregation to *move from one state or level of generosity to the next*. The environment we create is driven in large part by this: *pathways and opportunities*.

This is not to take away the responsibility a church has to manage money well and report on that to the congregation. It is not an either-or.

When we are talking about the environment a church creates, we could also refer to this as the *culture*. This field of inquiry is about what the church can do to shift the conversation and normalize talking about becoming generous in every possible way, including financial giving.

What can the church do to create environments where generosity can be green-housed? How can the church choose to do or teach something, challenge and encourage people, and add to its discipleship pathway?

These are the questions we must wrestle with so that we can consider changing the atmosphere of our churches. As already mentioned, it cannot just be teaching from the pulpit alone—we have decades of data to prove that this has limited effectiveness.

If we can establish these four categories (**transactional, organizational, spiritual and environmental**), we can then go data mining.

GOING MINING

The following quest for information is not meant to be seen as a pass or fail exam. It is a menu of data that could be collected or mined to provide "handles" for us to hold as we move ahead. It will help determine where we may have opportunities to disciple more effectively.

Notice that the first two categories (transactional and organizational) are not eliminated as unimportant—they still need to be monitored and managed well. But the fruit of this guide is to have a plan that incorporates the other two categories (spiritual and environmental) in a way that will produce discipleship growth.

We need to look at a more comprehensive picture of what is happening. Then, the interpretation of data can be a significant piece of the puzzle we are trying to solve. So before we go any further, it is time to go on a hunt.

DATA COLLECTION

Transactional (Annual For 3 Years)

The following figures are commonly assessed in a financial health scan of a church's giving records. This is basically asking the questions: how many households give, to what extent, and what does that add up to? The numbered rows are loosely based on MortarStone ministries' approach to analyzing "bands" of givers.

	Year 1	Year 2	Year 3
Total Annual/General Giving	$	$	$
% of Total via Digital Giving	%	%	%
Average Annual Gift	$	$	$
1 - All Givers (total units)	#	#	#
2 - Starting Givers ($1-200)	#	#	#
3 - Developing Givers ($200-1000)	#	#	#
4 - Core Givers ($1000-5000)	#	#	#
5 - Top Givers ($5000-15,000)	#	#	#
6 - Major Givers ($10,000+)	#	#	#

Figure 17.1

> ### Organizational (Annual For 3 Years)

Many churches will have an annual stewardship pledge, upon which they base projections. The figures below show the trends of the organizational arrangement of money at the top level—what is our budget versus our actual expenses? Further, what do our amount of savings, endowments, and debt say about our financial health?

Giving Totals

These facts and figures may be the most common. If a church is measuring financial health, they are more than likely looking at the items in this first cluster of datapoints. This top-level look is necessary for the backdrop to the next few discussions we need to have. It may also point out the level of urgency with which we treat this topic.

	Year 1	Year 2	Year 3
Total Annual Pledge	$	$	$
% Given vs Pledged Total Budget	%	%	%
Total Spending	$	$	$
Total Debt	$	$	$
Total Savings	$	$	$
Total Endowment	$	$	$
Total Missions Fund	$	$	$
Total Building Fund	$	$	$
Other_____	$	$	$

Figure 17.2

Giving Sources

The following checklist represents both the ways and methods giving channels can be diversified and "opened up" to givers.

	Yes	No	Notes
Cash	☐	☐	_____
Check	☐	☐	_____

	Yes	No	Notes
Offering plate/bag	☐	☐	_____
Offering box	☐	☐	_____
Envelope System	☐	☐	_____
Credit Cards	☐	☐	_____
Debit cards	☐	☐	_____
ACH	☐	☐	_____
Online Bill Pay	☐	☐	_____
Stock	☐	☐	_____
IRA Transfers	☐	☐	_____
Charitable Gift Annuities	☐	☐	_____
Family Foundations	☐	☐	_____
Donor Advised Funds	☐	☐	_____
Other_____	☐	☐	_____

Figure 17.3

Financial Practices

It also names the budgeting, pledging and reporting processes to see if these practices are in place.

	Yes	No	Notes
Annual Budget Process	☐	☐	_____
Annual Pledge	☐	☐	_____
Annual Financial Audit	☐	☐	_____
Annual Report	☐	☐	_____
Annual Members Meeting	☐	☐	_____
Giving Statements how often?			_____

Figure 17.4

Spiritual (Annual For 3 Years)

This category is the most underdeveloped at churches and the thesis of this book—that without an understanding of the pathway from baby steps to full maturity in generosity, a church will struggle to create generous disciples. The following are placeholders as churches will likely develop their own names and amount of levels (this is covered in detail in Chapter 15).

	Year 1	Year 2	Year 3
Pre-Givers (Level 1)	#	#	#
Periodic Givers (Level 2)	#	#	#
Proactive Givers (Level 3)	#	#	#
Percentage Givers (Level 4)	#	#	#
Partner Givers (Level 5)	#	#	#

Figure 17.5

Environmental

The environmental data is not usually measured by churches but gives a matrix by which we can start to see what creates a culture of generosity. It is about behavior, communication, and priorities. In many ways, these are the best dashboard indicators of an intentional approach to this area of discipleship. There are a handful of environments we create and nurture in the typical church setting.

IN WORSHIP	Often	Occasionally	Seldom	Never
Preaching Illustrations	☐	☐	☐	☐
Sermon Series	☐	☐	☐	☐
Offering Stories	☐	☐	☐	☐
Lay Person Testimonials	☐	☐	☐	☐
Celebration Videos	☐	☐	☐	☐
Impact Reports	☐	☐	☐	☐
Other_____	☐	☐	☐	☐

Figure 17.6

IN TEACHING

	Often	Occasionally	Seldom	Never
Personal Budget Classes	☐	☐	☐	☐
Groups Generosity Curriculum	☐	☐	☐	☐
Sunday School Curriculum	☐	☐	☐	☐
Generosity Pathway Taught	☐	☐	☐	☐
Planned Giving Seminars	☐	☐	☐	☐
Other_____	☐	☐	☐	☐

Figure 17.7

IN TRIGGERED RESPONSES

	Often	Occasionally	Seldom	Never
First Time Giver	☐	☐	☐	☐
Large Gift	☐	☐	☐	☐
Lapsed Givers	☐	☐	☐	☐
Year End Gift	☐	☐	☐	☐
Annual Pledge	☐	☐	☐	☐
Capital Pledge	☐	☐	☐	☐
Other _____	☐	☐	☐	☐

Figure 17.8

IN RELATIONSHIPS

	Often	Occasionally	Seldom	Never
Donor Updates/Meetings	☐	☐	☐	☐
1 on 1 with Top Givers	☐	☐	☐	☐
Giving expectations voiced:	☐	☐	☐	☐
for Members	☐	☐	☐	☐
for Leaders	☐	☐	☐	☐
for Staff	☐	☐	☐	☐
Other _____	☐	☐	☐	☐

Figure 17.9

IN SPECIAL CAMPAIGNS	Often	Occasionally	Seldom	Never
First Time Give Opportunity	☐	☐	☐	☐
Year End	☐	☐	☐	☐
Recurring	☐	☐	☐	☐
Capital Campaign	☐	☐	☐	☐
Crisis Relief	☐	☐	☐	☐
Benevolence	☐	☐	☐	☐
Missions	☐	☐	☐	☐
Tithe Challenge	☐	☐	☐	☐
Other _____	☐	☐	☐	☐

Figure 17.10

I am assuming that there are a few possible reactions to a chapter like this. One is that <u>it is overwhelming</u>—you never knew that so many things could be evaluated. And you may be not so sure you want to track all of these things. You are tempted to throw up your hands.

Another possible reaction is that you are <u>motivated but "behind"</u>—you are interested in doing a better job of tracking and understanding but just need some help knowing where to start. And you are not sure you have the time nor the personnel to attack this.

Let me encourage you with this: this book is meant to start you on a path of maturity as a church organization in the same way that we want individuals to go on a pathway of maturity as a generous giver. The first step is just knowing what the journey looks like. Then you can decide what the best next step is.

So what do you do with the data you uncovered? Here are a few suggestions. First, I recommend you and your team use a diagnostic exercise specifically for the generosity aspect of congregational life that asks the questions:

1) Where Are We?
2) Where Do We Want To Go?
3) What Will It Take To Get There?

You have already completed much of the answer to question 1. As you answer question 2, you can prayerfully and even playfully dream about what God could do with your church. And then question 3 usually implies some sort of change in behavior or practice. Change is challenging for most congregations. I suggest you follow a pattern I learned recently about the best order of change. People. Process. Technology.

First is **people** (who is the best person to take responsibility for this?), then **process** (what small steps could improve our process right away?), then often there is a **technology** or software that will help (do we have the right technology to help and not hinder this effort?).

But before you make any major changes, let's continue to peel the onion back another layer or two. We have come this far so we might as well!

The next chapter gives us a way to look at some of the environments and practices that make up our current culture. Stay encouraged. This deep diving will lead to some pearls.

CHAPTER EIGHTEEN
Self-Auditing Our Generosity Culture

I am a bit of a coffee snob. Or at least I thought I was; I have recently discovered there is another level of snobbery that has bested me.

Years ago, I began to notice that the coffee I liked the most was made by the small local roasters with a hole-in-the-wall coffee shop. When I traveled, I would try to discover a person who might know of such a place in whatever city I landed.

I started to roast my own coffee by buying green (raw) coffee beans at the Eastern Market in Detroit, and then used an inexpensive home roasting set-up to see if it was a hobby I would enjoy. For about twenty dollars, I bought an old-fashioned Whirly-Pop Popcorn Popper, a simple metal pot with a handle that turns a paddle inside so that the popcorn kernels (or in my case, the coffee beans) don't scald as you hold it over an open flame. I have enjoyed roasting beans from all over the world, and especially those from Ethiopia. If you have never had a cup of coffee made with beans roasted just a day or two ago, you are missing out!

But I found out that the next generation has sped past me to a new level of snobbery. They insist on water temperature and quality, specific weight and consistency of coffee grounds, and more. The younger guys in my network make me look like a truck-stop coffee drinker that uses powdered cream by comparison.

I discovered that there was a grid that people use to judge quality and excellence that I was not aware of. And that is what most church leaders discover when we talk about generosity development at a level beyond answering the usual questions like "how many giving families do we have?" and "how much money comes in each year to the general fund?"

Below are three grids presented from least to most complex. These are meant to provide lenses through which you can look at your church in terms of the features of its generosity culture. In essence, you are asking the questions, "Do we have some of the elements of a generous church? What are we missing? How can we move toward more generous disciple making?"

Let's call them the **Coffee Conversation**, the **10-point Inspection**, and the **NAE Deep-Dive**.

THE COFFEE CONVERSATION

The least complex analysis of your generosity culture is what I would do with you were we chatting over a cup of coffee. In the Coffee Conversation, I would ask about three categories:

1) **Preaching & Teaching** - how often and in what manner do you bring up the principles of generosity? In sermons, classes, seminars, staff meetings?

2) **Analysis & Awareness** - how cognizant are you of the givers & levels of giving? Do you track trends or do you have software that does that for the church?

3) **Giving Channels** - are you and your members aware of the possible ways that someone could give to the church and its mission? How do they find out? Is there intentionality behind graciously challenging people?

Quite frankly, I would also be secretly (or not so secretly) sizing up your comfortability with the topic as one of the church's leaders—particularly if you are the senior pastor. One of the chief indicators of a church's potential growth in this category is the senior leader's own health around the topic in terms of belief, behavior, and experience. More on that later.

In the meantime, the next level of analysis is to provide you with a discussion guide to use with church leaders. It is a set of lenses through which you can look at your own church. Allow a deacon board or key group of staff members to give a score for each of these. Better yet, ask a group of givers in the congregation to comment on or score these. In my experience, the "best practice" churches have ten things happening virtually simultaneously in their midst.

THE 10-POINT INSPECTION

I have summed up what best-practice churches do for the development of generous givers, in my estimation and experience:

1) **Teach Biblically** - There has to be a source of authority and though people may teach differently, the Scripture offers an enormous amount on this topic. Both Old and New Testaments have direct and indirect wisdom and principles that are timeless and deeply important for spiritual health.

2) **Hold Loosely** - People and their money, time, and talent do not belong to any church or church leader. If we expect people to hold loosely to their resources, churches need to model the same. Give things away regularly and people will catch the spirit. And the Spirit.

3) **Model Boldly** - Leaders compel people to follow. And if we expect people to follow the way of generosity, an example from a leader is a key factor. Teaching pastors, small group leaders, and staff are examples of men and women that will dictate (for good or for bad) the attitude of the rest of the congregation.

4) **Challenge Graciously** - In any discipleship relationship, there comes a time when someone needs to be challenged. Either they are complacent, inconsistent, or just have the kind of personality that needs prodding. But, saying nothing and presuming that people will simply change because we informed or inspired them is a recipe for stagnation, not growth.

5) **Inform Intentionally** - Churches that have a strategic approach to communicating the channels and platforms of giving see increased generosity. With a diversity of givers and styles, the church will allow for the practice of generosity when digital giving, planned giving, designated giving, campaign giving, and more are regularly highlighted.

6) **Thank Repeatedly** - In generosity environments, people are thanked to reinforce the gratitude that accompanies generosity. With the giving and receiving of gratitude comes more generosity. Remember that other organizations often do a masterful job of thanking people, so the church looks inattentive by comparison.

7) **Report Regularly** - There is no doubt that people will thrive more in generosity when they understand how the money part of church life works. Churches that report regularly keep gaps in communication small. They reinforce an open book approach, which only helps assure givers of the integrity with which money is being handled.

8) **Invest Widely** - So many people who love the church love it because of its ability to collectively create impact in the community and the world. Generous attitudes seem to increase when members of a church know that God's money is being used for both the sustaining of the church as well as the mission of God outside the church. This is especially true of younger generations.

9) **Remind Frequently** - Generosity is a spiritual discipline like any other. Churches that create a culture of openhandedness have rhythms and patterns of reminding us about our spiritual disciplines. Call it accountability or coaching, reminders in the most visible places (offering moments, website, etc.) help us create culture.

10) **Communicate Lavishly** - This principle is akin to reporting regularly (mentioned above). It also contains elements of reminding, cheering, challenging, and the rest of the 10 Actions. This refers to creating a constant and consistent environment of "keeping everyone up to speed" on plans, investments, and examples of how God has used the church to do His work in the world.

The final grid is a much more detailed analysis offered by the National Association of Evangelicals. Whether you use this formally or informally, the benefit is the approach. This is a comprehensive look at categories that you and I may not have remembered (or ever thought of) off the top of our heads.

NAE DEEP DIVE

The National Association of Evangelicals is a group that offers support, materials, and more for more than 45,000 local churches from 40 different denominations.

The NAE has a Financial Health division. As they aim to help coach churches in the category of generosity, they begin with a Church Generosity Assessment Survey. Like me, you will agree with many but not all of the practices or concepts outlined in their assessment. In my estimation, however, the value of this resides in its scope. It receives high marks for modeling a comprehensive approach to highlighting the practices and norms necessary to grow generosity.

Consider your church's practices as you glance down through these lists (which are actually in the form of questions on the survey):

Worship Services

- Biblical Financial/Generosity truths are shared
- Weekly generosity scripture verse appears in the bulletin or on the screen during offering
- A leader reads a weekly generosity scripture verse out loud before praying for the offering

- Worship songs on giving, generosity, and serving are incorporated
- Short videos with generosity teaching or testimonies are sometimes shown during the offering
- Digital giving options via text message/phone app and/or lobby iPad/kiosk available
- Giving envelopes are available in the pews
- Guest speakers are invited to preach on generosity/financial topics

Teaching Materials

- Financial class, seminar, or small group (i.e. Ramsey, Crown, or others) are offered
- Generosity devotionals for our church family to use are provided
- Short teaching videos on giving are included on the church website, during offertory, in eNewsletters or through other avenues
- Helpful financial/generosity articles, flyers, or cartoons are included in our newsletters, giving statements, literature rack, website, and other places
- Legacy/wills/trust materials, seminars and/or referrals or appointments with a professional adviser are offered

Donation Collections And Administration

- Online website giving and/or EFT banking is available
- Digital giving is available (by text, cell phone app, and/or iPad/ kiosk)
- Processes are in place to encourage and receive donated assets, property, stocks and gifts-in-kind and turn them into cash
- Mail out giving statements at least 3 times per year, so people can keep track of their giving
- Include a return envelope, financial info, articles and/or helpful reports with our giving statements
- Track and communicate with new regular givers (who have given at least 3 times) and unexpected larger gifts
- Provide our congregation with a list of "As God Provides" projects/costs that cannot be covered by our church budget

- Treasurer conducts an annual confidential analysis of our giving records
- Helpful written policies are in place concerning fundraising practices, borrowing, donor records, etc.
- Provide helpful financial/generosity training resources (webinars, ebooks, articles) for our church leaders/staff

Donation Collections And Administration

- Benevolence financial assistance is available for needy families in our church
- Recommendations and referrals are made to Christian budget or debt coaches/counselors for people struggling financially
- Resources and/or recommendations to provide career guidance help for unemployed and underemployed
- Christian Certified Financial Professionals or Estate Planners we can recommend to people needing this service
- Identify, connect, communicate, and minister to giving leaders and people of wealth in our church

Funding Projects And Campaigns

- A stewardship/generosity emphasis with helpful materials and sermons is executed annually
- An annual special offering is collected for the pastor(s) (e.g., October Pastor Appreciation Month, Christmas, birthday or anniversary)
- Benevolence fund offerings are collected to help people in our church and/or community
- Special donations are collected for missions, missionaries or short-term mission trips
- Collect donations or pledges for building funds or renovation projects
- Special emphasis to encourage generous year-end giving
- A way to receive funds for special "As God Provides" projects not included in the budget

- Mobilize people to reach out into our community with acts of kindness/service [66]

A Reminder About This Book's Purpose

To a great extent, this book itself represents a generosity audit. In a way, its major content sections (Theology, Discipleship, Strategy, Communication, and Integration) make up the categories of inquiry in a way.

Theoretically, the material you are working through becomes a kind of audit you could add to the three mentioned above as you ask yourself diagnostic questions about the work you have done so far.

Your church's Generosity Development Plan (GDP) is the goal of this endeavor. You will eventually create your GDP which contains statements of theology and practice: What do we believe? And what are we going to do about it?

The point is that you are doing what so few churches choose to do: **Be proactive in your approach to creating an atmosphere where generosity will be encouraged, affirmed, and celebrated.**

It is time to get things written down. We are doing this work so that over years we see a shift in culture and behavior. We need the long term plan. So next, we will be turning to the GDP.

---

66   https://naefinancialhealth.org/church-generosity-assessment-survey/

CHAPTER NINETEEN

Create A Generosity Discipleship Plan

Years ago, when I was a rookie road warrior, I began to gain weight. I would put on a pound here and a pound there, eating at restaurants much of the time.

When I visited my family doctor, Dr. Hollett, he told me I needed to get in better shape. I tried to jog and barely made it around the block my first time out. But some strange wave of persistence caused me to try that block again and again, and it wasn't long until I found myself signing up for my first 5k. My fellow Enneagram 3s or Strengths Finder "Achievers" know what is coming next in the story. After conquering the 5k, I decided to run a marathon.

Sparing you the details (us runners love to talk about running!) I entered an era of my life where I was able to complete dozens of races and five full marathons before a knee problem halted this hobby for good.

But here is the point: there is a key difference between deciding to run a marathon and being ready to do so.

And it is called *a plan*.

With the help of more experienced runners and a few key websites, I developed my plan. Step by step, I added distance and effectiveness to my runs until the day I was ready to cross the finish line 26.2 miles later.

You likely noticed a few hints in Chapter 17 for creating a plan for catalyzing a culture of generosity when *data collection* was addressed. In other words, if it is suggested, for instance, that a church track how much generosity is <u>taught in preaching</u>, then this is something that could be part of your Generosity Development Plan (GDP).

Since there was an inquiry about what the church does with <u>first time givers,</u> then that is something that can be systematized in your church's plan. And so on.

So, what were those areas?

The following is a reminder of the categories with an accompanying question to capture the primary intent of highlighting each area. Frankly, if your church leadership had even a very basic response to each of the following questions, they would be at least halfway to a complete Generosity Development Plan:

Worship - What will we include verbally, in video, and in print matter, and how often, to address those who attend Sunday or Weekend worship services?

Teaching - What content will be communicated, and how often, to those who attend groups, classes, seminars, and other gatherings for spiritual enrichment and discipleship?

Triggers - What action, commitment, sign-up, pledge, or type of gift by a member of the church will trigger a pre-planned response from the office or church leadership?

Relationships - In what ways will we converse with faithful donors, large donors, volunteer leaders, staff, and members in regard to the expectations and encouragement around giving?

Campaigns - What is the pace and what are the kinds of special giving initiatives we are likely to conduct throughout the year toward both internal and external opportunities?

Administration - What are the regular practices of sound financial management we will execute in regard to budgets, audits, policies, and reporting?

Discipleship - In what manner and pace will we remind the congregation about the priority of generosity and the pathway toward maturity in this category of their faith life?

Theology - *(though this is not in the data-to-be-collected section of Chapter 17, the first part of the book reminded us that ultimately all of this planning arises out of theological conviction—this is the first part of the plan)* What statements or assertions have we made about what we believe in regard to giving in the life of a believer, and what will our church institute to develop generous disciples?

The key to advancing generosity in the church is intentionality. Effective discipleship happens when the right ingredients are present. In a lot of ways, the plan is not the answer, but the plan allows for the Spirit to work in ways that tend to transform people to a new level of understanding and behavior. We do this in many other areas of the church, so leaders are likely way ahead of my line of reasoning here. The bottom line is that this takes pre-planning and prioritization—it cannot be an afterthought.

Let me encourage you with this: Your plan does not need to be as sophisticated as this book may lead you to believe. You do not need to add 55 new initiatives to create a culture of generosity. As a matter of fact, that would likely backfire.

Let's equate your plan to the building of a house. In that case, the book is trying to highlight a number of features in the house you can build—a menu of design options. It is about creating a floor plan but not necessarily finishing every room or decorating right away.

For instance, you may aspire to having a fully developed system for encouraging Planned Giving at your church. Following the house plan analogy, this would be equivalent to a finished and decorated room called the Planned Giving Room.

But, you may only have the energy and resources to design the room into the floor plan and put up the studs but nothing more. It is an unfinished part of your house—no drywall, paint, or trim yet. At first it will not have the furnishings you dream about. But you have the room in your plan!

For many churches, the first step toward a system for Planned Giving is simply the name of a person and their contact information. "If you are interested in planned giving options in support of our church, please contact Gary Clemmer at 215-321-5544."

For other churches that have been working on this for years, they have a more developed system that may include regular seminars, help with setting up giving vehicles like donor advised funds, charitable remainder trusts, and more. Using our house analogy, their Planned Giving Room is furnished and beautifully decorated. That room is "done."

This same church may have a highly organized plan or system for what happens in Worship (the room is fully furnished). They have a pattern of regular testimonials, teaching, and media that is built into the calendar up to a year in advance.

WHERE TO START WITH YOUR DESIGN

For a church just getting the ball rolling in creating a Generosity Discipleship Plan, there are a few areas that should be on the short list. In other words, tackle these six with as much energy as you can, and the impact on your culture will be significant. Then address all of the other things as you have time, energy, and personnel to do so.

On the short list are the following:
- The role of the senior pastor
- The significance of digital giving
- The potential in the 20%
- The opportunity at year end
- The primacy of church communications
- The importance of reporting impact

The Role Of The Senior Pastor

We will discuss the pastoral opportunity more in the last few chapters of this book, but for now it is important that an emphasis is placed on the cultural influence of the senior pastor. If he or she is the most vocal and visible leader in the church, then their approach to this area of the Christian life is critical.

What most pastors do, as was mentioned earlier, is only what is necessary (for the reasons we stated before). This often amounts to an annual sermon or sermon series. For denominations that conduct annual stewardship drives, this is where the teaching on generosity stays contained.

I would argue that the senior pastor in their own generosity (financial giving and in other ways) signals the level of priority of generosity in the life of a faithful participant in the church. *Leaders cannot expect people to go where they have not gone.* So, it will not be surprising that in both direct and indirect ways, the positive and negative attachments the senior leader has with money will have a significant influence on everyone else.

For instance, if the senior leader says, "I don't really like to talk about money," it often comes from a desire to avoid abuse or not wanting people to think that this is an unhealthy focus. Again, my critique of senior level leaders is rarely, if ever, that they are intentionally doing something unhealthy.

But regardless of intention, this signals the idea that money is a spiritual taboo or even dirty topic. Or if the senior leader has nervousness or anxiety around their own financial position or an unhealthy view of money, this will undoubtedly seep into teaching, side comments, or cynicism. And what about the implications of the leader and their spouse having tension in their marriage regarding money (not unlikely, since most of our marriages are stressed by the topic)?

This, like it or not, will influence the way many if not most of the congregation will view money and its role in the Christian life. What if the senior leader sees tithing as an obligation versus a privilege? Will this impact the generosity culture of a church? Of course it will.

I have often chafed at how much churches expect their senior leader to be a professional Christian and spotless example to their congregation. But the fact is that their influence is real. And churches that do not recognize this as a dominant factor in their culture are missing something significant.

The Significance Of Digital Giving

This is such a massive topic that it could take up a chapter by itself! Likely, you have been bombarded with information about this and have at least started the journey of making digital options available. Statistics tell us that 70% of churches in American now have this platform and the capability to receive a digital gift. But capability is only one part of the equation.

There is an aspect of digital giving that needs more focused attention. When I last checked, though about 3 out of 4 churches can receive a gift, less than half of church revenue arrives this way. Some churches have a very low percentage of digital giving that figuratively collects dust in the corner.

Understandably, churches have hesitations—some practical and some bordering on theological. Others are cultural convictions that something should be "put in the plate" as an act of worship. My main point here is that churches would do well to have a proactive stance. I am not trying to convince someone to use a methodology against their will or conviction. But I am asserting that the trajectory of economics points toward a cashless and checkless future, and we are gaining speed toward that future.

A number of questions about digital giving surface:
- Are we willing to explain and promote digital methods as legitimate options for giving?
- Have we informed people about the various digital giving channels and marketed them as a great option?
- What percentage of our givers operate in the digital giving way? What percentage of our overall giving is digital?
- Can we continue to cultivate digital methods without unintentionally delegitimizing the old-fashioned way?
- What needs to be fixed or refined in this area?
- How should we talk about e-giving during offering moments?

There are no real right or wrong answers here. The only posture I would urge you to leave behind is indecision.

The Potential In The 20%

Over my years of working with churches in financial giving, I cannot emphasize enough the importance of recognizing this reality: Pareto's 80/20 is alive and well. The Pareto principle states that "roughly 80% of consequences come from 20% of the causes." [67] In our case, *80% of giving*

---

67   https://en.wikipedia.org/wiki/Pareto_principle

tends to come from 20% of a given congregation. As much as I wish there was a higher level of engagement, my experience (and the giving records of most churches) will endorse Mr. Pareto.

Instead of resenting this (I used to) or spending a bunch of wheel-spinning energy on the 80% (I did that, too) it is important to know about the concept of working with the "willing disciple."

Spending Kingdom energy on the *willing disciples* is not to the exclusion or neglect of the rest of the congregation. But the good news is that in every church, there is a wonderful group of people that are willing to engage, willing to support, and willing to mature in their faith. They are not there to warm a seat. And in these willing disciples is where the spiritual and organizational energy of the church lies.

I suggest to senior pastors that they regularly tap into this group—gain strength from their energy and encouragement from their forward-leaning posture. And when it comes to people who will not only grow in their generosity but help you encourage others to do so, this is your team. Meet with them, ask them for their perspective (or even critique), and encourage them to be the ones to mentor others, lead small groups, teach Sunday School classes, and be on teams and committees. This is not *"preferring the rich"* but rather deploying into ministry those who are willing and engaged. Were I to go back into pastoral leadership, I would rethink which men and women I would put in positions of influence now that I know how much a generous posture links us to the heart of God.

The Opportunity At Year End

Years ago, I struck up a conversation with a coffee shop manager in our local mall in Kalamazoo, Michigan. One thing from that conversation sticks with me to this day. She said that in the context of a mall location, they made as much revenue between Thanksgiving and New Year's Day as they did the rest of the year.

This reality (in a less dramatic fashion) is one that lives in any organization fueled by charitable giving. This includes the church—at least in America, where tax incentives still play a role in giving motivation and amount. As much as having a consistent recurring gift from a member of the congregation is a kind of gold standard in church giving these days, the truth is that giving increases in the last 45 days of the year (and the last 4 to 5 days of the year). We won't spend the time on the reasons why, but will focus on the reality of the giving spike during the holidays.

This step has less of a direct link with discipleship, and a lot more to do with the importance of the practical opportunity at year end. It is about timing.

Other organizations will take this time to remind people of their mission, the results of that mission, and how important financial support is to that mission. I decided long ago that the cause of Christ was worth mixing into the year-end rumble. And my experience (along with the stats) has shown that many churches will see between 20 and 30 percent of their annual giving happen in this time zone! This is particularly true if there is intentionality behind how this is approached.

> **Hint**: Remind more than once, and do not wait until Christmas to start—other organizations have begun their communication in November.

The Primacy Of Church Communications

In the modern context, communications and media are deeply important aspects of church life. I know this is not breaking news. When I say primacy, I mean that it is essential. If communication is not effective, many areas of the ministry will suffer. Again, not a brilliant deduction, but it bears saying. When it comes to creating (and reinforcing) a culture of generous living and giving, the method and approach to communication is vitally important.

This includes the obvious forms of communication like preaching and teaching. But it speaks to "environments" as well. The lobby and hallways, the website, even leader training materials are examples of the potential influence of clear and excellent communication. These are environments that we create in the conceptual sense of the word. In regard to your church's communication, ask yourself these questions:

- Does our website make it obvious that we prioritize generosity as both a trait of an individual Christian and as a regular part of how our church responds to the needs of the community?
- Are there printed materials like brochures, hallway artwork or photos, and other displays that show our prioritization of giving and community impact?
- Does our communication effort support the nurturing of the many platforms and mediums of giving—from digital giving to planned giving to endowments or special causes?
- Does our email, direct mail, or social media activity include initiatives from our generosity development plan that reinforce how important this is to our congregation?

The Importance Of Reporting Impact

One of the questions that I am asked most often is "How should we report on giving? Should we put it in the bulletin each week?"

Reporting in the church is an extensive topic—and one of my favorites. Suffice it to say, that most churches (even the megachurches with lots of staff and resources) struggle to know what to measure and how to report it —including how to report on the generosity of the congregation.

You probably know by now that I try to avoid making our communication primarily about money or the church operational need. I also find that it is a rare person that will give "because the church is behind budget." And frankly, based on the spiritual principles we have discussed, the church budget *should* be low on the list of reasons to be generous.

Yet, without having any other options available, churches tend to either do nothing, or report "giving last week." I do not want to be overly critical when there is at least an attempt at transparency.

But, reporting numbers is not helpful to most people. And placing an amount in the program bulletin about *last week's giving* (for instance) is completely without context:

- Is this a good number or bad?
- Are we normally ahead or behind budget at this time of the year?
- Do we have an aggressive or conservative budget?

- Does this giving represent a trend that will need to be addressed by an organizational change?

The list of possible confusion goes on.

We will address this in a later chapter, but I passionately urge churches to report less on "input" measures like giving amounts and attendance numbers, and report more on *results* and *impact*. Input measures should be tracked, for sure. But a culture of generosity is enhanced when people hear regular reports of the use of money, its resulting impact, and how that supports your intended mission (outputs).

Again, the average non-profit or para-church organization models the way. They tend to be more apt to share stories of impact or examples of transformation. In their case, without signs of effectiveness, they will simply not exist anymore because donations will go somewhere else.

One of the reasons the younger generations are "checking out" of the church and giving minimally to local congregations is *not* that the church has lost its effectiveness, per se. But the church struggles to know and execute the right approach to celebrating impact. People tend to gravitate to the organizations that do this well.

NEXT STEP

If you are ready to wrestle this down, I suggest you write a Phase 1 draft of what will eventually become a fully formed Generosity Development Plan for your church (you can reference an example of a simple plan in the appendix).

Again, be encouraged! Picking up this book and writing a plan places you in a rare group of church leaders. You will be well on your way to developing a culture of generous disciples if you and a group of leaders agree to some statement about the following things:

- **Theology** - what are your core convictions?
- **Discipleship** - what is your generosity pathway?
- **Strategy** - what is on your generosity calendar?

- **Communication** - how will we communicate this?
- **Integration** - how will we (particularly the senior pastor) interact with people in regard to giving?

Just a page or two (in total) on these 5 areas will give you a fantastic start. Then, you can enhance it "on the fly." It is better to try something imperfect than to do nothing. You can adjust as you go and build the appropriate amount of complexity (over time and with experience) for your congregation.

NOTE:

There is no format that is necessary or required. Make it helpful and clear, not too long, and in the style and theology of your church and you will be well on your way.

Now that you have a plan, it needs to find its way into the life of your church. Sooner or later, we will need to locate and adjust the church calendar. Let's talk about that next.

CHAPTER TWENTY

Generosity Culture In The Calendar

In 2003, I went with Pat Graham—my boss at the time and the president of Cargill Associates—to a church just outside the nation's capital in Falls Church, VA. It was an amazing place—a large church with lots of programs and influence in the region.

As a fascinating side note to this story, the church was historic for a few reasons: One of them was that George Washington's name was on the historical record as a member of the vestry (a term used to denote a group of lay leaders in the church).

We had planned a training session on the church calendar for the leaders (both staff and volunteer) that would help execute a strategic finance campaign. When we announced our arrival to the receptionist and told her what meeting we were there to lead, she was confused and wondered out loud, "Oh—I thought you were coming here for the Men's BBQ. It is one of the biggest events of the year and most of the pastors and leaders are outside on the lawn."

The point of this is not to disparage that church (they don't deserve it). We were likely the culprits of not making our intentions clear: that without a solid place on the calendar, we would not be able to do the work we came to do. Who can compete with ribs and brisket on the lawn?

In the crush of events, programs, worship services, community outreach, and a myriad of other things that are the spinning plates of modern church ministry, there is little chance to create a culture of generosity if actions like the ones we are discussing do not own "real estate" on the church calendar.

Again, intentionality and proactivity are the key to any discipleship initiative. Very simply, the best way to begin to change culture and behavior at a church is when the leaders prioritize it. The first step is to decide what giving and generosity activities should be part of the rhythms of the church and place them on the calendar.

Setting strategic actions ahead of time into the church calendar means that we are not simply nurturing generosity as a response to a budget problem. Rather, it is a regular part of how we disciple people.

This includes classes, sermons, thank-you dinners, campaigns, offering moment testimonials, Impact Reports, and more.

The following three perspectives (from three different fundraising and stewardship professionals) offer a way to think through your planning:

1) A Month-By-Month Plan, Todd McMichen
2) A Seasonal Approach, Patrick Johnson
3) A Non-Profit Perspective, Gail Perry

A MONTH-BY-MONTH PLAN

Todd McMichen, Lifeway Generosity

Again, I turn your attention to some of the very practical examples given by Todd McMichen. Whether you agree with all of the elements of this example is not the point. What it shows, however, is that a church can have a commitment to proactivity:

January	Offer money management classes Send contribution statements (and cast vision) Send Annual Ministry report (gratitude, stories of success)
February	Create a calendar to celebrate generosity in worship (prayer time, scripture reading, personal testimony, etc.)
March	Conduct a church-wide serve day across your community Launch ministry to begin discipling high capacity leaders
April	Consider giving away entire Easter offering to a non-profit Consider receiving scholarships for camps and mission trips that will likely happen in the summer

May	Host a church-wide leadership event that is worshipful, prayerful and celebrative. Honor volunteers.
June	Give attention to your systems for counting, posting, reporting and budgeting. Discover what metrics you will measure to have defined targets for successfully developing generous disciples.
July	Begin to dream about the focus for your next fiscal year. Begin annual budget planning. Conduct a spiritual gifts discovery class to help people discern where God has called them to live generously.
August	Focused attention can be brought to generosity toward children and youth as school returns and athletics take shape. Adopt a school or league to bless with generosity.
September	Budget planning should be in full force.
October	Launch a message series and season of prayer on generosity. Do not make money the theme, but something like gratitude.
November	Host a church-wide celebration event. Show appreciation for the congregation for the impact they made. Cast vision and recruit volunteers. Print a full color Annual Ministry Report and create an inspiring video. Budget planning and ministry plan should be done. Launch a vision and generosity message series. Be prepared for the Holiday season—filled with benevolent opportunities.
December	Conduct a year-end offering toward a dedicated cause.[68]

Figure 20.1

68   Leading a Generous Church: Making Disciples without Chasing Money Todd McMichen
Rainer Publishing, 2015
Pp97-101

A SEASONAL STRATEGY

Patrick Johnson, Generous Church

For another way of framing the proactivity and calendar discussion, we will turn to Patrick Johnson, another influencer in the church generosity space. From the Generous Church website, you can learn more about his helpful technique to encourage any church to be fully conscious of the natural opportunities that present themselves throughout the year. I highly recommend the resources provided on this website, including the following graphic of the 5 Seasons model. [69]

Figure 20.2

If you would like, for instance, to do your planning at a seasonal or more macro level, you can consider Johnson's 5 Seasons approach. His "whole life generosity" teaching provides a wider lens through which we can train people about being giving disciples. It includes all of the ways that both the church and the individual can live in an open-handed way. And the year's initiatives become organized seasonally more than monthly.

Here is my adaptation of his seasonal approach:

FALL - In this *Season of Imagining,* the idea is to start off the ministry year and the back-to-school mindset by casting a vision for the congregation about generosity. "Could this be the year that we go to a new level in our generosity? Imagine what could happen!"

HOLIDAY - In this *Season of Inspiring,* the opportunity presents itself to capitalize on what happens in the last few months of the year in terms of people's posture toward giving. There are often opportunities both inside and outside the church for a special focus on how we live generous lives. "What could we do for our church or community at this time of the year to show the love of God and priority of building the Kingdom?"

NEW YEAR - In this *Season of Instructing,* the first quarter of the year provides the "fresh start" motivation for many. It is not uncommon for goal setting and resolution making to happen in January. Church leadership can teach and instruct on ways to redeem our goal setting by infusing it with the character and teaching of Jesus Christ. "What if this year became our year to go to the next level in our devotion?"

SPRING - In this *Season of Intentionality,* we can continue to provide formal and informal opportunities to graciously challenge people to make intentional choices that reflect a generous heart. With a few months before summer begins and people scatter on family trips and vacations, provide classes, seminars, and other ways to allow people to rethink their approach to life's priorities. "Have you taken advantage of opportunities to learn how to manage and invest what God has placed in your hands?"

SUMMER - In this *Season of Influencing,* many opportunities will present themselves to interact with members of the congregation relationally. Church leaders, pastors, and small group leaders, for instance, may have some opportunities for face-to-face coffee meetings and other more casual atmospheres for discussing the importance of generosity. "How are you doing in terms of the generosity aspect of your relationship with God?"

Here is an example of how this may look in the context of your church calendar:

SEPTEMBER-OCTOBER:
Vision Casting Message or Series
Include the possibilities of expanding impact and equating more generosity with more Kingdom activity and collaboration.

NOVEMBER-DECEMBER:
Year End Giving Opportunity
Review what God has done through the church in the past 12 months and ask for a year-end "extra" gift.

JANUARY-FEBRUARY:
Generosity Pathway Series
Allow for a self-assessment by each member of the congregation and graciously challenge them to make a "next step" in their growing generosity as a disciple.

MARCH-APRIL:
Digital Giving Initiative
Teach about the importance of prioritizing giving and especially emphasize recurring giving as a way to fulfill a faithful commitment and bless the church with consistent cash flow.

JUNE-AUGUST:
Summer Gatherings
Take the casual nature of summer for backyard or in-home gatherings of committed members of the congregation—to thank them, inform them, and discuss plans for the future (and receive feedback).

A NON-PROFIT PERSPECTIVE

Gail Perry, Guidestar USA

As you may have noticed, I keep my eye on *"secular"* fundraising professionals. I think church leaders can learn a lot from them.

Guidestar claims to be "the world's largest source of information for nonprofit organizations." There is a mountain of information and resources available through this organization, but for the sake of our calendar discussion, let me adapt and summarize a single example in order to spur your creative thinking.

As you read these month-by-month suggestions from Gail Perry, ask yourself the question, "Is this something we could adapt for church and place it on the calendar as part of our Generosity Development Plan?"

> **NOTE:**
> Some things listed below (like fundraising events) may have very little connection with your approach to discipleship, but there is still something (in principle) that we can learn from experts in this field. Consider Perry's advice to non-profit organizations:

January—Thank You

Research indicates that donors were far more likely to give again if they received a prompt, personal thank you. So go overboard and show your donors some love. Consider yourself in the gratitude business and elevate it to a high art.

Make the occasion of the gift an experience of joy and celebration on both your part and your donor's part. Studies show that first-time online donors can be particularly fickle. Go overboard with these donors to establish a warm connection quickly.

February—Major Donors

Are you systematically developing relationships with current and potential major donors? Set a firm goal for how many major donor visits you will accomplish each month. And then make it happen. Don't let anything stop you from making these visits—they're absolutely essential. This month, recommit to getting out of the office.

You can make many different kinds of visits:

- Thank you visits
- Advice visits
- Update visits
- "I'd love to hear your story" visits
- "I'd love to share our latest project" visits
- "I want your opinion and feedback" visits
- Asking (for a financial gift) visits

March—Social Media

Make sure your organization is present in social land—it's where you can make many friends for the cause. Social media helps your donors stay connected with you and your mission. Don't forget that people are social creatures. When your donors take part in the lives of others whom they are helping, they are happier and live longer.

This month, assemble and empower a group of smart young people who will drive the social media conversation for your organization.

April—Messaging

Just how snappy are your messages about your cause? Are they interesting? Imaginative? Full of energy? Are you using stories, pictures, videos effectively? Or are you still using that old lofty academic tone that so many nonprofits favor? Remember it's the story that evokes an emotional connection—not statistics!

Take a look at your newsletter. Revamp it into something that's full of pictures. Stop talking about you, your staff, and "organizational news"— instead fill it with stories about people you are helping and the difference you are making in the world.

May—Party Time

May is time to take stock of your events. Lay out the numbers. Figure in the costs of staff time and resources. Add up all the numbers—including staff. Then calculate your net profit for each event. What's the return you're getting on your investment (ROI)? Are all of your events really worth it? The average net cost from events is about 50 percent of each dollar raised. Mailing campaigns cost about 25 percent per dollar raised, and major gifts cost about 10 percent per dollar raised.

June—Retreat

Time to pull your board together for a one-day retreat to discuss the dreams for the future and the funding required to see them become a reality. Discuss, dream, plan and emphasize the personal giving growth of both board and individual donors—what is the strategy?

An annual retreat is essential for another important reason. Downtime outside of a formal meeting gives your board members a chance to socialize with each other and get to know each other. Social time helps knit them into a more cohesive group of team members.

July—Planning

If your fiscal year ended on June 30, you are probably entering a welcome lull. It's time to take a breath. And plan.

Reconfirm your fundraising priorities. What are you really raising money for? What do you need to promote? Can you find some new special donor-friendly projects to promote?

It's time to set new goals for the year. What kind of increase is really possible? If you plan for fundraising increases, spell out exactly how you'll make those goals.

August—Planned Giving

Planned giving doesn't have to be complicated:

1. First, identify people who are your best estate giving prospects they are your longtime donors who give consistently year after year.
2. Then plan to send them a note twice a year promoting an estate gift.
3. Get rid of all the jargon and simply chat with them about the idea of leaving a bequest.

September—Year-End

You're entering the major fundraising season—the year's end. If you are like most nonprofits, you'll raise most of your funding during the last quarter of the year.

Lay out a multi-channel fundraising effort—using direct mail, phone follow-ups, postcards, e-mail, and social media. Use the exact same message over and over in each medium. And lay out a sequence of appeals that reminds your donors over and over how much they care about your cause.

Also, be sure you let donors know your track record of producing measurable results. That just may be the number one reason donors will choose you over another charity.

October—Face-To-Face Asks

Don't forget to include face-to-face asks in your year-end strategy. Select 100 donors and map out a plan to see all of them during the year-end fundraising season. If you can't see all 100, then choose 50, or 40, or even 30.

November—Tweak Your Website

Some 59 percent of all donors are doing *"more research"* before making their gifts—and much of that research is happening online.

Add a Web page that says, *"Your gifts at work"*—with a pie chart of your revenue sources and how you use the money. Post your overhead percentage—that's what today's wary donors want to see, because they are less trusting than in the past.

December—Show Love

This month focus on appreciating everybody! Send holiday wishes to your wonderful donors who help make your work possible. Take time out to thank your board members for all they do for the cause. Board members are so seldom appreciated.

And be sure you thank the staff. An appreciated and acknowledged staff is also a high-performing staff. Remember it's the small thank you(s) and appreciations that make staffers feel appreciated.[70]

Here is an example of how the above NPO model may look in a church context (it comes from the sample Generosity Development Plan in the Appendix):

CALENDAR:

January	Annual Giving Statements
February	Personal Budgeting Class begins
March	Legacy Giving Seminar
April	Budget Process Begins
May	Digital Giving Initiative
June	Senior Pastor visits with top givers
July	Adjust/Finalize GDP for year
August	Annual Audit
September	Vision Cast Dinners with the 20%
October	Annual Generosity Pathway Series
November	Year End Giving Initiative
December	Annual Impact Report Distributed

Figure 20.3

---

70   Gail Perry, MBA, CFRE
On behalf of GuideStar USA, Inc. https://trust.guidestar.org/author/gail-perry

Is your highlighter busy? Or did you underline the things above that you will likely incorporate into your plan going forward? Perhaps various suggestions from all three models will be helpful as you process with your team.

Using any one of the models as a starting point to plan the generosity components into your church calendar will enable you to adapt, edit and re-shape it into something that fits your church. Keep in mind that it is better to start with small objectives and get early and simple *wins.*

For instance, if you are doing very little right now that resembles a comprehensive approach as in the examples above, you may not want to shift to doing something very complex or detailed. You may not even be ready to shift to an initiative every month. Perhaps you could try every other month.

The *5 Seasons* model may be a good ramp up for churches starting from ground zero. Doing too much beyond this may cause over-engineering or even over-emphasis in relation to other aspects of discipleship. When churches deploy too much too fast, the new-found focus on a generous culture will seem out of balance by comparison.

As Alex Calder and I started to pick up steam creating a full-fledged generosity ministry at Kensington church, we started to (unintentionally) get more attention than other very important ministries. We had to learn to pace ourselves so that our exuberance did not make our church leadership look like their primary ministry spotlight was always shining on financial giving.

By now, you have hopefully been able to sketch out your theology, draft your discipleship pathway, and think about the proactive approach to enveloping generosity discipleship into a normative day-to-day part of church life. But there are a few more things to tune up. We now turn our attention to the nuts and bolts of handling money in a way that continues to build trust with our congregations.

CHAPTER TWENTY-ONE
The Traffic Laws Of Church Money

I have lived just outside Detroit for two decades.

Throughout that time, I have heard some of the fascinating stories behind the development of the automobile. And what has been equally as interesting is learning about everything that changed because of the car. About a hundred years ago when the culture shifted from horse and buggy to these crazy new fast machines, new boundaries were needed. Take, for instance, traffic laws.

In the first decade of the 20th century there were no stop signs, warning signs, traffic lights, traffic cops, driver's education classes, lane lines, street lighting, brake lights, driver's licenses, or posted speed limits. Our modern protocol regarding making a safe left turn was not developed enough to avoid mishaps, and drinking-and-driving was not considered a serious crime.

There was little understanding of speed. A driver-training bulletin called "Sportsmanlike Driving" had to explain velocity and centrifugal force and why when drivers took corners at high speed their cars skidded or sometimes "turned turtle" (flipped over).

The transition from the horse age to the motorized age would prove to be very dangerous. At first, speeding vehicles were not a big problem, but as early as 1908, auto accidents in Detroit were recognized as a menacing problem.

As a result, the city would lead the nation in managing this chaotic, enormous challenge:

- Detroit was the first city to use stop signs, lane markings, one-way streets, and traffic signals.
- Detroit was among the first to have a police squad dedicated to traffic control, and second to New York City in creating a judicial

court for traffic violations.

- The city drew national attention for using a tennis court line-painting device to mark pedestrian crossing areas, safety zones, and parking spaces. [71]

So, the inclusion of the proper guardrails to allow for a powerful new wave of change was necessary in what would become the Motor City.

Guardrails are not uncommon in the church environment as well. They are one of the things that insures integrity in the way we handle money matters. And without integrity, it is extremely difficult to create a generous culture. This chapter is about building those guardrails.

Without the appropriate amount of safeguards and protections in place, we can unintentionally cause harm. Having traffic laws in Detroit did not stop all crashes or problems precipitated by the automobile, but it gave the city and its drivers a set of parameters that would reduce harm.

Many churches are ahead of the game on policy and procedure and behind the curve on discipleship in terms of modeling and mentoring generous practices. Still, this handbook cannot afford to skip over this discussion or presume that these guardrails are in place.

The following are the traffic laws that govern how money handling can stay between the lines. There is a splash of guidance about each area—there are longer and more complex treatments of each of these topics elsewhere (in other books, blogs, and articles). I encourage church leaders to benchmark what other churches have done before inventing something from scratch or drastically changing what they are currently doing in these important areas:

- **Policies**
- **Procedures**
- **Budgeting**
- **Audits**
- **Oversight**
- **Transparency**

71   https://www.detroitnews.com/story/news/local/michigan-history/2015/04/26/auto-traffic-history-detroit/26312107/

POLICIES

Most pastors and church leaders I know did not get into ministry because they were excited about policies. If you are anything like me, you may not even be reading this right now—you've skipped past the nuts and bolts chapter because it drives you crazy. But three decades into church leadership, I know now why it is so important.

Good policy breeds trust and it also protects good people from false accusations. Conversely, it allows us to uncover people who are intending to harm the church and then put them on a path to reconciliation and recovery.

"Trust is fragile," says financial coach and church consultant Bonnie Ives Marden. Because finances, if not handled correctly, can be a source of worry rather than security, she outlines seven policies that reduce confusion, build trust, and encourage generous support. [72]

Your church may already have similar policies in place or may have a handful more than the seven I adapted from Marden below. The point is that we are not only *talking* about the safeguards, but also documenting our decisions:

1. **Building Use Policy** - When a group uses church property, a building use policy clarifies expectations about access to the property and use of facilities, such as food preparation, sound systems, worship space activities and supplies, set-up and clean up expectations, safety, and insurance verification. Information on fees, keys, and emergency contacts are important policy elements. Any user needs to align with your missional purpose and to provide a binder documenting appropriate insurance coverage.

2. **Endowment Policy** - Language contained in your endowment policy should include a description of membership, the purpose of the endowment, an investment policy, and guidelines for amending the policy. Also known as a charter, the policy defines the goals, framework, and identified priorities for an endowment in your mission. Because of the legal responsibilities and financial

72   https://www.churchleadership.com/leading-ideas/7-policies-every-church-needs-for-trust-and-transparency/

accountability for managing invested assets and endowments, the policy contains language similar to language used in bylaws. Legal counsel is recommended to ensure that this policy complies with state laws impacting investments, endowments, and charitable giving by nonprofit organizations.

3. **Finance Policy** - These policies provide instructions for creating the budget, opening bank accounts, managing transactions, record keeping, and other aspects of financial management. Your finance policies orient leaders to mission procedures and expectations. While roles and responsibilities for financial management may be defined by denominational guidelines, these policies provide supplemental guidance for local operations.

4. **Gift Acceptance Policy** - This policy offers donors and committees guidance about the types of gifts accepted and how different types of gifts are stewarded, including refusing certain gifts. Especially appreciated by major donors, the policy provides helpful guidance describing whether valuable items or property could be donated to your mission. This policy helps your mission avoid gifts it can't use.

5. **Memorial Fund Policy** - Memorial funds receive gifts honoring a person's life. The memorial fund policy describes the purpose and stewardship of gifts, appropriate uses, and local traditions. Input from family members may be invited; however, the church retains the right to adopt or reject suggestions. Since families and members cannot create new designated funds, their input does not supersede the church's authority to make the final decision.

6. **Pastor's Discretionary Fund Policy** - This designated fund is often available to pastors for special needs or pastoral care emergencies. Models for funding, managing, and distributing discretionary funds vary. Pastors should never be sole signatures on a discretionary fund account because this practice puts both the

church and the pastor in a position of unnecessary risk and temptation. It is the church's responsibility to protect both its assets and leadership.

7. **Safe Sanctuary And Limited Access Policies** - Faith communities set expectations about protecting children, youth, and other vulnerable persons by adopting a Safe Sanctuary policy with guidelines for supervision, adult-child ratios, and transportation. Annual review and revisions, as well as ongoing education, are necessary after adopting a policy. In situations where previous violations of trust, convictions of illegal actions, or status as an offender of some sort exist, customized agreements or covenants set expectations for any level of access or activity. Such covenants need ongoing supervision and vigilance; they set appropriate boundaries seeking safety for all persons. [73]

PROCEDURES

It fascinates me that churches and nonprofits in our country continue to experience some sort of malfeasance: the soccer mom caught robbing the concession stand cash drawer or the finance director that has been embezzling from a parish for years. I suppose it shouldn't surprise me in light of my earlier comments about the power of money.

In an article prepared for Church Law & Tax, Laura Brown provides helpful checklists for churches when it comes to cash handling in particular. There are other procedures to consider, but the handling of cash seems to present a vulnerability for many organizations (not just churches).

Evaluate her suggestions in light of a few questions:
1) *Are we currently doing this?*
2) *Should we be changing or adding to our procedure?*
3) *Are the procedures written down?*

---

73   https://www.churchleadership.com/leading-ideas/7-policies-every-church-needs-for-trust-and-transparency/

Procedures for Cash Receipts

☐	For your offerings, enlist money counters (tellers) who aren't related by family and don't work at the same place during the week.
☐	Avoid selecting someone experiencing a financial crisis. This kind of responsibility may expose such a person to temptation.
☐	Rotate tellers periodically. Try using teams.
☐	When offering plates are emptied, have at least two tellers present. Ask them to count and bag offerings on church premises.
☐	Designate a teller to record the money received. Ask another to review and initial the record.
☐	On a regular basis, have someone other than the tellers reconcile the bank account and list of money received (to the bank deposit, donor records, and general ledger).
☐	Immediately stamp all checks "for deposit only" and place the funds received in a lockable canvas cash bag. Use a bag with only two keys—one you keep at the bank, the other at the church.
☐	Deposit cash daily in your bank account. Never keep cash on the premises unless you use a lock box.
☐	Compare deposits from the regular services to previous services, noting the consistency of amounts.
☐	Send periodic statements to donors detailing the dates and gift amounts received.

Procedures for Cash Disbursements

☐	Make all disbursements, except from petty cash, by check or draft.
☐	Require two signatures on all checks over a stated dollar amount.
☐	Prepare cash disbursements only when someone has approved and documented payment.
☐	Mark supporting documents "paid" to prevent resubmission.
☐	Lock up all blank checks.

> ☐   On a regular basis, have someone other than the individual preparing disbursements reconcile check registers to the bank statements.[74]

Figure 21.1

BUDGETING

Carl George famously observed "Leaders allocate the finite resources to the critical growth path." [75]

His point relates to more than budgeting because a church's resources are more than just its money. But what is powerful about the statement is that it presumes leaders know the critical growth path and are willing to arrange the use of all resources (including funds) accordingly. This is not always the case in churches that have allowed a budget structure to last for years without scrutiny or overhaul when sometimes that would be best. Year after year, many of us start from the same budget architecture, hoping that we don't have to change it much and that we can still issue the staff some sort of pay increase.

Most churches have a budget design and approval process in place. They may not see this as an urgent matter in their generosity ecosystem. You may have already realized that your church has bigger fish to fry than renewing your budget process. At the same time, it may be prudent to think through how a different approach may produce different results.

Among the great challenges in regard to budget, however, is that it is very difficult to set a budget for future ministry when forecasts are usually wrong.

So, why do you spend time making and setting a budget? There are a few reasons, as outlined by author and pastor Eric Geiger:

1. **Start with mission and strategy.**
    Jack Welch declared that strategy is merely resource allocation, meaning a budget is really a reflection of your strategy. It shows what you value and where you are putting emphasis and focus. Connect any strategic planning you do to your budgeting process. Disconnecting strategic planning from budget planning is not wise. Make budgeting about strategy, not finances.

---

74   https://www.churchlawandtax.com/web/2012/may/10-tips-for-counting-cash.html

75   https://www.visionroom.com/budgeting-for-the-preferred-future/

2. **Identify the biggest opportunities for growth and impact.**
   As you plan, look for the biggest opportunities for growth. Set
   goals in connection with those opportunities, and plan to finance
   the biggest opportunities generously.

3. **Find waste and reinvest it.**
   If you use the budgeting time to uncover expenses that could be
   better used elsewhere, you are often able to finance the big
   opportunities. Budgeting lesson: take funds from what is less
   fruitful to fund what could be more fruitful. To do that, you must
   read the next item:

4. **Don't straight-line.**
   A common mistake in budgeting is to take what you are currently
   spending in a category and project that for the next year (called
   straight-lining). Basically, current expenses are copied and pasted as
   next year's expenses. But there may be some unwise spending and
   waste within the category. If you straight-line, you may be straight-
   lining bad stewardship.

5. **Use the time to learn and relearn.**
   I learn something new every budgeting cycle. Because people are
   focused on the type of questions that budgeting raises, the
   conversations are quick and helpful. Approach the budgeting time
   as a time to learn and relearn how resources are allocated in light of
   your strategy.

6. **Form a contingency plan.**
   For the last decade, I have used budgeting to form growth plans.
   But I have also learned to use that time, the time when everyone is
   looking deeply into the finances, to form a contingency plan. What
   will we do if we need to cut 10% from our budget? The plans can be
   high-level and even on just one page, but I would rather think
   about a challenging scenario before the chaos of the scenario hits.
   File the plan away and hopefully you will never need it.[76]

---

76   https://ericgeiger.com/2017/08/6-ways-to-not-waste-your-budgeting-process/

Budget Increase Decisions

It is important for church leadership to have a way to talk about income forecasting. With each passing year, church giving seems to be more difficult to predict. More importantly, it seems like the default mode of most church boards is to anticipate growth, when the analytics reveal something else about the church's giving behavior.

For church leadership to set an expense budget, there should be a top-level discussion (before specific line items are addressed) about the reasons we may be setting the budget at a new level.

Consider the following terminology (or make up your own terms) to have this discussion. Some churches have accounting and finance personnel (or volunteers) who will use financial modeling that provide an analytical approach to financial forecasts—and this can be very helpful. Particularly when a board is justifying one of the following postures:

- **Aspirational Increase**   *(10% or more)*
- **Faith Based Increase**   *(5-10%)*
- **Cost of Living Increase**   *(3-5%) Increase*
- **No Increase**   *(0% - budget remains the same)*
- **Budget Decrease**   *(-5% or more below current)*

Likely, you do not need to create a new budget from scratch. However, you may need to audit and modify your budget to fit with the current challenges as well as your desired direction. The following guidelines will give you a few more rules of the road.

Budget Guidelines

The importance of the budget process is that contributors will respond more generously to an intentional and well-reasoned plan for forecasting.

Consultant and author Ashley Hale writes, "Almost all budgets are compromised, watered-down documents. The average budget provides no reason for generous giving and countless excuses for token giving. It is at best hesitant and fearful and at worst static and apologetic." [77]

---

77   Creating Congregations of Generous People Michaell Durall
An Alban Institute Publication, 1999
Bethesda, MA p39

This kind of budget is what we are aiming to avoid.

My colleague and friend Mike Gammill will often consult churches with a set of parameters that allow a church to assess the distribution of funds. Though he will treat church plants differently in regard to this advice, he contends most churches will need to think through staffing, facilities, programs, missions, and reserves. There are sub-categories under these, of course. But to begin the discussion, Mike will ask the church to consider the following parameters:

☐   **Are we investing too high of a percentage on staff (more than 55%)?** This can be an artifact of a day when the church was growing and hiring to manage the growth along with the belief that having a bigger staff will cause more growth, etc.

☐   **Are we investing too low of a percentage on facilities (less than 25%)?** This could mean that a church has no mortgage but is also not planning for deferred maintenance or seeding a capital fund of some kind.

☐   **Are we too low on programs and ministries (less than 15%)?** This is, of course, an important part of use of money and can sometimes mean that the church has lost control of fixed expenses and is underfunding programs that will fuel the mission.

☐   **Are we too high on international missions (more than 10%)?** Though this may sound counterintuitive—how could you ever spend too much on missions and missionaries—the point is that some churches have abdicated their own involvement in local missions. Churches can unintentionally de-activate members by simply allowing them to "write checks" as opposed to living out their faith in the church's immediate geography.

☐   **Are we keeping too little (less than 3 months' operating expenses) or too much (more than 6 months' operating expenses) reserve cash on hand for emergencies?** Too little or

Figure 21.2

> too much here is a discussion each church should have. Too much
> may indicate too much oversight or too much fear. Having too
> little may mean lack of planning and discipline, or too much risk.

Budgeting On 90%

Todd McMichen has been a leading voice in the church financial world
and is notorious for surprising church leaders with a powerful strategy for
financial strength. When most churches anticipate (and budget according
to) anticipated increases year over year, McMichen takes a different
approach:

*One of the first steps is to get spending in order. I would encourage you to
set a goal that your future annual ministry budget will total 90% of your
previous year's receipts (income). Then with this 90% establish 80% for
internal expense and 10% for cash reserves.* [78]

Imagine that your church spent the next five years using McMichen's
philosophy. With even small increases in giving, there would still be
substantial increases in savings and the ability to have both cash reserves
and deferred maintenance accounts in order. It wouldn't be long before you
could start new initiatives without the often-used planning model of "we
don't quite know where the money will come from but we are operating in
faith."

Here is a quick guide to McMichen's wise financial management

- Discern God's unique vision for your church
- Over time, focus all of your resources on that vision *(staff,
  buildings, finances, and ministries)*
- Say "no" to whatever is not in line with your vision
- Learn to live on 90% of last year's receipts
- Give at least 10% away to like-minded causes
- Put at least 10% yearly in cash reserves *(until you have 3-6 months'
  expenses)*

- Patiently wait, stick to the plan, and get ready to start saying "yes" to new ventures
- Grow generous disciples of all ages
- Possess a high leadership culture
- Pray, lead, and ask boldly [79]

AUDITS

Audit is another word that tends to not produce warm fuzzies in the hearts of those who hear it uttered. But I have certainly warmed up to the importance of audits over time. I liken it to the dentist—I certainly don't enjoy heading over there every six months, but what it does for the integrity of my ability to chew things is very important to me.

An internal audit can include things we do with our process and procedure to self-monitor. I suggest churches additionally welcome an outside party to do an *external audit*—to obtain reasonable assurance that their finances are not being mishandled or misreported.

The group conducting the audit will compare accounting procedures against industry standards and issue a statement (opinion) about what they found. When I was overseeing the finance and development office at Kensington Church, I was impressed with how helpful these audits were—not just for uncovering a problem (which rarely happened) but more for coaching us. It helped us make tune-ups to our procedure to protect employees and volunteers. Audits were never easy on our already busy team, but they proved to be enormously helpful as we continued to build up a robust approach to finances and generosity.

Audits are extremely important for creating a culture of generosity.

When you can look every member and donor in the eye and assure them that the handling of money has been scrutinized by a professional outsider, this is a significant step. It further establishes a culture where generosity can flow. This is my primary reason to suggest churches self-elect to have an audit every year.

---

79   ibid, p82

Secondarily, audits help us build up walls of protection, so that the church, its leaders and congregation, and its financial resources are not compromised. Churches that have never been victimized do not have the same incentive to audit as ones that have. But, the first thing every church leader needs to understand (and believe) is that their church is not immune to financial misconduct. The "we don't need to worry about that here" mentality is the reason why so many churches become victims of embezzlement. Even if your church isn't being victimized (that you know of), implementing a system of internal controls will ensure that your finances aren't at risk in the future.

Coming out of the economic downturn that began in 2008, one major church insurer logged 32 embezzlement-related claims in 2009, up 12.5 percent from the previous year. "Regrettably, financial misconduct tends to be more predominant in economic downtimes," says David Middlebrook, a Texas-based attorney specializing in church law. [80]

Fraud experts often refer to a three-legged stool for embezzlement risk: opportunity, need, and organizational ethos.

Opportunity often is born out of non-existent or poorly managed financial controls. And organizational ethos refers to the cultural environment of the church—is it a place where people feel under emotional strain and see mismanagement in other areas justifying their missteps?

In terms of need, church leaders must pay attention to hardships in the lives of their employees. The most common scenario for church fraud involves longtime employees who face an unexpected financial stress—a job loss for a spouse or an extended illness with hefty medical bills for a family member. "These employees don't start off thinking they're going to steal," Middlebrook says. "They think they're going to borrow from you and pay you back when things improve." [81]

Where do we start? Find an independent accounting agency who will conduct an audit if you haven't already.

Beyond that, please consider a few of the suggestions that come from CPA Kimberly Phegley, who was the Internal Audit Manager of LifeWay Christian Resources when she authored the article "Establish Strong Church Financial Review Practices."

---

80 & 81 A Guide to Internal Controls: Basic principles for keeping church finances safe. Tyler Charles | posted 12/26/2010

Review Of Records By A Knowledgeable Independent Party

The church, or other parachurch entity, should have a finance committee or knowledgeable deacon to oversee the organization's finances. This individual or group should review financial statements for unusual trends, balances, or relationships, and also review any supporting details to provide assurance that the financial records support the statements.

Vacations For Financial And Accounting Staff

Require all staff members responsible for financial and accounting matters to take periodic vacations. Train other staff members or volunteers to serve as backups to the accounting and finance staff. Fraudsters often refrain from taking vacation time to minimize opportunities for others to detect their improprieties.

Independent Review Of Bank Statements

Someone other than the primary accountant or bookkeeper should prepare bank reconciliations and review bank statements for large, old, or unusual reconciling items and suspicious transactions. Reviewing cleared checks or check images could detect checks fraudulently made payable to the accountant, or an entity or alias controlled by the accountant.

Security Of Signed Checks

Secure the church's signed checks to prevent access by the preparer or record-keeper. Signed checks not adequately secured could be altered, allowing the individual to cash them or apply the funds to a personal account, such as a utility bill.

Segregation Of Duties

Keep certain financial and accounting duties separate among staff members, and don't assign incompatible responsibilities to related parties.

Ensure that different individuals perform record-keeping, custody, and reconciliation duties. For instance, best practice dictates that one person would post disbursement entries, another person would have access to the check stock and signature plates or sign checks, and a third person would reconcile the bank accounts to the general ledger.

> ### Money Left Unattended Or In Only One Person's Control

Two or more persons should always count and confirm church offerings, and such monies should always be in a staff member's direct possession or stored in a secure location. These practices reduce the risk of allegations that can neither be supported nor refuted. They also eliminate the opportunity for theft.

> ### Detailed Budget Review And Reconciliation

Detailed budget inquiries serve as both a deterrent and detective control. Thieves look for opportunities where they are not likely to be questioned, call attention to themselves, or call attention to unusual activities.

> ### Checks And Money Logged And Posted By Separate Persons

Generally, the person who first touches the mail should open it and log incoming checks. The second person will then prepare the deposit. The remaining process depends on how many people are available in the office. If there is only one other person, the person who prepares the deposit can post the checks received, and then balance the totals posted with the person who logged the checks. If there are two additional persons available, a third person should balance the log and the summary of posted incoming checks.[82]

OVERSIGHT

Rob Faulk, who served as an executive pastor and now as a partner at CapinCrouse, a ministry consulting firm, recommends strong finance and audit subcommittees with specific responsibilities.

---

82   https://www.lifeway.com/en/articles/church-accounting-financial-review-practices

"Many church boards have two main areas of focus: the faith-based aspect of governance and the business and stewardship aspect. It's important for your church to balance the two, because a weakness in either can cause serious issues in overall governance." [83]

Your church should invest in hiring competent accounting personnel to ensure the basic records are well-maintained and accurate. It is also key to train the accounting staff on what information the board needs and how to prepare it accurately and on a timely basis.

The board should tend to financial health and strength, paying particular attention to:

☐	Protecting the overall health of the church by continuously analyzing financial conditions and trends
☐	Maintaining adequate levels of reserves
☐	Safeguarding investments
☐	Ensuring internal controls are in place to prevent fraud and protect assets
☐	Analyzing best use of funds
☐	Benchmarking other similar churches and their budgets
☐	Assessing financial health
☐	Assuring that appropriate financial practices are followed
☐	Seeing that an annual budget is created
☐	Making sure financial statements are prepared on a regular basis
☐	Seeing that policies are in place to ensure appropriate reserves are maintained

Figure 21.3

It's important to consider how to best plan for and establish the duties for gathering financial information and ensuring proper oversight. Keep in mind that in most medium-sized churches it can take a subset of elders or the finance committee a significant amount of time to be trained on how to properly monitor the church's finances.

---

83   https://www.churchlawandtax.com/web/2018/december/role-of-your-church-board-in-providing-financial- oversight.html

It is vital to put in the time and effort, however. When your church board is receiving the specific information it needs to monitor the church's finances and reserve levels throughout the year, it can make informed strategic decisions to help maximize your ministry.

TRANSPARENCY

One of the best ways to continually build trust is to be open about how money is received, managed and distributed. Though people don't always want to know the specifics of the dollars and cents, they do want to know that there is a process and a person that will help them with any questions they may have.

If church money management seems hidden or it appears that only a few people have the power to make decisions, it does not build trust. How do money decisions get made? By whom? If I have a question, is that perceived as disloyalty or a lack of trust on my part? When does the church report on the specifics of financials and how specifically? Can only members and financial contributors see financials or is this open to anyone?

Since 2008, church spending in America has come under great scrutiny by members who want more information about how their gifts are being spent and what difference is being made as a result of the use of those gifts. [84]

Later, we will explore the difference in generations and their view of transparency regarding church finances. Suffice it to say that with each successive generation, the expectation of transparency about how financial matters are disclosed continues to grow.

When Martin Luther King, Sr., assumed the leadership of Ebenezer Baptist Church in Montgomery, Alabama in the 1930's, he ended the long-held tradition of secrecy surrounding what people gave to the church. He opened the pledge records of the church for anyone to see. Anonymous gifts would be accepted but not recorded. "The practice of anonymous giving," he thundered from the pulpit, "leads to the practice of anonymous non-giving!" [85]

As bold as this move is by the senior Dr. King, that is not what we mean

---

84   The Church Budget: A Catalyst for Spiritual Formation, Ben Stroup, NACBA Ledger, Summer 2011
85   Creating Congregations of Generous People Michaell Durall
An Alban Institute Publication, 1999
Bethesda, MA p15

in regard to transparency. This would backfire considerably in the modern era. I love the story, though, for lots of reasons. The fact still stands that when there is an air of secrecy, it impacts the church spiritually as much as financially.

I remember John Maxwell telling the story that when he was a young pastor and could not find out why there was such an insistence on secrecy by the church board, he eventually realized that it was because the board was not giving. He did not choose Dr. King's method of revealing member giving, but if I recall, it involved something about demoting board members (the whole board, if my memory serves me well). But Maxwell learned that to bring money out of the closet was the best approach for the continued spiritual growth of individuals as well as the church.

Let me be clear: *I am not advocating a kind of transparency that involves revealing member giving.*

It is an interesting study, however, to look at the times in Scripture when the amount of giving was openly discussed. There is a part of me that wonders if we are glorifying or even deifying money when we speak of it with such hushed tones.

I am recommending the kind of transparency that Stu Baker prescribes in regard to trust building. He is another consultant who highlights the fact that the generation now stepping into adulthood is less likely to give to organizations that do not have an easily accessible way to see where and how money is being used.

Baker writes: "Opening up about money—how it is being used and where it is most needed—builds trust between you, your staff, and your church members. It gives congregations an opportunity to be part of the story of growth, financial blessing, and increase in the church and community." [86]

Our "traffic laws of money" discussion has been another opportunity to self-evaluate in light of the above concepts and points of advice. A robust, written, and agreed upon plan to address these six areas (Policies, Procedures, Budgeting, Audits, Oversight, Transparency) will provide the

---

86   https://www.newfiregiving.com/how-transparency-encourages-giving/

strong foundation for creating the guardrails needed.

At some point, we must address one of the critical components of healthy church life—the ways we communicate. It is important enough to be its own wave, and it's where we are headed next.

WAVE FOUR

COMMUNICATIONS

REINFORCE THE CULTURE.

How can we teach the importance of generosity?

CHAPTER TWENTY-TWO
Pinpointing The Communication Gaps

A wonderful couple moved next door to my wife and me just one month before the global pandemic in 2020. It took us a while to introduce ourselves since, in the early days of the "stay at home" order, very few of us knew how to socialize appropriately.

But then something amazing happened. The smell of food cooking on their backyard charcoal grill drew me like a moth to a flame. I am weak in the knees for food, as we have discussed already. And this smell was unique and unfair in its power. It wasn't long until I was crossing from my backyard to theirs to introduce myself.

We since have come to know them as delightful friends. They are Iraqi Christians, and Laith, my friend, will often treat me to a sample plate of his unique food. And it is delicious. Like most chefs, Laith is happy when I am pleased with his work. We also discovered that he has an instructional cooking channel on Youtube with tens of thousands of followers. One video has over one million views.

A unique dynamic of our friendship is that occasionally when Laith is speaking to me about food, home improvement, or the various things that neighbors chit-chat about, he will suddenly stop, smile at me, and turn to his wife for assistance. He will look at Amani and they will speak in Arabic for a few sentences and she will turn to me and say, "he wants to know how to fix the leak in the garden hose but didn't know the English for that."

It is always impressive to me (a one-language person) that until his smiling pause, I completely forget that he is speaking in his second language. The stunning fact is that there are only a few words or concepts that stump him; most of our conversing is smooth. He has been in the United States for only five years. His cooking channel is in Arabic, he and his wife speak in Arabic, and only when he is at work or needs to interact with his nosy and hungry neighbor does he need to practice using a different tongue.

I am suggesting in this book that there is a communication gap in the church. Many pastors and church leaders stumble when we get to the language of generosity. For most of us, it is not our native tongue. But—it can be learned. Some of us struggle because of lack of experience, and still others struggle because the experience we have has not been pleasant. Therefore, we choose to shy away from it—*once bitten, twice shy*, as they say.

Researcher and sociologist Robert Wuthnow reveals his experience with both talking with clergy about what they say about money and from examining the transcripts of their sermons. He concludes that clergy often tiptoe around the topic of money as if they were taking a walk through a minefield.[87]

One pastor said, "Money is probably one of the most divisive issues in the churches. It is an enormous pressure. I hate it. All it takes is one comment, and it sets me off. I absolutely hate it. When I deal with people's money, it is like touching a live wire. You get people that are, you know, *ouchy* about it. I wish I could be more open about it, but people are touchy."[88]

Though these are the words of one particular pastor, he represents what so many of us feel. Yet, the reason we are invested in this topic is to discover how to create a culture where the *ouchiness* lessens.

Is it possible to broach the subject in a way that is less of a trigger for both church leader and parishioner alike?

Consultant Loren Mead says that most congregations live with an unspoken rule:

1. The clergy will not address personal spiritual issues about money.
2. The clergy are allowed to talk—a little—about church budgets and contributions to the church.
3. Everything else concerning money and people's personal dilemmas about it is off limits.
4. The laity will respond by trying to make sure there is enough money to run the show.[89]

87   Passing the Plate
Why American Christians Don't Give Away More Money Smith, Emerson, Snell
Oxford University Press, Inc. New York 2008 p83
88   ibid, p73
89   ibid, p74

Mead's unfiltered assessment may sound biting to some, but they have a lot of credence. Silence seems to be everyone's modus operandi.

And the crazy thing about church communication is that even when we try to communicate clearly about a topic, it still gets confused or unnoticed by many of our congregants! No wonder the relative silence about the topic of generosity has the multi-decade effect of less than 3% giving in America.

The one complaint—the one problem—that nearly every organization or church puts at (or very near) the top of its list of challenges is communication. George Bernard Shaw, the famous Irish playwright, set us straight on this when he said: "The single biggest problem in communication is the illusion that it has taken place." [90]

Suffice it to say that there are some very wide gaps in communication when it comes particularly to what church leaders think, know, or feel, and how that may be different than much of the congregation.

Take, for instance, the reality that Presbyterian pastor Karl Travis highlights when he reminds us that because of growing life spans and active older adults, there are often multiple generations in one church at one time. He writes, "Add to this timeline the quickening pace of cultural change, technological development, and globalization, and we have a formula for disconnection. Not surprisingly, this disconnect applies to our attitudes about money." [91]

A SIGNIFICANT CONTRIBUTION FROM BARNA RESEARCH

In the last decade, the seminal research work on church generosity is in **The Generosity Gap**, by Barna. It involved rounds of interviews with Adults, Self-identified Christians, and Protestant pastors (all in the U.S.). [92] The results of this recent survey are particularly important to the topic at hand because the gap (or gaps) that Barna discovered affirm what those of us in ministry have known all along—the job of communication for church leaders is only getting trickier.

Barna's research concluded that there are four major gaps. For the sake of our work together, it is important that we study them briefly. Of course, reading the full report would be a benefit to anyone interested in the topic,

---

90   https://www.brainyquote.com/quotes/george_bernard_shaw_385438
91   Mind The Gap Karl Travis, 2014, First Presbyterian Church, Ft Worth, TX
92   The Generosity Gap - Barna Group, Ventura, CA 2017 www.barna.com/generosity-gap-sessions

but this chapter will serve as a primer:

The Mind Gap - how we *think* about giving.
The Heart Gap - how we *feel* about giving.
The Soul Gap - how we are *motivated* when it comes to giving.
The Strength Gap - how we *prioritize* our giving. [93]

The Mind Gap

This area demonstrates how we *think* differently about giving and generosity. Consider just a few important discoveries:

- Pastors tend to believe generosity is a matter of planning, discipline, and sacrifice, while many younger Christians think spontaneity and compassion are essential to generosity.
- Christians whose parents were generous during their childhood are more likely to highly value generosity as adults.
- Pastors talk about serving more than they talk about giving—with unintended consequences.
- The people who are most likely to serve or volunteer also tend to give most financially. [94]

In my lifetime, there has been a significant shift in the posture of people, including Christians, regarding the work of nonprofits and organizations that do good in the world. There used to be very little to decide in regard to giving, as the options were fewer than they are today.

For instance, my parents would tithe and give beyond that, often to individuals in need or to missionaries on furlough. But in the 1960s and 1970s, there were not thousands of NPOs vying for attention on a regular basis like today—not to mention the reality that many of these groups do a more effective job than the church in demonstrating the connection between giving and effectiveness.

More than half of U.S. adults surveyed told Barna that buying something for oneself at, for example, Warby Parker or Toms Shoes ("one-to-one" retailers that give away one product to someone in need for every

---

93   Ibid p12
94   ibid, p17

one purchased) is still generous because the effect, regardless of the giver's intent, is good.[95]

Barna's research reaffirmed the connection that those who give more are most likely to spend time serving others—but they are also more likely to say generosity is a frequent topic of conversation in their family. Two-thirds of Christians who consider generosity to be extremely important say they talked with their spouse (67%) or children (64%) about generosity within the past week, compared to fewer than half of all the others. It appears that an understanding and practice of generosity is developed at home.[96]

The Heart Gap

What the research group calls the heart gap has to do with intentions and ideals. Simply put, the heart gap is how people *feel* about their giving. Again, we are discussing a gap—so in this case the gap is how some people versus others value aspects of giving:

- Millennials are more likely than older adults to think of generosity in terms of hospitality and less in terms of money.
- Service or volunteerism is highly valued and more frequently practiced by Elders.
- People tend to think their preferred way of expressing generosity is more generous than other ways.
- Just one in 10 Christians say "to serve God with my money" is their ultimate financial goal. [97]

Back in the early 1990s many of us learned healthy relationship tips from Gary Chapman. In his *Love Languages* book and paradigm, we learned that we tend to want to give love in the way we like to receive it. The lesson was that if I feel loved by acts of service, I may misstep by presuming that my wife also feels loved by acts of service when that may not be her "love language." There is a parallel discovered in this research. We each have a *generosity language* and have a bias toward that.

Researchers found that people most strongly associate their own chosen

95   ibid, p19
96   ibid, p25
97   ibid, p29

means of expressing generosity with their ideal of generosity. If they believe monetary giving is the best way to be generous, they give money. If they believe serving is the best way, they tend to give through acts of service. Still others practice generosity by offering emotional or relational support to others. [98]

> ## The Soul Gap

This gap is the distance and difference between how people are motivated to handle money. These differing motivations drive how people behave and give and is ultimately tied to their primary financial goal or goals.

Many will attribute their financial decisions to a personal or spiritual commitment. Yet, the actions they take can be substantially different from their friends—even the ones with whom they attend church.

In what some may perceive as an oversimplification, for the sake of clarity Barna chooses to describe a money spiritual divide between Givers and Keepers. This is a study of the primary spiritual motivation and here is how the divide is described:

Givers are motivated by "others-focused" goals:
- To provide for their family (43%)
- To give charitably (23%)
- To serve God with their money (20%) To leave a legacy for others (14%).

50% of Christians are Givers

Keepers are motivated by "self-focused" goals:
- To support the lifestyle they want (42%)
- To be content (37%)
- To be debt-free (16%)
- To earn enough to show how hard they work (5%)

35% of Christians are Keepers [99]

---

98   ibid, p52
99   ibid, p47

Fifteen percent of respondents don't fall into either category because they are primarily motivated to meet their financial obligations, which researchers categorize as an "indeterminate" goal. These were respondents who were under-employed and struggled to keep up, so were not necessarily making a spiritual decision but an urgently practical one.

So, from the perspective of discipleship, we may conclude that it is an uphill battle for half of the congregation (both *keepers* and those who are struggling financially) in many churches.

Or we could surmise that givers (50%) plus keepers (35%) are all people that have room to grow on a continuum or pathway toward devotion to Christ in their posture of giving and openhandedness.

Either way, this explains what I have wondered for years about the statistic that around 40% of those who attend any church will not give financially to support that church. I have wondered out loud, "How could someone regularly come to a church, hear about its ministries and the opportunity to support those initiatives and never give?" This research has allowed me to soften my frustration with a level of compassion. Some people in the church are barely surviving. If anything, I should be contributing to solutions that can help them, not judging them as fully ungenerous in spirit.

And the following are some of the observations of the study in the Soul Gap category:

- A person's ultimate financial goal strongly correlates with his or her giving habits.
- Givers are more likely to be married, to have children and to be Protestant, while Keepers are more likely to be single, not to have children and live in a city.
- Orthodox Christian beliefs and regular church attendance correlate with more generous giving habits.
- Christians with giving goals give a lot, and Christians with keeping goals give less or not at all.
- Those with a higher level of Bible engagement tend to give more. The Bible-engaged have a "high" view of Scriptures and read the Bible four or more times per week.[100]

---

100   ibid, p52

Once again, when we choose as church leaders to dive into the complexity, we realize that the diversity of people we lead makes communication a challenge to say the least. But when we recognize the opportunity to create an environment for growth over time, there is hope for transformation.

The Strength Gap

The strength gap refers to how different groups of individuals choose to *prioritize* their giving and generosity. Intentionality is the key concept here. It will come as no surprise to the reader that people who consider generosity important give more consistently to their church and other ministries.

Those who give $2500 or more each year are the most likely to volunteer. Those who are more generous with their money are more generous with their time. And in my experience, this line in the sand (or the giving and volunteering records) will basically correlate to the 20% in the 80/20 principle—these are the people carrying much of the weight of the ministry.

And though half of all Christians say that giving and volunteering are interchangeable, pastors tend to not agree. Most pastors think that giving is not as negotiable as the parishioners do. This represents a strength gap or a difference in what some feel should be prioritized and others do not.

What is the most important contributor to strength in generosity in adults? The answer is that this person was raised by parents who modeled generosity. The actions of parents who were "moderately" generous were not as influential as parents who were decidedly or considerably generous— these are the parents linked with the children that became generous adults.

What may be helpful from the research in terms of developing an effective plan for creating generosity is a confirmation of the idea that individually asking individuals to give is more effective than asking groups. Coupled with the discovery that better givers tend to use electronic giving methods, and you are off to the races with at least two features of how we can approach encouraging generosity.

The urgency to close the four gaps, says the researchers, is increasing by the day. Without effort to close the gaps in your immediate community, they may widen. So, what do we do and can we start right away? There is good news here. You probably have the platforms in place already, and it will be a matter of strategizing how to use those communication platforms differently going forward.

Let's turn our attention to immediate opportunities to close the gaps.

CHAPTER TWENTY-THREE

Closing The Gap

D uring the summer of 2020, I took up a new hobby.
I have always loved being near water. And I have especially loved that water almost always drew me near to boats. I am not sure when I first became enamored with them, but it stands to reason; my father was in the Coast Guard and has grand stories of stints at sea in the 1960s.

When we were kids, Dad rented little fishing boats during our vacations to Lake Wallenpaupack in upstate Pennsylvania. Our other getaways were near the ocean—we called it going to "the shore" like most Philly-bred communicators. There, he would take us on fishing charters. My Scottish maternal grandfather, Adam Paterson, was often with us, pulling in flounder from the Atlantic off the coast of New Jersey. Yet, incredibly, none of us have ever actually owned a boat. My brother and I have talked about this tragedy for virtually our whole lives.

Something finally came over me in 2020 and I purchased a 1958 Wooden Boat—a runabout with the original 35 horsepower outboard motor and most, if not all, of the original parts to the boat. Very old parts.

My boat was unused for who knows how long. It was in need of restoration, the likes of which I would not understand until I was elbow deep in sawdust and sandpaper. I gingerly trailered it to my garage and stared at it, not knowing where to start.

So I just began. I would eventually completely disassemble the benches, shelves, floorboards, and more—and strip, sand, and refinish the surfaces before the boat got reassembled again.

I was quite the spectacle in my suburban neighborhood sitting inside an empty boat in the summer sun, working for hours like Noah preparing for a future that no one else could see or understand. But I was having a ball and the repetitive grunt work of restoration kept my mind off some of the chaos of the world that summer.

I am sure you are already ahead of me in identifying the potential hurdles of a first time boat owner choosing to purchase one that required this level of expertise—an expertise that I did not possess.

I spent lots of time on the Internet watching instructional videos, in marine supply stores talking to "old salts," and listening to advice from my 84-year-old handyman father-in-law in an attempt to swim my way out of my pool of ignorance. I didn't even know what I didn't know.

Certainly when it comes to basic elements of discipleship, there is a gap of information that needs to be closed. Seeing someone grow in faith certainly has an informational aspect to it—because like a rookie boat restorer, people don't know what they don't know. We need to communicate, teach, remind, and encourage—and use all of the methods available to us.

When it comes delivering information in order to create a culture of generosity, the streams most available to us are:

Sermons
Storytelling
Offering Moments
Groups & Classes
Digital Media

SERMONS

As simple as it sounds, many researchers on the topic point out that the primary driver for increasing revenue was the frequency of teaching about giving—90 percent of congregations who discussed or taught explicitly about giving weekly experienced growth. Yet, it is also clear that the vast majority of congregations (79%) only talked explicitly about giving in worship services once a quarter or less. [101]

I encourage teaching pastors to consider various approaches to talking publicly about generosity. It is too simplified to say something like "teach about this weekly" because each church has a different idea of what they mean by teaching.

---

101   https://www.churchlawandtax.com/web/2019/october/reliable-help-for-building-financially-healthy-congregation.html?start=5

I suggest a variety of angles and methods—a diversified portfolio of communicating about generosity. One of them is certainly preaching—sermons delivered in the main worship gathering. And in terms of appealing to action on the part of the congregation, this breakdown may help as you decide your approach to teaching:

Biblical

This teaching regards **what we are encouraged to do from God's word** regarding our living and giving openhandedly. There are a number of sections of Scripture that can be either stand-alone messages or developed into a multi-message series.

Financial

This kind of teaching goes specifically **to wise money management as an outgrowth of the healthy spiritual life.** The fact is, there is wisdom from both inside and outside Scripture for us to consider as we steward God's resources.

Spiritual

Another approach is to **zero in on the heart behind the generosity.** This teaching will be about motivation, attitude, and posture before God our provider. Scripture provides examples of how the heart of the giver and the level of sacrifice is the key to God-pleasing generosity (not just the size of a gift).

Anecdotal

There is power in teaching a series that allows us to **hear how others process generosity in their hearts or model it in their lives.** There can be great power to motivate and inspire a culture of givers when we are able to hear stories of faithfulness by others.

Visionary

This is the kind of teaching that **lives in the "what if?" in order to describe a yet-to-be-realized future.** This teaching paints a picture of what it would be like if we were all living in radical generosity—how our homes, churches, and communities would be transformed if people prioritized God's kingdom.

If you had to pick one of the above approaches based on what you think is the best next step for your congregation, which one would you choose? Did one of these strike you as either your preferred approach or "just what our congregation needs right now?" I encourage you to follow that leading as you are developing your teaching calendar in the coming year.

Patrick Johnson continues to provide great help to the church with his coaching and writing. I especially want to recommend to you his highly practical approach to the sermon component of our topic at hand. In an article entitled *Choose A Theme for Stewardship & Generosity Preaching*, he outlines a different approach (and includes specific curriculum suggestions):

Holistic Stewardship Series

More than just financial management, this series covers the stewardship of time, talent, God's Word, relationships, finances, and more. This may be good for a pastor who is preaching on the topic for the first time or who is wary of just focusing on money alone. It's also a good way to let members know you're not just after their money. *Example: the Generous Living Series by Fellowship Bible Church, Brentwood, TN.*

Holistic Financial Stewardship Series

Strictly on financial stewardship, this series covers giving, debt, budgeting, savings, and other principles from Scripture on how we manage money. It's another good theme for pastors wary of preaching just on giving, and it helps people in their day-to-day struggles to be good stewards. *Examples: North Point's (Atlanta)'s Balanced and LO$T series.*

Generosity Series

This series is strictly focused on the benefits of giving and generosity. Three options include:

- *Generosity: Moving Toward Life That Is Truly Life:* This four-week devotional by Gordon MacDonald is being used by churches as the basis for month-long sermon series, small groups, and personal devotions. Easy to digest, it's built around four "moving" themes—transformation, freedom, trust, and life—that inspire readers to the aspire to a life of abundant, joyful generosity.

- *Treasure Principle:* Many churches are taking the keys of this classic book by Randy Alcorn and preaching a 3-4 week series on these themes. This book presents the theology of eternal rewards in a very compelling way, so it's a great resource to share with your congregation to read as your sermon series progresses.

- *How To Be Rich:* North Point Community Church (Atlanta) presents this series each year, and it's one of the freshest and most compelling messages on generosity around. Based on 1 Timothy 6: 17-19, the series teaches that from a global perspective almost, everyone in today's American church is already financially rich, and we need to admit it. So the key is, it's not about learning how to *get* rich, but how to be rich in good deeds and generosity.

When it comes to crafting sermons, do not be afraid to talk about your own personal testimony with giving (including the parts where you have struggled over the years). Make a call to action that is gracious and unapologetic.

Remember to disentangle your own worth from how people respond to an appeal to greater generosity. If you point out God's work through your church and the impact that it is having and then appeal on that basis, a person choosing not to give is likely not going to be motivated no matter what. Just stay faithful to the authentic, gracious challenges that come from being a generous church.

STORYTELLING

I have the vantage point of being around the church for fifty some years. My mom was likely back to church as soon as possible after my birth. Little did I know when I graduated from high school that I would continue to track with the church and its evolution over the decades of my life as a pastor and consultant.

One thing that seems to be an old-thing-new-again is the effectiveness of telling stories about people or situations where God seemed to act in a powerful way. Our spiritual ancestors, the Jewish people, ostensibly operated in oral tradition alone until they wrote out the stories that make our Bible.

As we have come into this modern context, video has become almost a staple of compelling and emotional communication at churches. And live testimonials or interviews can be enormously powerful as well.

Again, the research from Barna indicates that the main reasons people say they have gotten involved in a cause in the past are primarily emotional: They believed they could make a difference (62%) or they saw or heard a moving story (45%). More than a third of adults remember being driven by an overwhelming sense of purpose (38%) or a relationship with someone who was already involved in the cause (34%).

Even direct pleas for donations may be more effective within the context of church attendance and faith commitment. Three out of ten (30%) practicing Christians (self-identified Christians who say their faith is very important in their lives and have attended a worship service within the past month) took up a cause because their church *"cast a vision"* for it.

Hope of making a difference continues to grow in the psyche of Americans. For example, when it comes to global poverty, a majority of U.S. adults (57%)—11 percentage points more than in 2011—say that knowing it is possible to end extreme global poverty would make them do significantly more to help bring that about. Among practicing Christians, the percentage climbs to 62%. It does not seem that this trajectory will change for the foreseeable future. [102]

---

102   https://www.barna.com/research/motivations-for-generosity/

OFFERING MOMENTS

A built-in teaching moment for most, if not all, worship services is the place where we choose to collect our offerings. Unfortunately, most churches want to "get this over with" and most worship planners see this as something that is an intrusion to the real objective for the day.

A lot could be speculated about the future of the "offertory" moment in a church service. Over time digital forms of giving will increase, physical put-it-in-the-plate forms will likely become extinct, and we will have to decide whether we will still talk about giving in worship if it is no longer a functionality of collecting financial gifts.

By now you probably know my take on this: If the only reason you are talking about generosity and giving is perfunctory (because you have to pass the plate), then there is already a significant problem with your generosity culture.

For the time being, however, churches will still be passing plates, buckets or bags in addition to providing links to text or transfer funds. Even offering boxes in the lobby need explanation during the service.

To create a teaching moment instead of simply a functional task, church leaders will need to consider:

- Talking about the "why" behind offering collections, not just how and when.
- Changing the place in the service or altering the words or prayers that lead into the offering.
- Connecting someone's generosity with the life-change in Christ that happens as a result.
- Utilizing a personal testimonial about stewardship from a lay person as the introduction.

Casey Graham, consultant and founder of the Giving Rocket (a resource for churches on growing giving), has been helpful to many churches by providing supremely tactical advice on how to do things like giving or offering moments in the church service. He writes that every giving talk must have:

1. **Clear direction.** This isn't a time for spiritual mumbo-jumbo. You need to be clear.
2. **A "connect the dots" moment.** Share a stat, tell a story, or explain a Scripture passage.
3. **A call to action.** This is the moment where you tell people exactly what you would like them to do. It's a clear and specific action step.[103]

Dan Mountney, a friend of mine and a former news anchor and media consultant, offers an encouragement to teaching pastors when it comes to the importance of crafting a thoughtful introduction of the offering collection:

1. Fight the tendency to make it the same words each week. People will tune out repetitive messaging.
2. Make "offering moment" a part of your preaching and teaching preparation each week. Budget time accordingly.
3. Tell yourself that you are not ready to preach until you have a thoughtful offering story.[104]

We have a distinct advantage over the nonprofit organizations in that most of our constituents sit in front of us every week (or at least a few times each month). Most NPOs would kill for a captive audience this often. If we craft these moments well, it can close gaps of understanding, celebrate results, and continue to encourage people to live and give abundantly.

GROUPS AND CLASSES

George Barna reminds us:
All ministries teach stewardship. Most do it poorly.

Churches that seem to be excelling in financial giving and developing giving maturity in their churches have a systematic plan for teaching in small groups. This can be a Sunday School class, small group, or special seminar, but the calendar is replete with opportunities that are targeted

---

103   THE WHY BEHIND THE WHAT, Casey Graham, Giving Rocket
104   from a personal conversation with Dan Mountney, used with permission

toward people taking a healthy step in the management of their financial lives. Generosity is regarded as important as other spiritual disciplines like prayer, study, etc.

When it comes to curriculum and content to teach at your church, there is a wide variety of resources available. Some will be produced by your denomination. Many are available because organizations that specialize in stewardship and generosity have developed their own. Each has a distinct flavor that needs to be vetted by church leadership and then promoted in the church. And I suggest it be practiced on a beta group or test class of trusted individuals before it rolls out to the entire congregation.

For instance, when I was in senior leadership at Kensington Church, both the executive and teaching pastors of all the campus sites and their spouses went through Dave Ramsey's Financial Peace University before another 3000 congregants went through the class. This was in part to test the material, and in part to model what we wanted everyone to experience.

Here is a small sampling of budgeting classes and generosity curriculum that can be used in your church:

www.crown.org
www.goodsenseministry.com
www.effectivestewardship.com
www.discipleshiptools.org
www.generousgiving.org
www.generouschurch.com
www.ron-blue.com
www.daveramsey.com

Warning: Some of these studies, in an attempt to help people in a desperate personal budgeting or money crisis, emphasize wealth-building and financial security as the highest goal. There is an unintentional slide into depending on money for our sense of well-being.

I have seen many participants in budgeting classes "freeze" their giving because of the serious nature of the teaching about getting out of debt and getting things aligned. An "I'll give when I have my financial house in order" approach seems justified by the curriculum when this slips into an excuse for lack of generosity.

I would teach, rather, that including giving in your financial behavior is getting your financial house in order—you give while you are right-sizing your spending, saving, and debt reduction.

DIGITAL MEDIA

Another place not to be overlooked as an opportunity for teaching generosity is your church website. Sermons and messages can be downloaded by topic, and teaching content can be available constantly. The opportunity to communicate has never been like this in history.

Consider just a few samples of the teaching on Kensington Church's website giving page as an example:

- *We're not shy about this hot-button issue. Neither was Jesus.* He zeroed in on giving because how we handle our money is the best thermometer of our faith. Taking steps to "heat up" our giving temperature is one of the goals of spiritual growth. Here's how we look at giving...

- *When it's upside down, money controls people and destroys lives.* It's the #1 cause of divorce, a top level stress contributor and common cause of suicide. However, when it's right side up, money is a tool of a generous life helping people grow closer to God and each other.
  It's a reflection of your heart. - Matthew 6:19-20
  It's a privilege. - 2 Corinthians 8:2-4,7
  It's faith in action. - Acts 4:32-35

- *It is About Setting Our Priorities*
  When we give, we are acknowledging three things: First, everything that we have comes from the merciful hand of God. Second, the quality of our life is not measured by accumulating wealth, but by wisely investing it.

Third, it is a privilege to be God's instruments on earth and distribute his resources to a broken, hurting world. When we give, we are actually making a conscious decision to exchange our plans, agendas and priorities for God's.

- *It is About Growing Our Faith*
Giving demonstrates our faith that the God who has provided for us in the past will provide for us in the future. It's the opposite of fear. Fearful people hang on with white-knuckles to anything they can get. Faithful people (or at least those who are growing in their faith) see everything in life as a gift from God—including their money. Every time we open our hands in generosity, we are saying to God, "This is yours anyway—please use it for your purposes."

- *It is About Making a Difference*
Nobody wants to live a wasted life. Being generous with our time, talent and treasure can make a difference now—by giving water to the thirsty, medicine to the sick, or shelter to the homeless. And it can make a difference in eternity—by sharing the saving message of Jesus. You can do both by supporting the people and programs of a high-impact church like Kensington. In a culture that's characterized by selfishness, giving expresses the radical compassion of Christ.

As another example, take North Pointe Church in Atlanta. Visiting their website, I found teaching from Pastor Andy Stanley as well as curriculum to go along with a financial health course.

- **Balanced: Gaining & Maintaining Financial Stability**
Want to learn what the Bible says about money? Need a plan to get out of debt? We have developed a new 6-week curriculum called Balanced.

  - Financial Overview
  - Giving Plan
  - Spending Plan
  - Debt Repayment Plan
  - Tracking Your Spending

The Importance Of Closing The Gap

Being a disciple implies daily following in the steps and teaching of a rabbi. In many of our churches, this ancient concept has lost much of its day-to-day grit and authenticity.

It has devolved into information-delivery in Sunday School and small group gatherings as well as preaching in worship services. These methods are certainly not bad (I recommend them) but may not be the most effective.

Research seems to indicate that the most generous people were discipled in a more effective way—usually by a family of origin where this was simply the water in which they swam.

But many of the people in the modern church have missed out on clear teaching and modeling so we are often operating from ground zero (if not sub-zero because of the *ouchiness* described in the previous chapter). We need to have ways to deliver information in a regular and normalized way, without making it a "special talk" once or twice a year.

Generosity increases when church leaders promote it as a serious and spiritual category of what it means to follow God. There is preaching, teaching, classes, small groups, and even personal budget counseling for those in crisis; there are informative websites and great brochures aplenty.

But beyond that, the people that attend these churches catch a "vibe" that the leaders expect that people will be more generous than those who are not intending to live a Christ-centered life. There is an aura of expectation—people that attend feel a bias toward acting out faith and not just theorizing about it. "Wow—the people around here put their money where their mouth is." And the church leaders don't shy away from closing the gap; they point out the connection between faith and finance on a regular basis and use every platform available to them.

I will continue to be unapologetic in my bias toward all-church campaigns that, in a special surge of energy and attention, challenge the congregation in a powerful way. I think campaigns are communication rocket fuel—so let's talk about them next.

CHAPTER TWENTY-FOUR

Campaigns As Catalysts

I wish we could reclaim and redeem the word *campaign*.
Let's just say with each passing year, having a "campaign" in a church may not be the wisest word choice. And you can't blame people. The word "campaign" often has a distasteful political edge to it.

In 1804, Aaron Burr, who was vice president and aspiring for higher office, killed Alexander Hamilton, George Washington's former secretary of the treasury, in a duel. Doubting Burr's judgment and patriotism, Hamilton had worked to deny Burr the governorship of New York. Burr was outraged over Hamilton's efforts to deny him the political success he craved.

It may have provided fodder for a great Broadway musical, but Burr's shot represented the early stages of what would become a long line of campaign-related violence in America. [105]

Add to this the assassinations of Dr. King and Robert Kennedy in 1968, the year I was born. The riots that erupted in my adopted city of Detroit around that time are still reverberating through its streets to this day. Campaigns and elections in America seem to go with riots and violence.

So a word like campaign is often associated with the ugly side of politics. I continue to hear people ask, "Do we have to call it that?" Absolutely not—call it what you want.

But if we cannot use the word any longer, we cannot throw out the concept. I believe campaigns are a critical part of creating a culture of generosity. Call it initiative, opportunity, or something else, but don't throw the baby out with the bath water.

You may remember in my introduction that this is personal to me. So (full disclosure) I may be biased. Having helped run about 125 capital campaigns at this point, I have a soft spot in my heart for what it can do in the life of a congregation. But, I am not addressing simply capital

---

105   https://www.scientificamerican.com/article/violence-has-long-been-a-feature-of-american-elections/

campaigns for the church. I did that in a different book.

I believe that that a church practicing generosity will have an opportunity to campaign multiple times a year and kick up the spiritual dust in doing so:

- Digital Giving Campaign
- Year End Giving Campaign
- Tithing Campaign
- Missions Giving Campaign
- Endowment Giving Campaign
- Summer Giving Campaign
- Crisis or Disaster Relief Campaign

Let me explain: *A campaign is a concentrated effort to use communication strategy to highlight an opportunity and allow people time to consider and a clear pathway to fund that opportunity.*

There has been a movement lately to *"never do capital campaigns again"* and roll up any capital initiatives into one fund. I am not a fan of this methodology for a number of reasons, but I am also not vehemently opposed. In some situations, this may provide a certain level of clarity and streamline a giving process for an established church that occasionally needs surges of capital for building upkeep. Perhaps it may work in a church with an endowment established for building maintenance and capital improvement. In these cases, a capital campaign for facility improvement or updating may be overkill if a line item can be worked into the budget for capital expenditures.

Because I view campaigns as an all-church spiritual recommitment retreat, I have a hard time wanting to eliminate this practice in our churches. Especially as people get more distracted and it takes a special explosion of communication to garner attention and participation. And because we see them as a kind of detox from cultural mishmash, these campaigns can catalyze spiritual growth, generosity activity, and a higher level of understanding of the ministries of the church. They are like "getting back to the gym" after a few months of sneaking Oreos while binge watching Friends on the couch.

What are we up against in terms of the clatter and clutter hitting the hearts of our congregation? How can we cut through the noise?

In my experience, campaigns cut through the noise and get people's attention in a special way. They are made by a recipe that mixes in these ingredients in tasteful portions:

- Biblical teaching
- Discipleship conversations
- Opportunities to serve
- Public relations
- Organizational Communication
- Vision Casting
- Reinforcement of Values
- Entryway for first gift or first involvement

I will not be the only church advisor to observe that vibrant churches who are serving their community and the world have a generosity fever that is fueled by regular opportunities for people to give and serve.

Short version: *Vibrant churches have campaigns.*

It therefore becomes a shame when I hear church leaders talk about "never having a campaign again" as if that decision was a big favor they did for their congregation. It makes me want to ask, "Do you not have a dream or vision for God so big that it will require the congregation to step up in a way that may rustle them out of their spiritual doldrums?"

KEY FEATURES OF CHURCH FINANCIAL CAMPAIGNS

There are some key features to campaigns of any kind that will produce spiritual and financial results.

Vision Clarity: When church leaders are headed toward asking for more money, they need to spend some time making sure the "why?" answers are in place. Why are we investing in this and how will it help our church fulfill its mission in a more effective way?

Long-Term Planning: Projects that require financial fuel often have multi-year implications—at least the results of them can. When we are investing in something tangible (like a building) or less tangible (like a ministry, initiative, or staff person), we need to explain how it is not a temporary fix, but a long-term strategy.

Communication Strategy: To engage an entire congregation, you will need the help of communication specialists. People who can help church leadership tell the story of *what* we are doing, *why* we are doing it, and *how* it will propel us forward are needed desperately during a campaign. These communication gurus often cause us to ask questions of ourselves and our church that, in a reverse direction, force even further clarity.

Everyone Invited: Campaigns are always an "all-play." Is it a campaign to increase our prayer intensity? A campaign to reach out to our neighbor with God's love? A financial campaign to address a need in our community? A tithing campaign to experience the power of giving at least 10% away? No matter what it is, it presents an opportunity for all—rich and poor, old and young, new and long-time Christian.

Leaders Lead: Church leaders cannot expect members of the congregation to do what they are unwilling to do. Great campaigns are led by the leaders of all aspects of church life—not simply the pastoral staff. Leaders are coached up on the details of the campaign before the rest of the congregation so they can shepherd people through the opportunity in a gracious way, so that no one feels strong-armed into participating.

Precise Ask: People need to know what you are asking them to do, how to do that, and when it should be done. Great campaigns lay out the vision for what will happen if we are successful and then invite people to respond to a specific challenge with a date of culmination.

- "We are asking you to tithe from now until the end of May."
- "We are asking you to commit to a 2-year pledge to build our children's wing. We will all respond on October 17th."

- "We are asking you to join us in praying every day for at least five minutes throughout the advent season."

So, as you can tell, I am a big fan of these periodic bursts through the doors of a church called campaigns. And they can take on many forms. The following represent a handful of the most common ones.

TYPES OF FINANCIAL CAMPAIGNS

Digital Giving: The goal to this type of campaign is to challenge more households to commit to recurring giving—the gold standard of consistent cash flow for the church and an intentional and faithful level of support by a member.

Year End Giving: The benefit of a campaign in the last 45 days of the year is the opportunity the church has to participate in the wave of giving that happens at this time. If churches do not ask for it, someone else will get it.

Tithing Challenge: Many churches in recent years have used the "training wheels" of a 90-day tithe challenge with a money-back guarantee that if the experience was not positive (defined differently by each church), the church will refund all of their giving. Some see this as gimmicky, and I can understand how it could be viewed as such. However, I have seen firsthand that it can cause people to increase their giving and continue even after the initial campaign period.

Missions Giving: The teaching and presenting that happens during a missions giving campaign allows the church to reinforce its value of outreach, spreading the gospel, and funding mission work locally and globally. This is a campaign that focuses on reminding the congregation about that priority as well as one that allows for extra giving.

Endowment Funding: Endowment campaigns often cause the church to have opportunities for planned giving workshops and seminars. This usually—but not always—applies to older givers who will likely have a more positive perception of what an endowment can do.

Summer Giving: The purpose of a summer emphasis on giving is that many people travel and attend church less in most parts of the country. Because our school systems run on the age old agrarian structure that allows for summers off, attendance and attention to giving tend to slump.

Crisis Relief: These initiatives are spontaneous because they are a response to an unforeseen disaster or problem in the community or the world. These are especially good for new and younger givers, as it seems like a direct application of the dollars they give.

The bottom line is that churches that practice generosity utilize campaigns to catalyze spiritual and financial growth. How, how often, and for what you campaign will be a product of your overall Generosity Discipleship Plan. Keep in mind that you want a tolerable pace for rolling out these ideas and initiatives.

The next aspect of clear and powerful communication has to do with how we relay back to our congregation the fruit of our mission. So many churches struggle with what to measure in the first place. So we will start there, before we tackle how to report what is being measured.

CHAPTER TWENTY-FIVE
Measuring The Impact Of Generosity

S eth Godin warns that sometimes we can't measure what we need, so we invent a *proxy*, something that's much easier to measure and stands in as an approximation.

TV advertisers, for example, could never tell which viewers would be impacted by an ad, so instead, they measured how many people saw it. Or a model might not be able to measure beauty, but a bathroom scale was a handy stand in.

A business person might choose cash in the bank as a measure of his success at his craft, and a book publisher, unable to easily figure out if the right people are engaging with a book, might rely instead on a rank on a bestseller list.

One last example: *the church that uses money raised as a proxy for difference made.*

You've already guessed the problem. Once you find the simple proxy and decide to make it go up, there are lots of available tactics that have nothing at all to do with improving the very thing you set out to achieve in the first place.

When we fall in love with a proxy, we spend our time improving the proxy instead of focusing on our original (more important) goal.[106]

Galileo once advised, "Measure what is measurable, and make measurable what is not so." Successful organizations exhibit this motto in their metrics and reporting. They invest in appropriate monitoring and evaluation and are constantly learning.[107]

When churches measure the *right things*, they will begin to cultivate an environment where generosity can flourish. In other words, if we can demonstrate that spiritual progress and kingdom impact are measurable at

---

106   https://seths.blog/2012/11/avoiding-the-false-proxy-trap/

107   The Giver and the Gift: Principles of Kingdom Fundraising, Peter Greer and David Weekley, Bethany House Publishers, Bloominton, MN 2015 p37

our church, we have eliminated an obstacle to more generosity. Easier said than done, right?

As we have already covered, churches can unintentionally make money about the functionality of keeping the organization afloat (a kind of self-preservation posture) as opposed to how money can be used to build God's kingdom.

When money is simply counted, reported, conserved, re-budgeted, and managed, the focus becomes on the money more than it should. This may sound strange to the reader as I have written a lot already about finding more and better ways to discuss and normalize it.

But here is the key and vitally important difference: **Money should always be measured and reported in the context of how it is helping grow our congregation and its impact.**

And if we are not measuring impact, ministry, and spiritual growth as a result of our investment of resources, money will tend to always be simply a data point on this question: Are we meeting versus not meeting the spending projections?

A reminder: *Jesus never talked about money financially.*

According to my friend and colleague Andrew Esparza, the founder of Kingdom Analytics, data collection regarding non-churched people still puts money issues at the top of reasons why they are reluctant to visit a church. In the United States, 55.7% of *non-church* attenders would tell you that the church is too focused on money.

When *church attenders* are asked about their reason to consider leaving, the "too focused on money" reason is cited by 64.7% of respondents.

We have heard this before, but I have come to believe that it is not that we are too focused on money, it is that we appear to be focused on money because of our lack of effort in measuring more than the input: how much money did we collect?

The days of only measuring inputs are over. Most churches need to catch up with this or they will eventually die. I truly believe this.

My passion for this (and perhaps my exaggeration) is in part due to the fact that there are so many more donation-based organizations that have perfected their ability to measure and report, giving the church a literal run for its money.

According to David C. Hammack of Case Western Reserve University, the meteoric rise of nonprofits in our country is due to at least these factors:

- The rise of wealth for Americans
- The impact of the Civil Rights movement on lifting restrictions on Social Services organizations
- The "marketization" of nonprofits

In the last quarter of the 20th Century, the pace accelerated and the competition for the charitable dollar reached a frenzied pitch.[108]

When treated as a single *"industry,"* nonprofits are the third largest workforce in America, behind retail and food services, employing 12.3 million people in 2016. There are twice as many nonprofit workers than there are in each of the nation's transportation, trade, finance and insurance industries, and they account for 10.2 percent of the country's workforce.[109]

The quick history lesson is to identify a challenge that most churches do not realize they have: **If there was a contest between the transparency and demonstration of impact that non-profit organizations communicate and what the church communicates about their impact, the church would lose in a landslide.**

I believe that most churches have a hard time with this *"contest"* because they are, by nature, supposed to be humble. Anything that smacks of bragging has crossed a moral boundary.

Perhaps this question is a great start to the conversation: *What, if anything, can a church reveal or celebrate about its impact without crossing some line of propriety and without appearing to pander for the charitable dollar?*

As the generations that invested in the church primarily because of loyalty are passing away, we are left with generations that have been wooed by NPOs that have done a great job of demonstrating value.

My former colleagues from Cargill Associates have continued their excellent coaching with other organizations—including Scott McKenzie

108   Introduction: Growth, Transformation, and Quiet Revolution in the Nonprofit Sector Over Two Centuries, David C. Hammock, https://journals.sagepub.com/doi/pdf/10.1177/0899764001302001
109   https://nonprofithub.org/nonprofit-content/what-the-growth-in-the-nonprofit-sector-means-for-you/

and Kristine Miller, who write about the usual "scare tactic" way of reporting giving for many churches:

> *Throughout the year, the numbers are red, and people are led to believe that the church is on the verge of financial ruin. Then comes December, the Christmas offering, and somehow, miraculously, the year is finished either in the black or close to it. But come the following January, the scare tactics start all over again. Someone on the finance committee decides that the best way to encourage people to give is to scare them with impending financial doom.*

They go on to cite other stewardship experts on the importance of measuring the most effective way. We can look, for instance, to J. Clif Christopher in *Not Your Parents' Offering Plate*, where he writes that one of the leading reasons people decide to give to an organization is the organization's financial stability and fiscal responsibility.

In his book, *Wit, Wisdom, & Moxie*, Jerold Panas says, "Tests emphatically demonstrate that citing the problems and challenges your organization faces is far less effective than talking about your opportunities, results, and successes.... Donors want to hear the good news, positive outcomes, and results that count. That's what will keep them giving. Don't talk about your needs." [110]

How Should The Church Measure Progress These Days?

But I am getting ahead of myself. We must talk about measuring before we can talk about reporting in the next chapter.

I am sure you have heard that, on the whole, attendance and giving at Christian churches in America is declining. In part this may be good news even though on the surface it seems alarming.

It has been exciting to see more talk about **engagement,** a qualitatively better thing than mere attendance. And in the last decade, the word **missional** has entered the conversation to describe churches that are not sitting passively waiting for ministry opportunities to walk through the front door. In the new way of talking about church progress, *Engaged*

110   https://www.churchleadership.com/leading-ideas/better-way-report-giving/

Christians are the ones who understand and *Carry Out Mission*—frankly, they carried it right out the front door.

Yet there is still a level of cloudiness to the definition of words like *engagement* and *missional*, and like a lot of buzzwords, the definition depends on whom you ask.

There is also the age-old challenge of identifying and measuring spiritual progress in individuals and churches. Measuring the spirit can be like nailing jello to a wall. And if measuring spiritual progress gets too clinical or mechanical, the beauty of metamorphosis is killed, like pinning the wings of the butterfly down to study it closely.

The church, like many organizations that deal with people and life transformation, has a much easier time with measuring input than they do output.

Why Is Input Versus Output Measuring So Important?

For the church, the end game is lives that are transformed by Jesus Christ—this is the desired *output*.

Jesus did not tell us to gather crowds and manage volunteers in order to do good works in our communities. He wouldn't necessarily disagree with those things either—he was all about justice and caring for our underserved neighbors.

But what he unequivocally directed us to do was to go all over the world and make disciples—by teaching, baptizing, and basically creating the "pass it on" multiplication effect that has transformed individuals for millennia.

In North America, individual churches have been marking progress by the standard of "more is better" for a very long time. It is partly cultural (America values progress and increase) and partly human (our preference is for growing, not shrinking) and partly biblical (when God is moving, the church tends to grow in number).

But taking the shortcut of simply looking at *input* (counting the people and activities of the organized church) does not allow us to be honest about the quality or effectiveness of our disciple-making which is the goal of the church in terms of *output*.

Though language like input and output seem to have an industrial or mechanical quality to them, the concept is still very important. Allow me to continue using them for the purpose of our work in this chapter.

Boiled down, it means this: a church can be spending a <u>lot of energy</u> doing a <u>lot of activity</u> with a <u>lot of people</u> and not necessarily be doing what Christ called us to do in terms of disciple-making. It's a tricky but important discussion because *not everything that can be counted counts, and not everything that counts can be counted.*

Here are a few ways to look at the differences using <u>marketplace language</u>:

INPUT MEASURE	OUTPUT MEASURE
Tasks needed to be done	Outcomes needed as a result
Resources Devoted	Program Production
Activities	Results
What We Need to Get Right	What Results Will Come
Service Provided	Achievement as a Result
Use of Resources	Level of Results
Resources	Impact

Figure 25.1

Here are ways to look at this concept using the <u>language of the church</u>:

INPUT MEASURE	OUTPUT MEASURE
Worship Attendance	Life Transformation
Small Group Attendance	Relationship Quality
Financial Giving	Generous Heart
People Serving the Community	Neighborhood Transformation
Attending Bible Classes	Changed Behavior and Attitude
Visitors to Members	Engagement with Mission

Figure 25.2

The distinction between input and output measures is an illustration to train us to start thinking differently. There is no need (nor suggestion) to stop counting noses in worship, for example. And we should still count the offering.

But the urgency being addressed now relates to going a step beyond those elusive and top-level input measures to figure out how to see effectiveness in discipleship in its further colors, shades, and depths.

Your church can start out with a phased approach to measuring impact. This will include inputs, but will be populated over time with more and more output measures as you learn how to best measure those. For instance, you may want to start with five categories and be certain that you have a consistent tool for measuring those things. Here is a Phase One suggestion:

1 ATTENDANCE, VISITORS, AND ASSIMILATION

In addition to measuring attendance at worship, events, and other ministries, there can also be measurements around how new people find those events and choose to stay or not. This category concerns the manner in which we identify, welcome, and assimilate visitors into the life of the church. It asks measurement questions about first-time and returning guests, follow-up, and the pathway from visitor to fully engaged participant or member in serving the mission. More and more, churches are also aiming to measure online attendance and digital engagement with podcasts, blogs, and other mediums as markers of engagement.

2 GIVING AND GENEROSITY

Churches will, and need to, measure the amounts and ways that financial resources are given to the church. Because this is a critical area of spiritual maturity, the giving numbers can paint a picture of spiritual progress of individuals in the congregation. Generosity focused churches can measure the increase of giving, consistency of giving, or average household giving. They can count the members who have taken personal budgeting classes or ones that participate in digital or non-cash forms of asset giving. This not only addresses the practical concern of organizational solvency but also faith growth as it is connected to increased generosity.

3 SMALL GROUPS AND CLASSES

Though they are called different things in different tribes—small group, life group, Sunday school class, etc—most of our churches have a way to mark how many people are in a small gathering outside the worship service (which would be considered a large gathering). The percentage of active adults in a smaller group or class, the health of the groups, the multiplication of group leaders, and the average attendance rate at the regular groups can be noted.

4 LEADERSHIP DEVELOPMENT

Ultimately, the power of a church to minister more effectively to more people is a product of their ability to identify, train, and empower leaders to do the work of the ministry. Churches with leadership pipelines and development methodology will count new leaders, trained leaders, apprentice leaders, and more. Churches with systems for identifying spiritual gifting, five-fold gifting (Apostle, Prophet, Evangelist, Teacher, Shepherd), and other personal development tracks can measure that as well.

5 SERVICE AND MISSION

This is the outgrowth, or living out a life of faith, in service both inside and outside the church—on a local, national, and global level. Churches will choose to measure the percentage of adults in volunteer roles, participation in local or global mission efforts, or dollars designated toward "outside the church" initiatives. This measurement is based on the platform of mission the church has chosen and may include national or international missionaries the church chooses to fund.

The next phases of measurement can include even more related to output and impact, but this often takes time to develop. Then again, you may want to make your own categories or even move some of the following to your own version of Phase One:

- New Disciples and Conversions
- Infant, Child, or Adult Baptisms
- Youth or Adult Catechisms
- Community Impact
- Spiritual Disciplines
- Mentoring and One-on-One Discipleship
- Reaching the Unchurched
- Multiplication (Church Planting, Campusing, etc.)

The benefit of measuring output as well as input is based on a few important assertions:

1. What you measure grows.
2. What you celebrate gets repeated.
3. Measuring outputs is the ultimate barometer of effectiveness.
4. Output measures are the best catalyst for more engagement.
5. Nonprofits are doing this very effectively, so the church looks comparatively "not effective" even though this is often not true.

Imagine with me a future where churches all across our country start to measure more of the right things and hold themselves accountable to the most important things of God.

What started out as a discussion about creating a culture of generosity may also turn into creating cultures of ministry effectiveness like we have not seen in a very long time. Now, let's discuss how to get this kind of reporting into the hands of our congregation.

CHAPTER TWENTY-SIX
Contribution Statements and Impact Reporting

With each successive generation, skepticism increases about the use of money in institutions of all kinds—and the church is at the top of the list. And I cannot blame someone who has a question or two.

The modern televangelist has taken advantage of people who are gullible, misinformed, and perhaps really trying to do the right thing. Couple that with a high trust and loyalty in older generations when it comes to their giving to the church and there is a recipe for malfeasance.

Because money is such a powerful force, it has caused more than a handful of greedy preachers to mar the reputation of the church in this category. This does not help the cause of creating an environment of generosity.

British satirist and media provocateur John Oliver reported on preachers like Creflo Dollar who convinced people he needed a $65M private jet or Kenneth and Gloria Copeland who fly their "preaching machine" (a jet) to luxury ski resorts and gaming trips to India to hunt exotic animals.[111]

It is also widely known that churches have a lack of clarity around how and to whom they report. For a number of reasons that we have discussed already, including the various ways that different age groups view giving in the church, the criticality of effective reporting is on the rise. When considering a gift to a church, the older generations tend to believe the best. The younger the person, the more likely they are to believe the worst.

You would think churches would snap into shape and get straight to the task of reporting effectively and consistently. But the truth is, only a minority of church leaders are scratching the itch for transparency and clarity about use of funds.

And by now, you will know that I am not suggesting printed copies of the budget or profit and loss statements—unless you are taking up the

---

111   https://www.thedailybeast.com/john-oliver-exposes-shady-televangelists-fleecing-americans-for-millions

ministry of providing kindling for the fireplaces owned by the members of the congregation.

Sometimes I wonder what would happen if churches had to fill out the IRS 990 form. This is the public document outlining overhead costs and salaries of their principal employees. I am not suggesting that we change the tax law, but there is something interesting to me about the reason approximately 1.5 million nonprofit organizations in the United States are required to disclose this information and churches are not. Churches need a different motivation to be transparent.

Did you know that there are large professional organizations that grade, monitor, and measure how donations flow into and out of nonprofits? Organizations like the BBB's Wise Giving Alliance, Guidestar, Charity Watch, and Charity Navigator are all great resources to see if an organization has historically contributed a majority of their donations to their mission and show the breakdown of those donations within that mission.

Since there is more to the story, many of these groups will also be more specific with their donor base about how funds given were used to accomplish objectives. This helps donors understand how their contributions fit in with the bigger picture.

When any organization provides insight into how donations are being used, it adds a depth and breadth to the mission that could not be gained any other way. This includes the church and Christian organizations who, whether they are required to or not, should report to demonstrate integrity in use of funds, and impact in accomplishing the mission.

Increasing transparency helps organizations demonstrate the value of the donations they receive. While it may not be easy to correlate dollars directly to actions, estimated costs allow donors to understand how their funds impacted the work that was made possible.[112]

There are 3 critical considerations when it comes to reporting that cultivates a generous culture:

- **CONTRIBUTION STATEMENTS**
- **IMPACT REPORTS**
- **ANNUAL REPORT**

---

112 https://solutions.yourcause.com/measuring-impact-why-impact-reporting-matters-more-than-ever

As we have covered, I believe a critical misstep most churches make is to report on money collected as opposed to how the money we have invested has generated impact. Without this, a member may ask (even to themselves) "Why am I continuing to give to this church when I don't see anything happening that looks like progress?"

How do we report on giving and spending and to whom and how often? Many churches will think of reporting in financial categories, which is understandable.

There are some basic financial reporting practices that may be required (balance sheets, budget categories, etc.) for congregational vote or awareness.

At the same time, churches encouraging generosity need to use easy-to-understand and often non-financial ways to picture giving and spending. The average person's eyes glaze over at a profit & loss statement; they have little interest in reading a budget. But there are much more engaging ways now to express conceptual or mathematical information in a way that people can understand:

- **Infographics**
- **Charts**
- **Photos**
- **Videos**

Suffice it to say that in many polls and surveys, churchgoers have expressed a desire to have more financial information from their churches. Charles Zech, the director of Villanova's Center for the Study of Church Management, summarized his research in this way:

> *We asked the question in a number of different ways, and each time the answer came out the same. Parishioners want more say in how their parishes are run.... They want to be consulted and have direct input into decision-making processes. In parish financial matters they expect accountability and transparency.* [113]

Those findings are consistent with studies showing that congregants at more transparent churches are more generous. This chapter is about

---

113   https://churchtransparency.org/why-church-transparency/

transparency, in a way. But more specifically, this chapter is to outline the importance of the actual reporting and how and how often we do that.

CONTRIBUTION STATEMENTS

Most churches know that contribution statements are required once per year, but I recommend at least three times a year, if not four.

Writer Ben Stroop has been contributing to the generosity scene for years now and I have admired his clarity and practicality on many of these matters. I am adapting and including his treatment of contribution statements because it did not need to be re-written but rather shared:

1) **Personalize the address.** Any piece addressed to "Member" doesn't work. Printing technology has advanced to the point that variable data printing is cost-effective even for small churches. People want to read something with their name on it.

2) **Give me a reason to open the envelope.** Direct mail fund-raising still produces the highest return on investment. The same rules apply to contribution statements. If you don't give me a reason to open the envelope, then I'll never see what's inside. You could be creative or boring. Any copy on the outer envelope will achieve higher "open" rates than blank ones. Even adding "Please verify our records are correct for tax purposes" is better than a plain outer or carrier envelope.

3) **Design matters.** Make sure the mail piece AND the contribution statement are appealing to the eye. If it looks like a tax return, I won't read it. If I've opened the envelope, then you've overcome the most difficult obstacle. Don't fumble the ball when you are on a touchdown run with no opponents chasing you.

4) **Tell me a story.** Very few people are motivated by financial reports. I've met those people before. There is a glimmer in their eye when they are flooded with data and numbers. Guess what? Those people

are weird and not normal. The person opening the envelope wants to hear a story. Do more with this mail piece than just offer a standard, record-based print out.

5) **Leverage the letter.** Use a cover letter as an opportunity for the pastor to retell the story of the church over the previous quarter, especially highlighting measurable moments of ministry impact. Then, close the letter with your dream of what God is going to do over the next 90 or 180 days. Most people never see the "big picture" like the pastor and staff do. Help them see and feel what you see and feel on a daily basis.

6) **Include a comparison to previous year giving to date.** People like to keep score. Even my preschooler, who participates in a soccer program that doesn't declare a winner or loser after each game, knows if his team won the game or not. The people in the pew are no different. It's easy to forget to tithe when you are traveling on business or vacation. Seeing my current year giving next to my previous year giving becomes a subtle reminder to be faithful with what God has freely given me.

7) **Ask me to do something.** At the end of the letter, tell me exactly what you want me to do. You want each member to: review the information, submit any necessary changes, and/or make a gift. You can even include a statement on the reply envelope that indicates additional giving options such as online giving. (Note: You can add a sense of urgency to the reply envelope by printing a message like: "Please process this piece immediately." or "Immediate Attention Required.")

8) **Include a postage-paid response envelope.** Include an already addressed reply envelope. For even better results, make sure the reply envelope is postage-free for the member. When I don't have to search for a stamp, it becomes an easy, quick decision. You don't want the mail piece to get shuffled into a pile where it will be lost forever. You want the member to act instantly without hesitation.[114]

<u>REPORTING ON IMPACT</u>

Reporting needs to feel a lot like a celebration.

Short of dental surgery, there isn't much that is more painful than church financial meetings and bland spreadsheet reports. The people in the pews feel like they are chewing sawdust and most church leaders do it out of obligation.

What if there was another way? What if reporting on giving and expenses felt more like a celebration than a dirge? What if financial data was more photo or graphically driven? What if we asked people what encourages them and in what format?

International Justice Mission does this by attaching stories of men, women, and children that have been directly helped by their organization. It is one thing to know you gave money to help widows provide for their families—it's another to see the faces of those widows and their children.

People like to be part of a winning movement. Showing that investments of church money turned into spiritual and congregational victories encourages giving that is larger and more consistent.

One way to accomplish the reporting need in a church is to update friends and congregants in dinner meetings, coffee and donut round-tables, and large gatherings that feel more like a party that highlights God's work in our midst. We will highlight this methodology in Chapter 29.

Storytelling is the best communicator of life-change and the best motivator for givers that have invested their lives in this church. In these settings, "sneaking in" a quick financial update makes sense and is in context of ministry.

When churches name an event, "Annual Budget Meeting" people run for the hills. And most churches I meet just presume that this is just a given —that poor attendance at church budget meetings is part of life we deal with like death and taxes.

Let's be honest. Does anyone, including the pastor, want to go to a budget meeting? They feel like death or taxes to most of us.

Let's figure out how to conduct these more quickly via a streamed meeting, or change the structure of the polity, necessary votes, and church business meetings that were designed for a time when this was a significant part of church participation. But I suppose changing your church's bylaws is a different pot of coffee for another day.

With the media options available to us, including video, streaming, and digital reporting of all kinds, I believe the annual meeting should be more like a celebration or party and the reporting can be done in very effective visual reports that can be accessed or distributed throughout the year.

In fact, I felt so strongly about this, in 2019 I started **The Impact Report Company** (TIRC) so churches could have a partner when addressing the challenge of celebratory reporting.

Our small team coaches a church leader through the decisions regarding what to measure and how to report it to create a culture of generosity and engagement. Many churches simply need help deciding what to measure in the first place. Once they begin to measure, TIRC will help them create custom infographic-style reporting on a regular basis to encourage and inspire members. See sample reports below.

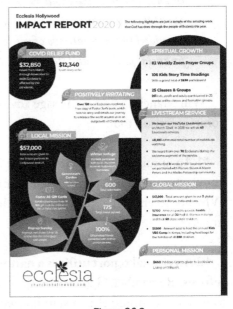

Figure 26.1   Figure 26.2

TIRC urges churches to start out by dipping their toes into the impact reporting world—not by tackling too many measurements at once. They encourage, as articulated in the previous chapter, a collection and celebration of impact that looks at the categories of Attendance, Giving, Groups, Leadership, and Mission, with custom graphs that model both input and output measures. Once the church catches their reporting stride, then they can graduate to other more nuanced measures and even more creativity.

ANNUAL REPORT

You've heard of annual reports, but have you thought of creating one for your church? The point of course is not to imitate a common corporate practice, but to leverage every opportunity to cast vision. As we scan a few reasons why you should do this, let's start with a definition.

Wikipedia: *An annual report is a comprehensive report on a company's activities throughout the preceding year. Annual reports are intended to give shareholders and other interested people information about the company's activities and financial performance. The details provided in the report are of use to investors to understand the company's financial position and future direction.*[115]

Will Mancini offers some sage advice on why you should leverage this communication tool:

#1 An annual report creates a great "excuse" to cast vision. Most people know what an annual report is, but don't expect their church to provide one. Why not leverage the "placeholder in their mind" to make a positive impact?

#2 An annual report utilizes a natural rhythm for reflection and refocus. Remember, God created the cycle of a year. Since you use the year to define everything else in your life, why not use it to nourish the vision for people in the church?

---

115   https://en.wikipedia.org/wiki/Annual_report

#3 An annual report is a great tool to retell your best stories.
Hopefully you've been sharing stories of life change throughout the year.
Now tell them again. As a leader, it's important to know your "folklore"—
the stories of God that are worth sharing over and over and over.

#4 An annual report is an act of gratitude toward God. What if you
saw the process like writing a thank you note to God? Even if your church
didn't have the best year, you have something for which you can express
gratitude to God. Use the report to honor God and point people to Jesus.

#5 An annual report is a helpful accountability mechanism. I get the
fact that accountability is not always fun. Sometimes you don't like
prepping sermons. But this Sunday keeps you accountable. Chances are, no
one is going to wake up and bug you for that 2021 annual report.
That's what makes this point a big deal. You can initiate the commitment
and hold yourself and your team accountable to this kind of vision casting.

#6 An annual report builds credibility with people. While an annual
report is not everyone's "love language," some people will take a giant step
forward because you took the time to provide this tool. It shows the
leadership's willingness to be honest with financial information and
communicates the deeper "whys" behind ministry decisions and direction.

**#7 An annual report is a perfect project to experiment with some new
talent and creativity.** Since this communication tool is not weekly or
urgent, you can recruit some people who are new or uninvolved and see
what they produce. If you haven't done a report, you have nothing to lose by
trying. Ask them for something fresh and different.

So, we are almost there. We have articulated our theology, created
process and practice to maintain high integrity, and designed a pathway to
disciple people to new levels of generosity. But this is not a one time
renovation. It is an ongoing practice that, ultimately, is about the life-giving
relationships that are part of a healthy church body. This is why the fifth
and final wave has to do with walking with the people of our church day in

and day out to generate the kind of congregation that sees generosity as normative in their lives and in the life of the church.

WAVE FIVE

INTEGRATION

WALK WITH PEOPLE.

How can we best lead our congregation?

CHAPTER TWENTY-SEVEN

Generational Differences

M y dad is sneaking up on 80 years old. He is pretty savvy for an old dude. He reads voraciously and deftly transfers from a physical book one day to a book on his iPad the next. He uses an app on his iPhone for his workout routine—it links to the exercise machines at the YMCA. He pays his bills via the bank's electronic payment option. And he has been known to travel through Facebook with the greatest of ease. He worked for IBM in the era that they battled with Apple for which was the best "home computer." I was groomed to despise Apple back then like my Detroit-bred wife was told to avoid foreign cars like the plague. But Dad will also tell you that he is not up for Instagram or "all the rest of that crap." And he would prefer that you don't add too many more options to his phone or computer—most of it appears wasteful and superfluous. He still watches television regularly and consumes news primarily through that method. My parents have a landline phone. He and Mom are faithful and tithing members of their church.

I am in my early 50s and grew up with a computer. We were the first family I knew who had a home computer sitting on Dad's desk in the early 1980s. I was also part of a "special program" in our public school that enabled a handful of us to program a Radio Shack TRS-80 computer where we saved our data on cassette tapes. By the time I went to college, I actually had a computer with me when I arrived. My first job in high school was at Hansen Properties in Horsham, PA, a real estate office that bought an early version of the fax machine. It was the size of a photocopier and stood like a massive piece of furniture in the middle of its own room. I have watched television my whole life: from antenna-received TV to cable in all of its iterations. My wife and I only recently "cut the cable" and have begun to watch Internet TV exclusively. I grew up being taught to answer

the landline "Gibbs family. This is Greg. How may I help you?" I also
watched the Bible version wars (was the KJV or NIV the one to be read?)
and the Worship wars (are praise songs actually from the devil?). My wife
and I were both raised by generous parents who were very connected with
the church. We have been giving at least 10% to the church since the day
we were married in 1990—by personal check for the first 25 or so of our 30
years.

My 22-year-old son is graduating from college and readying himself for
the world of work. He has had a smartphone since middle school; he
cannot remember *not* having one. He rarely buys anything (including
clothing) in a brick and mortar store. He and his friends exchange money
(when they need to pay each other back) via apps on their phone. He does
not know what it is like to watch a movie or television show with
commercials interrupting the story. He hasn't watched an actual television
show since he was a kid. He has never filled out a bank check. Nor has he
answered a landline phone or had to wait for a sibling to get off the phone
so that he can make a call. He has never referred to an encyclopedia for
information. My most serious and spiritual exchanges with him and his
younger sister have actually been via text message. His regard for the
church is respectful but disengaged—he has a playful banter with me about
how the church uses his "tithe money" for stuff that doesn't make sense. I
remind him that he is not tithing so his comment doesn't make sense. We
laugh together and then I wonder how many young people feel this way
right now.

ME, MY FATHER, AND MY SON

More and more material about generational difference is being written,
blogged about, and discussed than ever before.

And many seem to agree that the younger set is more connected with
social justice than anything else. And they certainly deal with money in a
virtually 100% electronic way. I am not embarrassed that my children could
not fill out a check properly—they do not need to know how to do that.

At the same time, the Boomers will be the ones that participate in the
largest transfer of wealth in world history as they give organizations as well

as leave their offspring their wealth.

Some generations see construction of buildings as a sign of ministry success. Others see touching the lives of the under-resourced as a truly worthy cause.

And most churches have a mix of three or more generations in one place! Churches that understand these differences will be more effective in crafting the messaging regarding giving and see more ownership at every generation.

As a church, what capacity do we have to deploy a strategy that communicates differently with each of us—to me, my father, and my son. One of the problems that currently exists in the church is that people my age and older believe that Millenials (Gen Y) and Gen Z are being either stingy or disloyal when they do not seem to give as much.

The gracious older people believe that the younger ones are motivated to give more, but it must be just a factor of income—that when they make more, they will give more. Therein lies the problem: all of these assumptions may be off the mark when it comes to Millenials.

Based on the way this discussion usually starts when I am visiting with church leaders, this chapter could have been entitled, **"Why won't the young people give more?"**

This is the question I get most of the time. It comes from both a frustration with the lack of engagement by younger people, as well as the sense of fatigue that older members of the congregation feel. "We have been carrying the weight of giving for decades. We are now on fixed incomes and no one seems to be stepping up like we did years ago."

Well, the difficult news is that there are no magic bullets or foolproof techniques to increase generosity in all of the generations that will follow us. But the good news is that having this discussion will cause us to think about a lot more than offerings and income—it will force us into conversations about the relevance and effectiveness of our ministry for the future generations.

By way of review, here are the basic breakdowns of the generations that sociologists study. The years can vary depending on which organization you refer to, but they are all very similar:

Gen Z is born after the mid to late 1990s (some say '96, others '98) and Gen Alpha is born after 2010. The years are fuzzy in the more recent groups as these are still forming and the "lines" as to when one starts and another begins are still being debated.[117]

Generation Y is synonymous with Millennial. This group is significant for a handful of reasons as this book is being written. They are emerging as the largest group as the Boomers pass away. They are also becoming the leaders of organizations, businesses, and churches. Business Insider describes the basic difference between younger donors and older donors:

Younger donors described themselves as much more random and peer motivated in their giving, in contrast to older donors who described themselves as more premeditated. Specifically, younger donors are more likely to support a charity when friends/family ask versus the charity asking them. They consider much of their giving relatively random based upon their emotional reaction to something in the media, or based upon who asks.

Older donors have a well-established commitment to their primary charities. They have a budget set aside for charitable giving, and know the organizations they plan to give to. This suggests that it is harder for a new charity to break in with older donors, but once you secure them, they are quite committed.

Younger donors represent relatively open targets. The best way to reach them is either through inspirational stories in the media or better still, via their friends.[118]

Given that a vast majority of charitable marketing efforts today are directed towards direct donor engagement and solicitation versus stimulating peer-to-peer engagement and general media exposure, it would suggest that those marketing efforts are poorly aligned with what younger donors say motivates them to give.[119]

ADVICE FROM A MILLENNIAL FUNDRAISER - WHAT NOT TO DO

In a clever approach to teaching me and my "older" tribe of church and organization leaders how to understand millennials, fundraiser and writer Allison Bonner Ness offers us advice on what not to do:

---

117 & 18   https://www.businessinsider.com/generation-z
119   The Next Generation of American Giving, www.convio.com

As a fundraiser, it can be tough work attracting people in their 20's. As someone who is both a millennial and a fundraiser, I know that people in my generation have plenty of good excuses for their apparent lack of generosity: Too many student loans, subpar employment opportunities, no tradition of giving. But they are just that—excuses.

If fundraisers take the right approach, it is possible to secure meaningful support from young people. Here are five things fundraisers should **stop doing** (along with some advice about what to do).

Talk at me instead of with me.

Communicating with millennials requires going well beyond the scope of television, radio, print news, or vanilla e-mails. Our communities—for better or worse—exist almost solely in the virtual space. We were raised sending instant messages to our friends and stumping our teachers with our ability to find arcane information on the sprouting Internet.

Now that we are adults, we embody the notion of interconnectivity. That's why nonprofits need to find creative ways to use social-media platforms like Twitter, Facebook, Pinterest, and blogs that spark us to action. Smart nonprofits should recognize that young people embrace social media as a two-way channel that allows us not only to stay abreast of the world around us but also to share our views about it.

Send me junk mail.

While direct-mail campaigns may still be a useful way to secure gifts from GenX and baby-boomer donors, they are unlikely to capture dollars from young adults. Few of us receive any meaningful "snail" mail. We pay and track our finances online, and we move so frequently we can barely keep up with updating our billing address.

When we do open a piece of mail, it's usually hand-addressed from someone we can identify by the return address label. If that's not you, you can pretty much count on that piece of mail making its way directly into the trash.

But, for the sake of argument, let's assume your direct-mail piece is so compelling that it gets us to open it. Here, you face the additional hurdle of actually getting us to give. If you're asking us to put our information on a donation form or write a check and put it in the mail to you, leave all hope behind.

We know that smart people don't write their credit card information down on pieces of paper and put it in the mail. Further, even if you do have a link to your online donation page, you'll need us to be patient enough to navigate your mobile-unfriendly site from our smartphone. If direct mail is a must, at least use a quick-response code our smartphones can read and make it easy to use your donation page on a mobile device. But, if you can find us and connect with us online first, you'll increase your odds of actually getting us to give.

Stay silent about your business model.

In earlier eras, nonprofits could appeal to a donor's sense of morality and get a check. But the ease of access everyone has to data means that young adults expect your organization to outline the cost and value of your work.

If you want your millennial supporters to give as generously as possible, don't ask them to consider a gift to the annual fund. Instead, ask them to support specific projects and make clear exactly what it costs the organization and how it contributes to achieving your mission. Building systems that allow your organization to break down its costs and value in a granular way can seem daunting, but the best way to start is one program at a time. When you make one program with concrete figures the centerpiece of your online appeal, your millennial donors, and plenty of older supporters, will be sure to notice.

Undervalue my capacity to give.

Because most nonprofits don't know how to reach millennials, they assume young adults just don't give, so fundraisers settle for asking for small gifts. But millennials know that $25, unless it's raised through Kickstarter, doesn't amount to much. When solicited for such small amounts from an established nonprofit, millennials don't see how a gift of that size can actually have an impact.

But it's possible to jump this hurdle, too. Take the $1K Club at the Washington Area Women's Foundation, which asks "emerging philanthropists" to pledge to give $1,000 to the foundation over two years. With a monthly auto-draft giving program, a mechanism many millennials prefer, this comes out to about $40 a month, the same most spend monthly on a gym membership, or Starbucks lattes.

Not only does the $1K Club leave its members feeling as if they are making a meaningful contribution, it also allows the foundation to cultivate them as future big donors and estimate accurately how much young donors will give.

Never ask for my advice.

It's not just fundraisers, but employers and managers who too often fail to seek meaningful feedback from people in our generation. Because millennials have been raised to expect a community of information sharing with constant feedback loops, we tend to get frustrated and overly critical when we aren't asked for our ideas and input. And we aren't content simply to respond to an annual survey. We want to be asked what we think about something that matters, and we want you to put our ideas to work. [120]

SUGGESTIONS FOR THE FUTURE OF GIVING

First of all, the above essay by Alicia Bonner Ness is a treasure of ideas for you to consider. In summary, I will state her clever "don't do this" approach in a positive manner:

1. Consider alternative to snail mail
2. Respect me as a potential large giver
3. Ask for my advice and involvement
4. Explain your business model and overhead costs
5. Have a conversation with me and other millenials

Second, it is clear that the days of giving by simply cash or check are

---

120   https://www.philanthropy.com/article/5-things-charities-do-that-turn-off-young-donors-like-me/

over. The days of simply doing a "give via the website" will also look old. As cash apps, text to give, and whatever is next (bitcoin?) come into the norm for exchange of currency, we may see the "count team" in the back of the church office going the way of the landline telephone.

By now, you know I am not an advocate of simply eliminating the old ways and replacing them with the new. I believe we are in a transition period that involves my father, my son and me. So, if the church has capacity to do so, it should open up more giving and communication channels.

WHAT IS BEING DISCOVERED

- That the heavy bias towards direct mail no longer makes sense.
- That the solicitation channel and the transaction channel may be different (for instance a donor may get a direct mail piece and choose to give online).
- That donors who are acquired via one channel (e.g. the Internet) may prefer to continue giving via another (e.g. direct mail).
- That websites are often consulted before checks are written.
- That a donor might learn of a cause, or be motivated to support a cause, based on something a friend posts on their Facebook wall, but then write a check or donate online. [121]

While direct mail dominates giving by Matures, the percentage of Boomers, X's and Y's who respond to postal mail declines steeply with each successive generation. The other generations report a variety of channels such as e-commerce, online giving, event fundraising, tributes, monthly debit programs, and mobile/text donations as important giving methods. The younger the donor, the greater the number of ways they give.

A QUICK BREAKDOWN OF METHODS

- Giving by mailing a check is the most common method for Matures. Give by mail is also still prevalent with Boomers and Gen X, although at a lower rate.

---

121   The Next Generation of American Giving, www.convio.com, March 2010

- Giving on a website increases with the younger group so that for Gen X it is nearly equal to mail, and for Gen Y it is greater than mail.
- Giving by mobile/text and social networks are emerging channels for Gen X and Y.

FOCUSING IN ON MILLENNIAL GIVING

As much as you may need to understand more and more about the generations that follow Millennials, the concentration of your time (particularly if you are in a "catch up" mode) should be on this generation because of the reasons stated above.

Here is a review of what we can learn from the research:

1. Build and maintain trust by developing personal connections with Millennials showing clearly how support can make a difference.
2. Articulate where dollars go and how they are managed.
3. Create opportunities for Millennials to get involved through volunteering and participating in conversations related to strategic direction.
4. Connect real and specific stories of impact to gifts.
5. Create opportunities for face-to-face requests and peer fundraising.
6. Recognize that Millennials tend to give many small gifts rather than single large donations.

INVITING MILLENIALS TO GIVE

David Kinnaman asks, "are you thinking and praying together with members of your church family from different generations? My friend Chris Kopka likes to ask if we are doing church to Millennials or with Millennials?" Any internal generosity review your church undertakes must include the input of both younger and older Christians.[122]

Pastors seem reluctant to personally invite people to give. Only one-third say they make a personal, one-to-one appeal twice a month or more

---

122   www.millennialdonors.com REPORT 2011 p66

often (32%). Those who lead large and growing churches, however, appear to be more comfortable with a personal "ask." [123]

Millennials are more likely than older believers to appreciate being challenged, to welcome opportunities to rise to the occasion. [124] Millennials' giving showed a preference for personal, traditional requests over any single technological approach. 59% percent of respondents gave in response to a personal ask and 30% gave after receiving a letter via the mail, compared to the 49% that gave online and the 25% that gave via email. However, this doesn't necessarily reflect how they *prefer to give*.

When asked how they prefer to give, 58% of them pointed to online giving as their preferred method. Still, 48% do prefer to give as a result of a personal request. A similar action-preference split appeared again when it came to giving via mail and email: While 30% of respondents gave after receiving a letter in the mail, only 21% said they prefer to give in response to a mailed solicitation. [125]

The idea of understanding generational differences can be daunting. The task of opening up different channels of giving and communication with younger generations can seem overwhelming. But, to some degree, the ability for your church to thrive beyond its current collection of congregants depends on this.

The next best step may be to create a team of advisors to address this challenge made up of the people that are in this age group. Guide them with the wisdom that comes from years of experience, but listen well—there is so much to learn and adjust.

One of the most powerful forces in church life, particularly when it comes to moving or shifting culture, is the group of men and women that lead. And when it comes to generosity, it is axiomatic that generous congregations are led by generous leaders. Let's look at the impact of leaders next.

---

123   ibid, p58
124   ibid, p63
125   ibid, p65

CHAPTER TWENTY-EIGHT

Don't Underestimate the Impact of Leaders

n the opening of Malcolm Gladwell's book *Outliers*, he tells the story of a group of Italians who were famous for living a very long time—a whole group of them that generation after generation were long on the earth. This group lived way past life expectancy by anyone's measure. They were defying norms and shattering records. What was it that caused this particular group from a particular region in Italy to stay alive so long?

Of course, the studies began—there is nothing like discovering the fountain of youth to motivate research. They studied everything from the wine they drank, to the amount they walked each day, to genetic predisposition and more. If you've read Gladwell, you know the rest of the story.

It was finally concluded that there was a sociological reason for their good health. Where they found themselves as "outliers," or uniquely set apart from the rest of humanity, was in their propensity to talk out, work through, and process life with their peers. That's right; in groups around dinner tables, campfires, and wine tasting, they *talked*. It was determined that without bottling up their inner angst, they were able to navigate life more effectively and with less stress. The result? Long life.[126]

In the 1980s and 1990s especially, the small groups movement in churches surged to recast what people had been experiencing in various forms since the dawn of time. God designed us as social creatures, and some of the most effective discipleship comes via peer groups that assemble. This is not to knock the power of large assemblies or gatherings nor formal worship services.

Among the most well-known phrases coined by a famous mega church 20 years ago that echoed through the living rooms of America back then is: "Life change happens best in small groups."

---

126   Gladwell, Outliers, pp 3-11

In my experience in integrating a culture that celebrates generosity, it has become evident that this concept of life-on-life small gatherings can be a powerful tool. These groups motivate, inspire, reinforce values, and allow for members of the congregation to process through one of the more difficult aspects of a growing faith—how to wisely invest the money God has entrusted to each of us.

God created humans to best understand each other with a give-and-take exchange of ideas. And, one reason Jesus modeled mentoring (discipleship) as the primary strategy for life-change was because this kind of interaction is key.

Shawn Reilly, the Minister of Stewardship & Generosity at the amazing Peachtree Presbyterian Church, has spent many years interacting with people around this topic in both Southern California and now in an affluent section of Atlanta.

He reminds me, "You can have all the systems, classes, and processes in place, but without people in the church who will model generosity for others, it will be difficult to see real change. By far, the most progress will be made through very personal conversations that intentionally broach the topic as an act of discipleship."

If you take nothing else from this chapter, please remember that one-way lecture style communication is not the ideal format for discipleship or life-change. As pastors, we know this intuitively—but at the same time, we sometimes rely too much on the formal large gathering to produce transformation in people. And then we wonder why change is so slow or non-existent.

In a short book I wrote called *5 Reasons Not To Preach About Giving 10% (Even If You Believe It and Practice It)*, I highlight this challenge:

> *It seems like it is time to admit that the responsibility for anemic giving cannot all be laid at the feet of the congregation. Preaching the tithe seems to be one more case study for the definition of insanity: doing the same thing over and over and expecting different results.*

The provocative title of this little book is basically urging pastors and church leaders to not expect that a great sermon series on giving once each year will drive increased generosity. As we have noted, it is one ingredient in the cake. But there are other things to mix in.

There are a few ways to see results by way of the influence of volunteer and staff leaders in your church without a great deal of change to the flow of church life. Particularly since a form of discipleship is a man or woman leading a team, group, class, or even informal discussion in the hallway. Generous leaders will beget generous followers.

In other words, there is already leading and following going on in your church. The question is whether or not leaders are helping or hurting our attempts to create a culture of generosity.

J. Clif Christopher finds it odd when he runs into churches that actually brag about not having the Senior Pastor involved in finances. This attitude is 180 degrees from what it should be in his view.

"What I have seen in fast growing churches is the Senior Pastor always has an excellent grasp of what is happening with his donor base." What happens when a pastor doesn't know? Christopher says lots of things—and most of them are bad. For example, when choosing leadership, the pastor often selects whom he or she perceives to be good leaders and stewards, but they may just have big mouths.

In my experience both as a consultant and a pastor, I have seen these similar concepts on display: *like attracts like* and birds of a feather flock together. In a sociological dynamic I cannot prove, I have found that leaders who do not want to be generous will find followers who feel the same way. If these leaders are allowed to have influence, title, or authority, they will create a tribe that is a stronghold against generous living. These are the tribes that self-affirm excuses for lack of giving and make waves about church leaders "talking too much about money" as a way to deflect attention away from their own unwillingness to look in the mirror.

Perhaps there were one or two, but I cannot think of a time in my 30 years of ministry that a good and faithful giver (especially the ones that give consistently at higher amounts) has ever confronted church leadership about talking too much about giving. The issue of this complaint is almost a telltale sign that someone's inclination to give is low. This occasionally includes people on staff. It almost always includes people on boards and committees.

How can we encourage giving in leaders and then encourage them to integrate relational discipleship into the fabric of church? Let's flesh this out by looking at the following:

- Holding High Expectations For The Staff
- Making Generosity A Prerequisite for Leadership
- Linking Generosity To Leadership Training
- Essential Elements of a Generous Culture

HOLDING HIGH EXPECTATIONS FOR THE STAFF

One of the challenges that some churches face is a result of not being clear with the staff about expectations around generosity and giving. Often this is because senior leadership is hesitant to address the staff about issues related to their own giving, seeing it as a kind of conflict in the supervisory relationship. In the world of the church, however, lack of clarity about the in (giving) and out (spending) of money never leads to productive ends. I have found that people who have felt the call to ministry can have particularly disorganized thoughts about money.

This includes the issue of transparency about church finances, where there is often an odd cloud of confusion because of lack of information delivered to the staff.

Based on the principle of *"the most visible and vocal leaders of any group affect the culture of that group,"* the attitude and posture of the staff becomes critically important.

Most senior leaders have felt at some time in their tenure the sting of hearing that a staff member showed only tepid support for a church initiative when a member of the congregation asked about it. Some have even felt the pain of disloyalty or even sabotage.

The point here is that if a culture of generosity driven by grace is being prioritized, it can be completely derailed by a staff member who has a hallway conversation that is less than honoring.

The ones who will tend to do this have their own set of money hang-ups, as a general rule, which can derive from a number of reasons:

- They believe they are underpaid
- They struggle with generosity
- They have a personality tendency toward fear of the future
- They believe that they don't need to model financial giving because they have already modeled generosity in choosing a vocational ministry career
- They have a spouse that discourages giving to the church

I do not believe that staff members are in the regular habit of being intentionally stingy or grumpy about generosity in the church. But sometimes, they cannot help talking about the topic in clumsy ways because of personal frustrations or even lack of mentoring in this aspect of their spiritual life. After all, we have evidence that pastors, parents, and even seminaries seem to under-serve this category, so what should we expect? This is the reason senior leadership needs to have candid conversations about this topic regularly that sound like coaching more than chiding. People need grace. And they also need help.

A helpful tactic is to, a few times each year, walk through a teaching on any number of topics that feel less directed at a particular staff member and more about becoming a well-equipped minister. Under the umbrella of "how to mentor and disciple people toward generous living," the staff may personally benefit from such training in applying it to their own regard for giving.

MAKING GENEROSITY A PREREQUISITE FOR LEADERSHIP

Another aspect of integrating generosity culture in a church is to continue to add training and expectations of the men and women who lead others.

This may be a small group of people compared to the overall size of the congregation but these are the ones with direct spiritual oversight, teaching, or influence over the disciples in the congregation. It is amazing to me how many churches will allow someone without basic Christian growth and maturity in areas like giving to have authority and influence over the spiritual health of the church body.

Think of the special opportunity these leaders have to move people in a positive spiritual direction:

- Small Group Leaders
- Sunday School Teachers
- Children and Youth Teachers
- Worship Leaders

But it also refers to those who hold positions on committees or service teams because volunteers work alongside these leaders and are deeply influenced by their spoken and unspoken communication.

It will come as no surprise to you at this point that I am highly recommending that the generosity and giving of an individual be considered as a prerequisite for virtually any leader in the church.

The best outgrowth of establishing a culture of generosity at the volunteer leader level is that the workload and opportunity to influence the congregation no longer rests solely on the shoulders of the teaching pastors. A culture of generosity is a team sport.

LINKING GENEROSITY TO LEADERSHIP TRAINING

If you will buy into my presupposition that the power to disciple others in the church rests in the hands of lay leaders, then we must teach and mentor those leaders and hold them accountable. It is a critical aspect of transforming a culture that often includes hundreds if not thousands of individuals. The leverage point is where people have direct contact with a leader and more often than not, this isn't the senior pastor. The character and spiritual maturity of lay leadership is paramount to the mission of the church.

This may catch some churches a little flat-footed in the area of Leadership Development and Training. Many pastors have inherited a system of identifying leaders that has little to do with character or competency. In my experience, even the most sophisticated churches are behind the curve on a pathway for men and women to be *identified, trained* and *released* to leadership in the church.

Again, I would suggest that you do what you can with what resources and energy you have. If you have a leadership process or pipeline, make sure expectations about giving and generosity are part of that. If you do not, then begin to slowly shift your culture toward one that goes about granting leadership in a different way. I highly recommend the work of my friend and colleague Mac Lake. His leadership pipeline coaching and writing is at the top of the list in terms of being helpful to churches aiming to organize more effectively.

Again, we turn to Rick Warren's pointed and helpful coaching as he aims straight at the character issues that need to be present in the life of a leader:

> *One skill that we pastors are never taught in Bible school or seminary is how to teach people to give generously and abundantly, in an over-the-top fashion.*
>
> *It is important, then, that we overcome these deficiencies and teach our leaders to operate in a healthy manner. I have been in ministry for many years now, and I have come to the conclusion that if you want the power of God in your life, it takes three things: integrity, humility and generosity.*
>
> *Vision, I believe, is not the key to the power of God. I will take someone with integrity, humility and generosity over a person with vision any day of the week. Vision can be a product of wrong motives, personal agendas and inflated egos. But if we want God's blessing on our lives and ministries, we must have integrity, humility and generosity.*
>
> *The reason is because those character traits are the three antidotes to the world, the flesh and the devil, or the lust of the flesh, the lust of the eyes and the pride of life. The values of this world are passion, possession, and position (1 John 2:16–17) and the only antidotes to these destructive forces are integrity, humility and generosity.* [127]

John Richardson writes that generous leaders are one of the key attributes of a generous church. In order for a whole community to be generous, it has to be led that way.

He gives some provocative examples like:

- Cornerstone Church in Simi Valley decided to dedicate one-half

---

of all their resources to their neighbors.

- Lloyd Shadrach asked the people of Fellowship Bible Church in Nashville to give away their shoes—at the end of the service, he took his shoes off and left them at the alter and 2500 other people went home without the shoes they were wearing.
- Barnabas sold a field and gave the proceeds away and soon others followed his lead and the early church became known for its generosity. [128]

In addition to public acts of generosity, Todd McMichen recommends that day-to-day choices are being made by leaders in the church to move the culture forward. He urges self-evaluation questions. Leaders need to ask themselves, "Are you…"

- Talking about generosity weekly in your staff meetings?
- Setting aside at least 10% of church donations to give away?
- Spending less than you are receiving, so you can be prepared to say "yes" to God's surprise opportunities?
- Regularly praying for people to be blessed at work?
- Regularly praying for those who are struggling?
- Personally thanking people for their generosity?
- Regularly showing people the impact their generosity is having?
- Constantly evaluating your expenses and financial processes?
- Having multiple training opportunities for the least to the most generous? [129]

The power in any organization lies in the world of what we do, say, and focus on the most. One of the ways the team at Auxano guides the discernment process whereby a church uncovers their identity is to ask the question: What does the leadership think about, pray about, and focus on? What keeps them awake at night or gets them up in the morning?

If creative ways to be generous as an act of God's love to the world never gets discussed by leadership, that says something about whether a culture of generosity will evolve or ever exist to its full capacity.

---

128   Generous Leaders (7 Attributes of a Generous Church) John Richardson, Leadership Magazine, September, 2011

129   McMichen, p42

ESSENTIAL ELEMENTS OF A GENEROUS CULTURE

I have taught for a very long time that the essential elements of an environment of generosity are:

- Trust in Leadership
- A Compelling Vision
- A Sense That God is Blessing

In essence, you can develop generosity in virtually any context, but the ideal scenario has these three things going for it.

Trust In Leadership comes from leadership repeatedly operating with integrity and doing what they said they would do as well as being open to the leading of God and wisdom.

A Compelling Vision is when there is clarity around what the church is doing, how it is accomplishing its mission, and what they are aiming at in the future.

A Sense That God is Blessing is the idea that people should invest their lives in something that has signs of God's involvement by way of fruit bearing. Henry Blackaby taught us to find out where God is moving and then get behind that. Churches can easily encourage generosity when people can see evidence of God's hand on their ministry.

My caveat to the above teaching is that if there is not trust in leadership, the other two don't really matter. So leadership does have a place of importance in the generosity equation in each church.

A study of Millennial donors discovered what motivated them and it is another endorsement of the importance of leadership operating with integrity. The 2011 Millennial Donors report found that they were motivated to give most by:

1. Compelling Mission/Cause
2. Personal Connection with leadership
3. Friend or peer endorsement [130]

The study further revealed that for this group, the way to earn their trust

---

130   https://casefoundation.org/wp-content/uploads/2014/11/MillennialImpactReport-2011.pdf

was "opportunities to meet leadership." If the leadership is not perceived as open, accessible, and full of integrity, the suspicion would be too great for a financial gift toward the organization.

Ninety percent of those surveyed said they would stop giving if they did not trust the organization.[131] The first step in the journey to giving growth is a "heart check" of the leaders that most influence church life and culture. Our problem as church leaders may be looking back at us in the mirror.

In addition to focusing attention on the development of leaders toward lives of generosity, there are things that each church must incorporate into the regular rhythm of leading and discipling the congregation, to which we now turn our attention.

CHAPTER TWENTY-NINE
Nurture and Challenge

I n the late 1980s, three former football quarterbacks started to go to the gym together to workout. They were all just turning thirty or so, worked on the same church staff in a traditional denomination, had similar dreams and frustrations, and had that confidence that comes from competitors. Eventually, the three guys and their wives (and a few kids, if I recall) left to start a new and risky adventure.

Long before I ever met these three couples that started Kensington Church near Detroit, they were plotting their church plant together that would start officially in 1990 and was thirty years old at the time of the writing of this book. I was blessed and fortunate to join them for years 2006-2016 because of the foresight of my friend and colleague, Kyle Nabors.

Kyle had worked in the early 2000s at Mercy Ships, a worldwide organization that managed tens of millions of dollars of assets and funds to serve the needy around the world. Mercy Ships converts cruise liners into seaworthy hospitals that can port in cities around the third world. Volunteer medical professionals commit to spend time on these ships, conducting surgeries and meeting the extraordinary medical needs that those regions tend to have.

Here is the point: The reason Kyle brought me to Kensington was because of the ridiculously ambitious vision of the founding pastor, Steve Andrews. Steve dreamed of and prayed for a future that included church planting and global ministry that would demand an equally ambitious amount of funding. Kyle, having been exposed to development professionals at Mercy Ships, knew that there needed to be a focused and intentional strategy to nurture giving. It could not be a business-as-usual approach to the offering collection. Steve's vision would need a level of sophistication that most churches do not have the resources to execute, but then again, most churches did not have this level of ambition. They went hand in hand.

The idea of a Stewardship Pastor or Generosity Pastor is not a new thing at this point—especially for very large churches. But it felt fairly new to me, and I was excited to take on the challenge. And it proved to be a decade of creating and honing a team and a process at Kensington that would create a culture of generosity.

We borrowed, copied, studied, and trial-and-error tested things from university and nonprofit fundraising. We went to seminars and workshops. We used much of what I had learned on the road with Cargill Associates. We took advice from Kyle and others who had experience with larger organizations with fundraising professionals. And we ran it all through a culture and theology grid to make sure it was kosher.

In many ways, the 5 Wave process in this book is a culmination of learning for nearly twenty years, but especially the ten I spent with my colleague Alex Calder at Kensington (to which I have referred many times so far in this book). What we learned was that ultimately it was about nurturing relationships with people who were on a spiritual journey, a journey that included their generosity. It was about intentionality specifically related to *nurture and challenge*.

Fortunately, I took a risk on hiring Alex, at that time a young college graduate, that God used in a powerful way. Alex's relational skills are top-notch, so his wiring was a hand-in-glove fit with what was needed.

For example, part of his relational genius is simply finding multiple lanes through which he (and the church) can express gratitude. Alex reminds us of the importance of thanking people beyond just trying to motivate the "next gift":

- Thanking people shows humility on the part of church leaders.
- Thanking says, "I don't take you for granted."
- Thanking affirms the partnership of people with resources investing in ministry initiatives.
- Thanking people for being a conduit of God's provision is a healthy spiritual posture for church leaders.

- Thanking begins or cultivates the relationship between church leaders and the congregation.
- Thanking communicates that the gift is needed and will be utilized for the church's mission.
- Thanking begins or cultivates the relationship between church leaders and the congregation.
- Thanking is free (email, phone call) or only a few cents (hand-written, hand-stamped card in the mail)!

In his book *The Spirituality of Fundraising*, author Henri J.M. Nouwen has packed a lot of punch into a very short work. He writes that fundraising is ultimately relationship building.

People have such a need for friendship and for community that fundraising has to be community-building. I wonder how many churches and charitable organizations realize that community is one of the greatest gifts they have to offer. Fund-raising must always aim to create new, lasting friendships.[132]

To keep alive the idea of funding the vision and developing relationships along the way, at Kensington we basically created what in a university setting would be called a Development Office. This is a group of people and a process that leads toward the cultivation of more funds for the cause—in this case, our church.

I fully recognize that a vast majority of churches in America cannot justify paying one staff person for such a position, let alone a team of two or three. But the activities and processes can still be executed at whatever level your church can prioritize and resource. And there are a number of these activities that could be right-sized to fit the scope of a volunteer role. At a very basic and bird's eye view, here is what our team did for Kensington. Again, I would suggest you use this as a kind of diagnostic tool and think of what your church does in each of these categories.

Another way to look at each tool is to evaluate whether or not a volunteer could be tasked with the responsibility:

1. **Contribution Statements** – on a quarterly basis, each giving

---

household receives a contribution statement accompanied by a vision cast (usually a cover letter) and often a celebration of some aspect of the ministry. The frequency allows for an opportunity to thank people as well as remind them of the importance of their gift.

2. **Day-to-Day Donor Care** – when anyone had a question about their giving, the church's use of funds, or anything that had to do with "money," there was a commitment to respond within 24 hours. This included times when we would say, "I wanted to call you back and let you know I am pursuing an answer to your question and will get back to you as soon as possible."

3. **Reporting & Celebrating** – in a systematic pace, the reporting of God's work through the church both locally and globally presents an opportunity to celebrate the fruit of ministry. This includes video updates shown in worship, the Annual Report, and more.

4. **Campaigning** – campaigns include large-scale capital campaigns, general fund focused campaigns (based on the discipleship pathway), year-end giving campaigns, digital giving campaigns, and humanitarian relief campaigns. Some are spontaneous but most are planned into the Generosity Development Calendar at least 12 months in advance. All are seen as a positive spiritual step—a way to engage people to either start giving or give sacrificially beyond what they currently give.

5. **Celebration Gatherings** – regularly the development office budgets for and hosts meetings of 15-50 people and often there will be 20 or more of these each year. The purpose is a no-ask gathering of supporters to thank, cast vision, and answer questions about church direction. These are done by campus, so the campus pastor attends the ones for that region as well (more specifics on this are coming a few paragraphs below).

6. **Organic Connections with Donors** – there are always

opportunities to invite donors to meetings that are occurring in the flow of church life that give them more ownership of the ministry. This includes staff meetings or lunches, ministry training seminars, and benchmarking trips to see what other churches are doing.

7. **Meetings with individual givers** – there is a regular and scheduled rotation of meeting with donors to the church by the pastors and development office senior staff. This can be as simple as a meeting in a coffee shop or as formal as a dinner between the pastor and his spouse and the donor couple.

8. **Ambassadors** – Development office ambassadors are mature givers who are not only generous but willing to be trained to speak on behalf of the church. They help with events and donor care, and become a de facto advisory team to the Director of Development.

9. **Vision Trips** – A few times each year, the development office invites high-capacity givers to see firsthand the work of the church in remote places. These international trips include one of the founding pastors and the Director of Development and produce deeper relationships and more understanding about the need for substantial gifts toward the vision.

10. **Legacy Giving** – the development office uses an outsource partner to educate donors on the potential benefit to their family and their church with planned giving. This includes non-cash giving now as well as will, trust, and bequest arrangements. The church development office absorbs any costs related to this training and process.

11. **Personal Budgeting Classes** – along with the Finance Office, the Development office provides regular opportunities for households to be trained in financial management in order to be a better steward and a better giver.

12. **Responding to Triggers** – processes are in place to allow the development office, sometimes with the help of the pastoral staff to respond to certain giving "triggers." This includes thanking a first time giver or recognizing a large gift (a gift that exceeds an amount the office deems out of the ordinary), or a stock transfer. It also includes reaching out pastorally to a family whose giving has lapsed.

GATHERING GIVERS IN NO-ASK MEETINGS

Over the years, we have called them Celebration Dinners, Celebration Gatherings, and other things. But far and away the approach that Alex Calder and I get asked about the most from around the country is what we do regarding regular meetings with donors where there is no ask for money.

As we have mentioned, the key principle in creating a culture of generosity is ultimately linked to relationships. Relational dynamics change considerably from the worship service (large gathering of people usually sitting in rows) to a small gathering (less people usually sitting in a circle at a home).

Over the years, I have adopted and adapted the concept of an in-home meeting to serve the purpose of normalizing talk about generosity in a church context. And I have yet to meet a pastor who did not absolutely enjoy this unique opportunity to meet with members of the congregation.

In short, I think senior leaders should gather regularly with whomever they want (but particularly those in the engaged and giving 20%) to thank, report, and answer questions in a casual and "no-ask" meeting about how the church is using financial resources.

These meetings are virtually failure proof in that they contain food, transparency, gratitude, and then celebrate what God is doing through the church. Add to this the social and relational benefit of getting together and it is a slam-dunk, at least in my experience. Here are the steps to organizing, hosting and facilitating a no-ask celebration meeting:

Step 1 – Decide How Many Meetings To Host

In a certain segment of time (whether it be a semester, season or year) decide how many gatherings would be attainable with the energy and time you are willing to invest.

For instance, if you would like to meet with 200 families this fall but that would require 20 meetings, you may want to reconsider this in light of how much time that would take. But if, for instance, you conducted 6-8 meetings this fall or in the 4th quarter of the year and then another 6-8 in the first quarter of the following year, you would meet with many (over 100) households in a stretch of six months.

Step 2 – Find the Hosts and Settings

The next step is to find the hosts that you know are an engaged part of the congregation and are viewed as a positive influence. It is particularly helpful if they have a home that is large enough to host up to 15 people in a living room. You likely already have names and faces in your mind where it would be an appropriate setting and couple to handle the logistics of hospitality—food, beverages, etc. like any other social gathering or party.

Often, the host or host couple is willing to provide the dessert or snacks and beverages. Depending on the setting or circumstance, the church may want to pay for the hospitality expense. If it is possible to do so, these meetings are better suited for being in the home of a member of the congregation. But, in some cases, I have used the church building, a small restaurant with a "side room," or other setting. My preference, however, is to move away from buildings and institutional settings and move toward a family's living room.

Step 3 – Determine the Guest List

To a great degree, the guest list is determined by the size of your congregation. If your congregation is made up of 100 regular attenders, I would recommend doing enough small gatherings to include everyone—perhaps 7 or 8. As congregations get larger, it is more likely that you will take a portion of the congregation (like the top 20% of giving households, for instance) and utilize these gatherings as a way to report back to and thank them. Again, this would be based on your desired amount of meetings in a particular time frame.

NOTE:

When I worked at Kensington Church, we would vary the target of the invite and it would not always be the larger givers. There was often a strategic or discipleship reason to go "lower" on the giving list and the nature and content of the meeting can remain virtually the same.

Many churches will assemble an invitation list for each gathering that is 35-45% more than you would expect to come to the meeting. The size of the home or venue determines the size of the guest list, but keep in mind that a meeting of 10-15 can sometimes be more effective than 20-30 or more. As a general rule, the smaller group will increase individual participation in the conversation. For example, if you have 8 meetings and invite 12 households to each meeting:

- Up to 2 people are invited per household (depending on marital status)
- Max individuals invited to a home would be 24, but with those who decline, it is usually attended by half of this total
- 96 Households (often 150 people or more) are invited
- 10-12 Individuals is the likely size of each gathering

Step 4 – Invite and Follow Up

Once the hosts, settings, and guest lists are determined, it is time to create custom invitations. For instance, if you were hosting 8 meetings in the fall semester, you would find eight different dates that the Senior Pastor could spend an evening in a gathering like this. Then, the invitations can be made (with custom date and address for each house holding a gathering).

For example, the pastor could have a schedule like this:

Smith Home	Thursday Sep 10
Jones Home	Monday Sep 14
Willis Home	Tuesday Sep 22
James Home	Saturday Sep 26

Hurst Home	Monday Oct 4
Walter Home	Wednesday Sep 6

Figure 29.1

The invitations should be elegant and simple, hand addressed and hand stamped. They should be mailed out all together, and then followed by a phone call to get an RSVP. Ideally the host is making the phone calls.

The phone calls should be framed as "Will you be joining me?" but should also have an alternative (if possible) so that the host can say, "If you can't make this, are you interested in attending one of the other gatherings on [DATE, PLACE, TIME]?"

The basic text of the invitation will flow like this (this can be edited/altered to your church or pastor's style):

Pastor Jacob Novak would like to invite you to a small gathering of friends from First Church to be held in the home of

George and Michelle Cortizo
123 Main Street, Arlington, VA 10101

August 2nd at 7pm

Dessert and coffee will be served
We will call to confirm your attendance

Step 5 – Agree on an Agenda for the Event

This meeting is facilitated by the senior pastor (usually) so that the hosts are taking care of the hospitality details and do not have to concern themselves with any of the meeting content or flow.

The time limit should be set by the hosts and the organization and should be kept. A 90-minute event is ideal; a dinner event will require longer. As there is an official close of the meeting, people can linger as they wish, but leave if they want. It is better to be succinct and end on time to honor the guests—many will have work in the morning or babysitters at home.

If there are any handouts or reports, the pastor should bring enough for every participant. If a video is to be shown, the host needs to be made aware of the video requirements and this must be tested ahead of the guest's arrival.

A sample agenda is as follows:

7:00–7:30	Arrivals, Drinks and Dessert
7:30–7:35	Gathering of guests into the meeting room ("Let's all gather in the living room…") The ideal situation here is that people are seated in a circle and not in rows (lecture seating). Ideally, it feels more like a family gathering chat than a speech, class, or sales presentation.
7:35–8:00	Pastor begins the meeting with a relational ice-breaker
8:00–8:15	Pastor presents a re-cast of the vision and celebrates progress toward achieving that vision, delivers handouts, and/or shows video
8:15–8:45	Q & A
8:45–9:00	Time of prayer or closing prayer

Figure 29.2

TEACHING PEOPLE ABOUT GIVING

After a number of no-ask times, at some point there comes a reason to ask. I offer you Rick Warren's reasons people give to your church for some encouragement during those times. He contends that the dual goals of discipleship and more money for ministry can be achieved when we recognize that:

1. **People give when they trust the leadership.** John 10:1-11 says, "The sheep listen to [the shepherd's] voice. He calls his own sheep by name and leads them out. … He goes on ahead of them, and his sheep follow him because they know his voice. But they will never follow a stranger; in fact, they will run away from him …. The good shepherd lays down his life for the sheep. The hired hand is not the shepherd …" Study after study has proven that in the hierarchy of giving, people give first of all to people they believe in. Then they give to purposes. Finally they give to programs. That means the most essential elements in teaching people to give are relational, not functional.

   Even if you use a consultant to help you raise money, the pastor still needs to be out front. And if you are a pastor and you are not the most trusted person, then you have a leadership problem and you're not ready to teach people to give yet. You need to be the most visible because the person who is the best qualified to ask for money should be the person who's the most trusted.

2. **People give when they catch a vision, not when they see a need.** The Bible says, "Where there is no vision, the people perish" (Proverbs 29:18 KJV). Did you know that Ivy League schools usually receive the largest endowments? And they are the schools that need the money the least. Why? People give to success. They give to vision. They don't give to needs. That's why in fifteen years we have never had a bulletin with our financial reports in it along with how much we need. Why? Because bills do not motivate people to give. People give when they catch a vision and they get the big picture.

You must be very clear about what your vision is. At Saddleback, we've never had a vision for a building, but rather for what the building can help us do. We've never had a vision for raising money, but rather for what the money can do. Emphasize the lives that will be changed as people give—the marriages that will be saved, the broken people that are going to be put back together, the people who will break addictions, the changed lives that will happen. That's the vision!

3. **People give to experience the joy of generosity.** It feels good to give generously—it really does. A person who doesn't understand that has never given generously. The happiest people in the world are the most giving people. Guilt never motivates people to give. Giving that is motivated by guilt only lasts as long as the guilt does. So you never use guilt to motivate people to give. You use joy to motivate people to give.

    I absolutely do not accept the health and wealth theology, which teaches that God wants everybody to be rich. But the fact is, there are more promises in the Bible related to giving than any other subject. You cannot out-give God. If you're going to be Christlike, you've got to learn to give.

4. **People give when they are inspired by models.** We learn best by watching models. That's why a testimony about giving is a thousand times more effective than a sermon on giving. Models motivate us. Giving is contagious. So I encourage people to write down and send me their testimonies, how they decided to give, and what they were giving.

5. **People give when they are involved.** Paul told the Philippians, "I thank my God … because of your partnership in the gospel …" (Philippians 1:3, 5). The fact is those who are most involved in a capital campaign, for instance, will be those who sacrifice the most. One of our gauges of involvement at Saddleback is how many people have completed our classes. And the more classes people

have completed, the more involved they are, and the more they tend to give. The average gift from an attender during one of our giving campaigns was about $7,000. For the people who had gone through class 101, the average gift was $8,500. The average gift from people who had been through class 201 and 101 was over $11,000. And the average gift of people who had been through 101, 201 and 301, which usually indicates they are actually involved in the ministry of the church was over $15,000.

6. **People give when you ask them to give.** James says, "You do not have because you do not ask God" (James 4:2). The Bible says ask and seek and knock. God asks people to give. The fact is we're doing people a favor when we ask them to give because they grow in faith, they grow in love, they grow in sacrifice, they grow in commitment, and they grow in character as they learn to give. They will be blessed in return. Never say no for anybody. Your church will be hurt more by those who would have said yes and were not asked, than by those who were asked and said no.

7. **People give when you make it possible for them to give.** Second Corinthians 8:12 says, "For if the willingness is there, the gift is acceptable according to what one has, not according to what one does not have." That means you need to make it possible for people to give in as many ways as you can. Teach people how to want to give, and they'll figure out how.

    Teach people that they can either give by reason or by revelation. Giving by reason means this—I look at what I have, I figure out what's reasonable, and I commit that amount. It doesn't take any faith to give by reason. I just figure out what can I afford to give. Giving by revelation means I determine my gift by praying "Lord, what do you want to give through me?" This requires faith. When you give by revelation, you're committing an act of worship and saying, "How much am I willing to trust God?"

8. **People give when their gifts are appreciated.** The whole book of Philippians is just a thank-you letter from Paul for their offerings,

for their financial support. Figure out seven ways to thank people for their gift—a card, a call, a banquet, etc. A little appreciation goes a long way in encouraging people to be generous for the long haul. [133]

Once you have given yourself time to draft a way forward that includes some of the above suggestions in your Generosity Development Plan, you will want to include at least one more discussion with your team. It is in reference to a specific segment of the congregation that are wealthy and what we feel led to do regarding their nurture, care, and encouragement toward further generosity.

One of the most frequently asked questions we quickly referred to in Chapter 11 has to do with how these principles of discipleship apply to the wealthy in our congregation. It is actually a topic that demands more attention, so it is the subject of our next chapter and a significant part of this wave.

133   8 Reasons Believers Give to Your Church, Rick Warren By Pastor Rick Warren
https://pastors.com/8-reasons-believers-give-to-your-church

CHAPTER THIRTY

Discipling The Wealthy

I n the early 2000s, I worked with a number of churches near our nation's capital. When you are anywhere near Washington D.C., there is a high likelihood that you will meet someone in a position of power, influence, or success. In the context of the churches I worked with, I met white house staffers, television moguls, and people who were enjoying the very affluent lifestyle of Northern Virginia.

I had heard from the Senior Pastor at one of the Methodist churches I was working with that there was a gentleman in the congregation that was not only wealthy but also inclined to be generous. He was one of the founding partners of a large restaurant chain that everyone reading this would easily recognize. After building this restaurant to a national level and household name, he and his partners sold the chain.

For whatever reason, we were having trouble getting in contact with him. However, I discovered that he lived within a mile or two of the church in a 20,000 square foot home. What I did next is not part of my consulting services. I had never done it before and have not done it since. I drove to his house and knocked on the front door.

What ensued was a wonderful and respectful conversation during which I asked him to consider a very large financial gift to his church. He gave that gift and much more—both to his church and to other organizations doing God's work in the world.

We have become friends; our wives and children have spent time together, and we stay in contact to this day. My knock on his door was a monumental moment in my understanding of interacting with people of wealth. *(I am, of course, aiming to protect his privacy by not mentioning his name nor his restaurant chain.)*

When the apostle Paul wrote to Timothy in 1 Timothy 6, he taught we should enjoy the wealth that God has entrusted to us because every good and perfect gift comes from the Father above.

In reference to people who possess wealth, he coaches young pastor Timothy to "command them to do good, to be rich in good deeds and to be generous and willing to share. In this way, they will lay up a treasure for themselves as a firm foundation for the coming age."

But aside from the idea of simply *commanding* (wow—that word demands some further exegesis) or encouraging people of wealth to be generous, there is a significant pastoral opportunity.

Most pastors know this if they have ever interacted with high-net-worth individuals in their church. My friend Bevan Unrau is the Senior Pastor of Seabreeze Community Church in Huntington Beach, CA. He reminded me recently that over his long tenure as a pastor he has heard of only a few pastors who attempt to disciple the wealthy.

This is unfortunate, in his view, as these men and women are very often isolated from meaningful spiritual input and accountability because they intimidate most people in the church, including the pastors.

He wrote in an email to me: *I can't think of a better opportunity for a meaningful pastoral conversation than a one-on-one coffee with a person of wealth in the congregation. My experience has been that much of the time is spent talking about personal matters. And when the conversation turns to the topic of money, it drives a deeper conversation about much more than money. I used to bristle at the idea of such a meeting, but now it is one of the most energizing things I do.*

Bevan's experience dovetails with mine as I have found that people of wealth are able to talk about it very directly and openly with their pastor. These are often fascinating people with a story of God's work in their lives, when given the opportunity to share.

I have learned that wealthy people are often eager to have an honest, open conversation. So I tactfully say something like, "God has given you the ability to make and manage a lot of money. That is a world I don't understand but I'm curious about it. Let's talk about how you are doing with all of that. What has been difficult? What has been rewarding?"

Again, when you portray a level of comfort with the topic, that demeanor seems to produce even more trust relationally so that the conversations are fruitful.

I had always suspected that these conversations were only difficult because of my inability or fear, and rarely about a wealthy person being unwilling to talk to one of their pastors about the specifics of their life and resources. I never knew how to articulate this, and then I discovered a short and powerful book by Henri Nouwen. It was so intriguing to me because I rarely think of Nouwen in this category.

I am quoting a section of his writing where he specifically addresses asking for money, though I am not saying that meetings with wealthy people should always be about asking. I actually believe that a minority of these meetings should be about asking. But the spiritual principles in the following paragraph apply, even if the nurturing of a relationship does not contain an ask. See if you agree with me:

> *If our security is totally in God, then we are free to ask for money. Only when we are free from money can we ask freely for others to give it. Money is a taboo subject because our own insecurities are connected with it, and so we are not free. We are also not free if we are jealous of the rich and envy their money. In this, we reveal that money is still our master and therefore we are not ready to ask for it.* [134]

He casts a vision for a new way forward by admonishing that "when we have gained the freedom to ask without fear, to love this as a form of ministry, then fund-raising will be good for our spiritual life." [135] And ask, at some point, we must—for the sake of the giver, the asker, and the ministry we are fueling. Everyone benefits when these discussions include a gracious challenge. Sometimes I wonder if one of the plots of the evil one is to keep pastors and ministry professionals afraid or intimidated by wealth so that resources get directed away from kingdom initiatives. And in so doing, we remain shackled by a topic that should not be taboo.

As Aesop wrote long ago: *wealth unused might as well not exist.*

And we can ask a similar question from the Christian perspective: Why would God bless someone with surplus resources if not for God's purposes on the earth?

---

134   Nouwen, p23
135   Nouwen, p7

In the same sense, Andrew Carnegie calls philanthropists *administrators of surplus wealth* and Warren Buffet refers to wealth, such as his own, as "claim checks" that should benefit society.

Put differently, it might be said that if the vast enterprises of medieval philanthropy depended on a vow of poverty, the equally vast enterprises of modern philanthropy depend on essentially what is a vow of wealth.

And though this "vow of wealth" concept may seem like a modern concept, there is also historical-biblical evidence that wealthy people have had a hand in supporting efforts to spread the gospel. One scholar suspects that Lydia was a gospel benefactor when he wrote, "There is also considerable evidence that Paul's missionary strategy involved not only an urban focus but also a practical focus on converting high status persons who could be sponsors for a fledgling Christian community, including housing it. Lydia fits the profile nicely." [136]

How Wealthy People Decide

Imagine if we could figure out how to more effectively partner with people of wealth to make a difference in the world? How many more people could be saved and served? What would it take to understand the unique circumstances and decision-making challenges our wealthy congregants face?

In my limited experience, I have found that people of wealth understand organizational leverage. They know that there are certain ways that a gift from them can exert a kind of beautiful force on a project or a church. I have partnered with a handful of wealthy people to pay for a new initiative, creating a matching gift, or to "make up the difference" between what the congregation gave and what the need is. These are all ways where they can feel that their unique circumstance has been used by God to propel things forward.

David Weekley, a businessman and philanthropist, has made a commitment to give 50% of his income to works of God around the world and shares his approach. The principles he shares are completely relevant to what church leaders must consider if they are to minister more effectively to the wealthy. Consider how his methodology may inform your next steps.

---

136   Witherington, B., III. (2011). Paul's Letter to the Philippians: A Socio-Rhetorical Commentary (p. 8). Grand Rapids, MI; Cambridge, U.K.: William B. Eerdmans Company.

He explains:

Before I give, I try to ensure that a particular organization has:
1. A unique and well-defined mission
2. Excellent programs or services that clearly advance the mission
3. A clear way to measure the results
4. A three-to-five year strategic plan
5. A business model and cost structure demonstrating that the organization will make a greater impact in a more efficient way as it grows
6. Strong executive talent
7. A strong and effective board of directors [137]

I usually make larger gifts to build capacity in a nonprofit—their reach, scale, growth plan, or facilities. I have found that this is not as effective to make large, ongoing operating gifts. I usually will limit an operating gift to no more than 5 percent of an organization's annual budget, and a capital gift to not more than 20 percent of the capital needed. [138]

Transformational giving can occur when an organization has every element in place for positive growth and change—clear goals, a compelling mission, adequate staff and infrastructure, wise visionary leadership, strong communication, established procedures for accountability and reporting—everything except the necessary funding to take action. Though you and your church may not be vying for a contribution from the David Weekley Family Foundation, it does give us a sneak peek at how some major donors think about leveraging their wealth for something long-lasting and not short-lived.

When fundraising consultant Albert Mueller encourages high net worth individuals, he tells the story of Joan Kroc, the McDonald's restaurant heiress, and her final gift of $1.5 billion to the Salvation Army. We would benefit, as church leaders, to hear the kind of advice wealthy people are

(1) Start with small gifts to test how faithfully donations are handled; Kroc had previously given $92 million to the Salvation Army and

---

The Giver and the Gift: Principles of Kingdom Fundraising, Peter Greer and David Weekley, Bethany House Publishers, Bloominton, MN 2015 p70

138   Ibid, p76

was satisfied with the community center they had built in San Diego.

(2) Consider using larger gifts to fund capital projects, designating some of the funds to cover a portion of the operating expenses; by funding a community project yet only providing for some of the budget, the giver allows the community an opportunity to participate in a plan that benefits itself.

(3) Give to those ministries that are faithful to their vision and efficient with their funds; the Salvation Army has an excellent track record of efficiency.

(4) Maximize the impact of your donation by giving to existing ministries rather than spending money on the establishment of new organizations; the expense of running foundations diverts money that could otherwise be used to help the needy.

(5) Be actively involved; decide before your death where the money will go. [139]

David Thoroughman, Co-Founder and CEO of Mortarstone interacts with churches across the nation and has a unique vantage point.

In addition to their popular giving analytics software, he and his team spend a significant amount of time helping churches set up legacy and planned giving programs. Because of this, he has interacted with many high net worth Christians.

He says, "Across the church landscape there is one kind of person that eludes a common name or title. From church to church they are called many things from top givers, generous donors, financial leaders, loyal donors, and more."

He goes on to explain his privilege in helping churches understand how to interact with this segment of the church that is, in many ways, the most underserved. Pastors will ask, "David, I want to do this more effectively, but

139   Super-Sized Gift: Lessons to Learn from the Largest Gift Ever Made to a Faith-Based Organization Albert J. Mueller. Excellence in Giving, 2004.

where do I start?"

He recommends that pastors understand more about the life and decisions of the wealthy in order to serve them well. As an example, he recommends some training to gain a cursory understanding of wealth transfer. Particularly since in the 2020s and 2030s, we will be experiencing a wealth transfer of trillions of dollars as boomers pass away.

Pastors need to recognize at least some of the terminology people are using when they are deciding about what to leave to children, grandchildren, churches and charities. There are significant spiritual challenges that accompany these decisions. Is there a biblical framework for handling inheritances? How can family foundations help with wealth transfer? How much is too much to leave to your children?

Consider the fact that Warren Buffet is one of the wealthiest people in our generation. When asked why he gave his wealth to charity and not to his kids his response was "I want my heirs to have enough money to do anything, but not so much to do nothing."

When discipling wealthy people they know that there will be three benefactors of their wealth: their children, the IRS and the Kingdom. Without planning and education the only two sure recipients are their children and the IRS.

I highly recommend the resources that come out of the National Christian Foundation (www.ncfgiving.com) as well as Generous Giving (www.generousgiving.org), as both organizations continue to lead the way in education and tools to navigate this well.

Our Church Can't Handle The Kind of Money I Can Give It

Jim Baker, pastor and now church consultant and coach, wrote about a time that profoundly changed his understanding of what affluent church members consider before allocating their dollars to the church, charities and non-profit organizations.

Jim had noticed in the newspaper that a friend who was a member of his church had recently made a multi-million-dollar donation to a local college and had pledged even more in the future. They were close enough that Jim took him to lunch to find out why. He writes:

So, the next time we met for lunch I got up the nerve to ask him why, though he supported our church generously, had he never given even close to that amount to our church, the church where he was raised and served as a deacon. I didn't have an answer for his reply, "Jim, our church can't handle the kind of money I can afford to give it."

When Jim asked his friend to explain more, he went on to share how the college president had invited him to dinner and shared a compelling vision and strategy for an entrepreneurial initiative that he was passionate about. He shared how the church had no such compelling vision and strategy and he feared if he gave the church that size of a gift we would spend months arguing about how to allocate it. [140]

How to Deepen Your Relationships with Major Givers

"Sometimes I think that the only people in this country who worry more about money than the poor are the very wealthy," says Robert A. Kenny. "They worry about losing it, they worry about how it's invested, and they worry about the effect it's going to have. And as the zeroes increase, the dilemmas get bigger."

Kenny, who is trained as a psychologist, says that extreme wealth can take away some of the basic joys of living. For instance, some wealthy people don't look forward to the holidays, "because they were always expected to give really good presents." When you're a millionaire, Kenny says, expensive gifts merely meet expectations. *That was a pretty good present*, the recipients might respond. *But last year, you gave me a car.* [141]

I encourage pastors to meet regularly with major donors for relationship building, pastoral care, and advice. Often these men and women are world-class organizational consultants and are right under our noses. And they do not always know how best to contribute their time or giftedness to their church in light of their busy schedules. So advice or perspective from them can be extraordinarily valuable.

Also, as a "corner office" person in the work context, they are often alone with the inevitable stress and pressure that comes with the job. And they

140   https://sacredstructures.org/money/church-money-management/
141   http://www.theatlantic.com/magazine/archive/2011/04/secret-fears-of-the-super-rich/8419/

really cannot process this with employees, which would be inappropriate, and try not to burden their spouse with a "dump" of work issues, which would be tiresome in many marriages.

Like a lot of other areas of developing a generosity culture, this one may be a "just try something" kind of approach. Because this is not a natural part of most church leader's training or experience, we need to practice. I suggest you start with the wealthy person or couple you know the most, as this will feel like a smooth take-off. With some courage, you could even circle back later and ask them how you did.

While most ministry leaders will go through a whole career without having a meaningful conversation like this, you can choose to pray, trust God, and invite a wealthy member out to coffee. I will bet you the cost of that cup of coffee that it will be a powerful and encouraging meeting for both of you.

It is now time to finish our project, the Generosity Development Plan. My suspicion is that you are almost done before the final chapter of this book, which is great news. Let's look at the components of the GDP one more time to give you the tools you need to take your congregation to a new level of generosity and devotion.

CHAPTER THIRTY-ONE
Generosity Discipleship Plan

As pastors, we were taught that we should be ready to "preach, pray, or die" at any moment for the cause of Christ.

In Detroit, there is an addendum to the preacher's readiness: Always be ready to preach, pray, die—or talk automobile manufacturing theory. Relating to many people in Motown requires that you are ready to "dial up your auto industry talk" at social gatherings because likely the engineers in the room (there are always a few) can veer quickly into lean manufacturing or process improvement chitchat.

For the uninitiated (like me), I had to learn over time that these discussions may have been an outgrowth of Henry Ford's influence in the first part of the 20th century, but were definitely connected to influence of the Japanese in the second half.

Henry Ford is often mistakenly thought to be the inventor of the automobile—he was not. But what he created was enormous. Books are written about how he created a high volume, low cost opportunity for Americans to own a car. Many say he built the middle class in America by doubling the hourly pay of workers at the time. He also turned cars from a luxury for a few to a necessity for the masses.

In the decades following WWII, however, the American auto industry was deeply challenged by Japanese engineering. In 1958, Toyotas and Datsuns were imported into the U.S. for the first time, and American automakers began losing market shares to the well-engineered, gas-saving, and affordable foreign vehicles. By the time The Beatles were on the Ed Sullivan show, the new ways of Japanese automakers were being discussed around every water cooler in Detroit.[142]

There was much to learn from Japan, and many of these approaches have

142   https://www.investopedia.com/articles/pf/12/auto-industry.asp

lasted to this day. The *5S approach* is one of those methods. It is an easily adaptable method of *creating a better system*. Each of the S words is rooted in a Japanese term and applies to so much more than just car manufacturing. Consider this quick distillation of the words and ideas:

- **Sort** - remove the unnecessary (Seiri means tidiness)
- **Set In Order** – Organize and make efficient (Seiton means orderliness)
- **Shine** – inspect and scrub regularly (Seiso means cleanliness)
- **Standardize** – create operating procedures (Seiketsu means standardization)
- **Sustain** – assign responsibility and track progress (Shitsuke means discipline)

Those who teach this methodology are fast to point out that without writing down what you decide or discover, it will help very little. When you write things down, try them out, and adjust when things are not going as intended, you are on your way to creating a new environment.

It has been said that "If it isn't written down, it didn't happen." The plan that 5S thinking produces can be modified from its original, but must be drawn up.[143]

I am fascinated by organizational structure. And I love the idea of the 5S theory. Can you imagine if we took some of the disjointed things we do in our churches and *removed the unnecessary, organized, inspected, creating procedure, and assigned responsibility?*

This may sound too business-speak to you. But, I classify this under leading the church well and stewarding the organization with excellence. You don't have to use this Japanese methodology, but you have come this far in our process, so I encourage you to finish strong. Put in place what is necessary to see life transformation and have the courage to remove things that just are not serving the mission to disciple people in the ways of Jesus.

The purpose of this book is to inform and inspire. But, its ultimate aim is to use the five waves to allow for a newly articulated (written down) approach to creating generous disciples. It is time to draw up a plan. And, if it is not written down...

---

143   https://www.graphicproducts.com/articles/what-is-5s/

GENEROSITY DISCIPLESHIP PLAN

We have linked an increase in generous behavior to the discipleship of a Christ following person. And the previous chapters provide both the theological impetus behind this discipleship, as well as the practical decisions that can be made to create the right environment for this to thrive.

Dr. Jack Wilson, a good friend and organizational guru would challenge an executive team I was a part of by saying, "I don't consider any decision to be real until it is in writing." He knew the propensity of the team was to talk about things and solidify and execute very little unless we wrote it down. Plus, writing thoughts, ideas, and decisions out gives a more tangible (less verbal and conceptual) explanation to others that may have to follow or cooperate with the decisions. You can literally show it to someone and ask, "Does this make sense?" Or "What do you think will be our challenges in executing these ideas?"

Some readers are way ahead of me. You knew this was coming and wrote out your draft before you even arrived at this chapter. For others, you may want to start now—get out an old-fashioned scratch pad or sit right down at your computer. You will likely pull this together quickly and then refine it over time. *(There are examples in the Appendix)*

Theology

Start with just a few basic assertions about giving and generosity. Use short definitions of terms (generosity, stewardship, etc.) as well as the Scripture that undergirds your belief. I recommend benchmarking other churches whose theology you trust and whose website may have a generosity theology. Another starting point is the www.generousgiving.org website.

Discipleship

This part of your GDP can include the steps (or levels) of your discipleship pathway along with the supporting explanation under each level. Many churches will create graphic icons to represent the steps as well as other media. Include this in your finalized plan in order to systematically evaluate the congregation and their movement toward maturity.

Strategy

The nuts and bolts of your plan are often articulated in this section. It can include your 12-month Generosity Calendar. It can also include the "traffic laws" or the policy and procedure that you will follow to maintain integrity and protect the people of your congregation. Some churches may choose to include their budgeting procedure in this section as well.

Communication

In your initial write up regarding generosity discipleship, it would be helpful to spell out your approach to the various suggestions in this wave: Preaching, Offering Moments, Digital Strategy, and Reporting. This is helpful particularly to those who may be responsible to execute this and test its effectiveness periodically.

Integration

This is ultimately a philosophy of pastoral leadership. This position states what both clergy and laity will do in leading others toward a generous life. It may include a statement of what we will "not do" as well as a statement of what we "will do." This gives protection to pastors and leaders who may be moving into new territory in their leadership.

A NEW WAY FORWARD

I trust it has become abundantly clear that being intentional about how we nurture generosity is a massive spiritual growth opportunity for the entire congregation—including for those of us who lead churches.

Jesus people are generous people. And when generosity is not one of the markers of our lives, we have a spiritual problem. Organizational solutions are fairly easy compared to the change of heart and behavior that can only be done by God. As church leaders, we are simply trying to remove the human obstacles and create an ideal environment for a spiritual renovation to happen.

Patrick Johnson reminds leaders to "consciously step back from the immediate demands of funding programs to see a person's entire life—all the fruit on all the branches." He writes that this fruit inspection usually uncovers "uncharitable relationships, stinginess with time, a self-centered view of vocation, and a lack of empathy for the hurting. Seeing the whole tree of a person's life radically changes the leader's goal from temporarily replacing one bad fruit—boosting giving—to transforming the entire tree by going deeper—cultivating disciples who are generous in all areas of life." [144]

I was struck by the results of a particular inquiry about what makes people live lives of generosity. It was an informal analysis of 100 individuals who ended up in a career in social services and other organizations for the common good. These are men and women that often face daunting and complex circumstances and receive less than ideal remuneration. But they are motivated to live a life of others-serving and self-giving.

What struck me was the connection I see between their lives and how a thriving church can encourage such a posture. In this analysis, I see again the potential influence of the church to radically change the world.

Though this study was not about "church people" per se, the findings seem to be entirely relevant to our journey. Laurent Park Daloz, who conducted the study, wondered if there was some experience that all of these generous people shared. He wondered, "What are the factors that cause people to live a life like this?"

Chronicled in a book he co-authored called *Leading Lives of Commitment in A Complex World,* he cited several factors that seemed to appear in the first three decades of a generous person's life:

- The experience of being "seen" as a child
- Having at least one publicly active parent
- Growing up in a home that is hospitable to the wider world
- Living in a safe yet diverse neighborhood
- Actively participating in religious life
- Having contact with adults in the community who model commitment

144   Generosity Reset: From Fundraising To Disciple-Making In The Local Church, Patrick Johnson, GENEROUS CHURCH EBOOK, page 7

- Participating in youth groups
- Having mentors

Can you see what I see? Participating in religious life, being "seen" as a child, contact with adults that model commitment, youth groups, mentors, active parents—incredible! This is the environment afforded by a healthy church. Those of us who have seen a church operate in such a way know that it can be one of the best organisms to serve as a greenhouse for spiritual growth in many things—including generosity.

It is encouraging to remember that a multitude of hospitals, orphanages, and social service organizations over the centuries have been motivated by a Christian understanding of how love is acted out. It seems like an obvious link to say that if people are shown the way of Jesus, it leads to generous acts that benefit the world.

When I first began to understand the power of creating generous disciples twenty years ago, I was inspired by the dual benefit of both increased financial resources for kingdom initiatives and increased devotion by God's people. **Anything that could raise more money for ministry and more faith and engagement by church members was enormously attractive to me.**

I still believe that this is possible. And to that end, I pray that you and your church will experience what I have seen time and time again—the growth of disciples of Jesus who are deeply generous.

APPENDIX A

Sample Generosity Discipleship Plan

Generosity Discipleship Plan
Assertions & Actions for
Creating a Culture of Generosity

Church of Champions
WWW.CHAMP.ORG

Creating A Culture Of Generosity
PROCESS PHASES

● Theology	● Discipleship	● Strategy	● Communication	● Integration
Re-affirm and clearly articulate our convictions about generosity	Describe generous disciples and name steps on a pathway of maturing in generosity	Deciding what we will put into place as a proactive plan for cultivating generous living	Regularly communicate expectations and gratitude - then report impact	Practice nurturing generosity relationally in various ways throughout church life

What is our belief about God in regard to generosity?

- Essence of God is giving (John 3:16)
- God created everything and governs it
- God is the provider of everything
- God gives dominion and authority out of his benevolence
- God gives redemption, healing and prosperity
- The Story of Redemption is about God's generosity

What are the generosity principles of Scripture?

- The primary message of Christianity is giving
- Believers surrender everything in repentance and response to God's mercy – before we could give, He gave.
- We have the marker of 10% (tithe) as a baseline for our generosity
- Giving a tenth is following the concept of first fruits.
- God created the garden and gave Adam and Eve responsibility for "good use" of his good gifts.
- The gospel is transported on the theology of tithing.
- The law was fulfilled in Jesus Christ, but the morality of the NT is based in the OT. We are not compelled by the law to give, but compelled by love.

What is our belief about God in regard to generosity?

- Essence of God is giving (John 3:16)
- God created everything and governs it
- God is the provider of everything
- God gives dominion and authority out of his benevolence
- God gives redemption, healing and prosperity
- The Story of Redemption is about God's generosity

What are the generosity principles of Scripture?

- The primary message of Christianity is giving
- Believers surrender everything in repentance and response to God's mercy – before we could give, He gave.
- We have the marker of 10% (tithe) as a baseline for our generosity
- Giving a tenth is following the concept of first fruits.
- God created the garden and gave Adam and Eve responsibility for "good use" of his good gifts.
- The gospel is transported on the theology of tithing.
- The law was fulfilled in Jesus Christ, but the morality of the NT is based in the OT. We are not compelled by the law to give, but compelled by love.

Slide 5

What is the role of the believer in terms of generosity?

- One of the hallmarks of Christians is a giving life.
- A generous believer is outward focused.
- They re motivated to give themselves away (not live for self).
- Living as a resource to give away rather than living in the poverty of self.
- We are not to be imprisoned by our own concerns.
- A life of generosity is one of joy and peace.
- The way we see things is the way we think and act.

What is the role of the church in developing generosity?

- To manage it with integrity
- To invest it in God's kingdom purposes
- To minister to the poor – equip them, help them, bless them
- Handle money for the kingdom and in dominion (how we handle money on earth will determine where we serve in heaven)
- How you perfect your order (government and management of things on this earth) will determine your level of influence in the kingdom to come
- The church should be the greatest resource in the community (we use the model of the temple in the OT)

Slide 6

What is the expectation of growth in this category?

* Every disciple will be on the move – maturing in their generosity.
* People will be blessed because they are continually pursuing and practicing generosity.
* People should be honest with themselves about their belief and behavior regarding generosity.
* People should see money as a tool for good not a source of identity.
* People should see this as part of their spiritual life and not something separate.

What is the role of spiritual leadership in cultivating and challenging generosity in the congregation?

* Leaders need to speak to this topic in the Christian life/walk as much (or more) than any other topic, following the example of Jesus.
* We have to raise up leaders who reclaim the language of generosity and not be afraid of it.
* Not being generous disqualifies someone from leadership in the church.
* Leadership have to be ahead of the congregation in their maturity in this category. We need to lead them into a blessed, generous, and well-ordered life.
* We need to speak about this as a regular practice (not doing it is not the whole gospel).

Slide 7

Generous Culture Discipleship Pathway

Mission
Nurturing beliefs and practices that create a culture where generosity is expected and celebrated

Values
Others-Focused
Demonstrated by faithful people who are motivated to not serve self but sacrifice for others

God-Driven
Demonstrated by an awareness that our devotion to God is demonstrated in our life of generous giving

Abundance-Fueled
Demonstrated by a belief in the provision of God for our benefit and flourishing on the earth

Community-Aimed
Demonstrate by regular acts of service and giving that impact our immediate surroundings with God's love

Slide 8

Generous Culture Discipleship Pathway

Strategy
Teaching in Worship
Instruction in Classes
Discipleship through a Pathway
Proactive Process

Measures
Am I consistently giving first to our church?
Am I using the tithe (10%) as a benchmark to hit and surpass?
How is my generous spirit reflected in my service to the church?
Is there a recent example of generosity to a person or place outside the church?
Am I living in poverty of spirit or enjoying the abundance of God's provision in my life?

Slide 9

NEXT MOVE SERIES

LAUNCHING THE GENEROSITY PATHWAY

Week 1	INTRODUCTION	2 Corinthians 8:1-7 Conduct the Self-Assessment
Week 2	CAST VISION	2 Corinthians 8:8-15 Begin to explain the pathway
Week 3	TEACHING OF JESUS	Mathew 6:19-21 What could the church do with more?
Week 4	NEW ADVENTURE	2 Corinthians 9:6-12 Conduct Commitment Exercise/Pledge Card
Week 5	CELEBRATE	Encourage the congregation with results and give direction for the next steps.

Slide 10

Slide 11

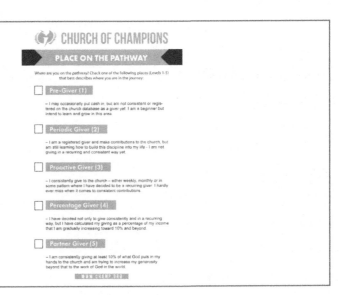

Slide 12

CHURCH OF CHAMPIONS

NEXT MOVE

My / our primary NEXT STEP is:
(check all that apply)

NAME : _____

EMAIL : _____

PHONE : _____

I/We discovered that I/we are at **Level** ____ and
want to try and move to **Level** ____ with God's help.

WWW.CHAMP.ORG

- ☐ Registering with the church by making a gift
- ☐ Signing up for a Personal Budgeting class
- ☐ Beginning to calculate and give a percentage of income
- ☐ Increasing the percentage given to the church
- ☐ Practicing the 10% (tithe) giving model for 90 days
- ☐ Signing up for a Will & Estate planning seminar
- ☐ Proactively modeling generosity to mentor others
- ☐ Explaining our giving and beliefs to our children
- ☐ We came up with our own NEXT STEP: _____
  _____

Slide 13

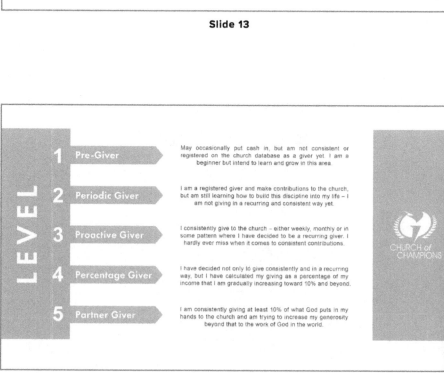

LEVEL

1 Pre-Giver — May occasionally put cash in, but am not consistent or registered on the church database as a giver yet. I am a beginner but intend to learn and grow in this area.

2 Periodic Giver — I am a registered giver and make contributions to the church, but am still learning how to build this discipline into my life – I am not giving in a recurring and consistent way yet.

3 Proactive Giver — I consistently give to the church – either weekly, monthly or in some pattern where I have decided to be a recurring giver. I hardly ever miss when it comes to consistent contributions.

4 Percentage Giver — I have decided not only to give consistently and in a recurring way, but I have calculated my giving as a percentage of my income that I am gradually increasing toward 10% and beyond.

5 Partner Giver — I am consistently giving at least 10% of what God puts in my hands to the church and am trying to increase my generosity beyond that to the work of God in the world.

CHURCH of CHAMPIONS

Slide 14

Strategic Components to Creating a Culture of Generosity

2021-2022

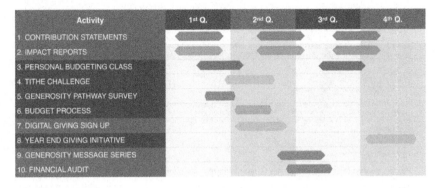

Activity	1st Q.	2nd Q.	3rd Q.	4th Q.
1. CONTRIBUTION STATEMENTS				
2. IMPACT REPORTS				
3. PERSONAL BUDGETING CLASS				
4. TITHE CHALLENGE				
5. GENEROSITY PATHWAY SURVEY				
6. BUDGET PROCESS				
7. DIGITAL GIVING SIGN UP				
8. YEAR END GIVING INITIATIVE				
9. GENEROSITY MESSAGE SERIES				
10. FINANCIAL AUDIT				

Slide 15

Communication

Email Updates
KEY FEATURE: *Consistent Updates*

Though email runs the risk of being overdone or potentially unopened, it still remains a requirement of communication regarding financial giving and spending. Setting this in sync with quarterly contribution statements provides a consistent pattern of information regarding financial health and investment in mission.

Offering Moments
KEY FEATURE: *Connection With Mission*

Churches have an opportunity (either in physical or virtual meetings) to regularly connect with the people that care most about their mission. The time we choose to talk about the offering is a prime opportunity to link giving with mission. Putting in regular appearances of lay people to update on an aspect of mission is recommended. Telling stories of life-change and mission activity should be a regular occurrence at offering time.

Giving Portal on Website
KEY FEATURE: *Multiple Giving Channels*

The giving portal or page on the church's website can also be an instructive tool. The church should add copy/narrative that explains the use of money and the belief regarding the importance of giving. It should also have user friendly and clear ways to give and a name and email of a contact person if there are questions of any kind. As COC continues to utilize Impact Reports, those reports can be posted on the giving page as well to reinforce the effective use of the funds.

Slide 16

Communication (cont.)

Contribution Statements
KEY FEATURE: *Vision Casting*

Contribution statements are required when the calendar year is complete but are useful to send out multiple times each year. Some will use the quarter system, but COC will be using January, May, August and November as the times for statements (each for different reasons). January is required. May will be to encourage giving during summer. August will be to "kick off" the new year with ministry goals attached. And November as a part of the Year End Giving initiative. Each statement is an opportunity to cast vision with a cover letter.

Impact Reports
KEY FEATURE: *Celebrating Progress*

In an attempt to be humble, so many churches fail to point out the instances of missional impact that can and should be celebrated. Giving God the credit, a church can highlight stats and lists that show how people are engaging with the mission and how lives are being changed. Failure to do this regularly puts the church behind other organizations who regularly demonstrate progress to their contributors.

Pastor's "Family Chat"
KEY FEATURE: *Transparency*

For many churches, they are operating at a deficit of trust. Sometimes that is earned and sometimes not. The point is that it will go well when we are transparent about where our giving and financial health stands. And in the case of COC, if Pastor Hutchins has a candid and transparent update about how things are going with the church being resourced to do its mission, this will enhance trust and credibility when the church is also asking for generosity to be directed at its mission.

Slide 17

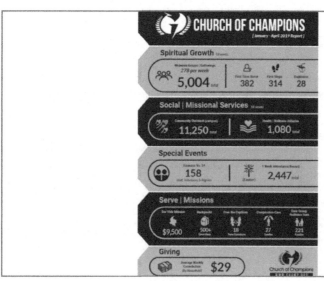

Slide 18

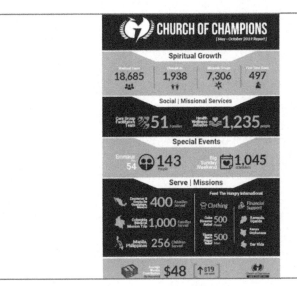

Slide 19

ONGOING INTEGRATION ACTIVITIES
Year Round Practices That Reinforce Generosity Culture

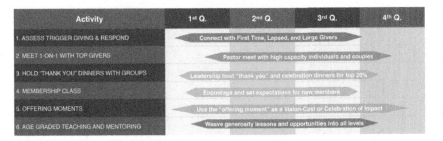

Activity	1st Q.	2nd Q.	3rd Q.	4th Q.
1. ASSESS TRIGGER GIVING & RESPOND	Connect with First Time, Lapsed, and Large Givers			
2. MEET 1-ON-1 WITH TOP GIVERS	Pastor meet with high capacity individuals and couples			
3. HOLD "THANK YOU" DINNERS WITH GROUPS	Leadership host "thank you" and celebration dinners for top 20%			
4. MEMBERSHIP CLASS	Encourage and set expectations for new members			
5. OFFERING MOMENTS	Use the "offering moment" as a Vision-Cast or Celebration of Impact			
6. AGE GRADED TEACHING AND MENTORING	Weave generosity lessons and opportunities into all levels			

Integration is the idea that generosity is better caught than taught and is a long-term discipleship plan. As this is one of the most difficult areas of development for most Christians, it requires more life-on-life and face-to-face conversations at every level fo the church. Leaders, elders, staff and members need to understand that it is an important part of the church's value set and culture. Conversations about money and giving need to be normalized in the life of the church and committing to do this regularly is highly important.

Slide 20

APPENDIX B

Sample Generosity Pathways

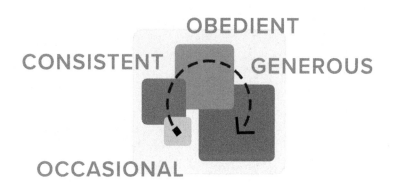

OBEDIENT

CONSISTENT GENEROUS

OCCASIONAL

generous
growing
engaged
emerging

Generous Giving Model

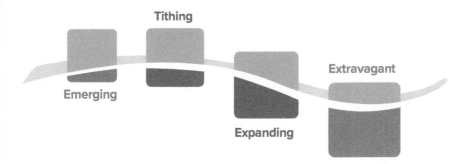

Tithing

Emerging

Extravagant

Expanding

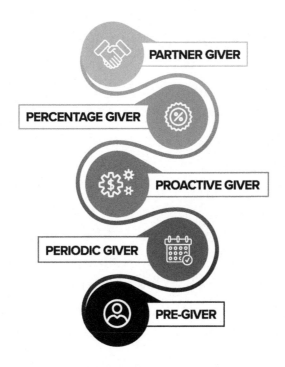

PARTNER GIVER

PERCENTAGE GIVER

PROACTIVE GIVER

PERIODIC GIVER

PRE-GIVER

APPENDIX C

Sample Impact Reports

Ecclesia Hollywood
IMPACT REPORT 2020 〉

The following highlights are just a sample of the amazing work that God has done through the people of Ecclesia this year.

COVID RELIEF FUND

$32,850 raised from March through November to assist Ecclesians affected by the pandemic.

$12,340 Given away so far.

POSITIVELY IRRITATING

Over 150 local Ecclesians received a free copy of Pastor Jon's book, which tells his story and details our journey to embrace the world around us as an outgrowth of Christ's love.

LOCAL MISSION

$57,000 Total amount given to our 8 local partners in Hollywood and L.A.

Genevieve's Garden
480 lunches served.

Winter Refuge
Ecclesia partnered with local churches to serve Hollywood's homeless.

Foster All Gift Cards
$2450 raised to purchase 98 $25 gift cards for children in the LA foster care system.

600 Total volunteers.

175 Total meals served.

Pop-up Sunday
7 groups met all over LA on 3/8 to serve the city and engage with people.

100% Of homeless friends connected with DMH or LAHSA services.

SPIRITUAL GROWTH

- **82 Weekly Zoom Prayer Groups**

- **106 Kids Story Time Readings**
  With a grand total of **5830** participants!

- **25 Classes & Groups**
  261 kids, youth and adults participated in 25 special online classes and formation groups.

LIVESTREAM SERVICE

- We began our YouTube Livestream service on March 22nd. In 2020 we will do **40** Livestream services.

- **48,303** estimated total number of individuals watching.

- We heard from over **78** Ecclesians during the welcome segment of the service.

- For the first **8** weeks of the livestream service we partnered with Pastors Steven & Nicole Peters and the Malibu Fellowship community.

GLOBAL MISSION

- **$41,000** - Total amount given to our **3** global partners in Kenya, India and Laos.

- **$2100** - Amount paid to provide **health insurance** for all **30** Fadhili Women in Kenya and their **60** dependent children.

- **$5500** - Amount paid to host the annual **Kids VBS Camp** in Kenya, including food bags for the families of all **200** children.

PERSONAL MISSION

- **$650** in Micro Grants given to Ecclesians Living on Mission.

ecclesia
churchinhollywood.com

YEAR-END UPDATE

CHURCH OF CHAMPIONS · 12922 CUTTEN ROAD | HOUSTON, TX 77066

REPORTING PERIOD
JAN - DEC
2020

 Day we went virtual: *March 15, 2020*

CARE TEAM:

Ministered to 62 families **affected** by COVID-19

Mailed out 242 Cards to family members affected by COVID-19

Provided Cleaning & Care boxes to 62 families **with COVID-19**

CREATED ONLINE SANCTUARY PROGRAMMING TEAMS:

 973 **hours of edit/production time to produce video content**

 94 **hours of video Teaching/Preaching**

 222,683 **views of Virtual Church content on social media platforms**

 28,490 **hours of Virtual Church watched on YouTube**

 Food Bank
Served over 9800 lbs. of Food

Connect Groups
359 People in groups

Prayer Team
64 weekly prayer meetings online

 Benevolence
$29,594

ChampKids City
Exterior Remodel Completed - $55,000

 GIVE
Contributions:
Down from 2019
$127,501.49

 $
Expenses:
Up from 2019
$288,397.35

CHURCH *of* CHAMPIONS
WWW.CHAMP.ORG

First Baptist Church
Prairie, CA

Reporting Period
Jan - Mar
2019

Check out the Reno Youth Mission Weekend!

From February 20-22 | **44** High School Students | **went** to Reno, Nevada | **to** serve an Inner-City Mission | **by** cleaning, painting, & serving other ways!

They *led a worship service* on Sunday morning for the residents. *Our church also gave a $20,000 gift* to the Reno Mission as it is one of our mission partners this year.

On average
803

people joined us for Sunday service.

514 Were adults.

65 Were youth.

224 Were children.

Actual giving by month.

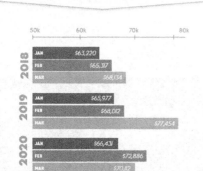

2018	JAN	$63,220
	FEB	$65,317
	MAR	$68,134
2019	JAN	$65,977
	FEB	$68,012
	MAR	$77,454
2020	JAN	$66,431
	FEB	$72,886
	MAR	$70,112

Discipleship.

14
Adult Small Groups

10
Adult Sunday School Classes

20
Serving Teams

ImpactReport
TheImpactReportCompany.com

ST. ANDREWS
COVENANT PRESBYTERIAN CHURCH

ATTENDANCE

450
AVERAGE ONLINE
ATTENDANCE

# of streams
The streams record at the beginning through the end of the video.

PRE WORSHIP	WORSHIP
STUDY SESSION	
f 30	f 50
▶ 30	▶ 82
🖥 71	🖥 109

SOCIAL MEDIA

f FACEBOOK

4,674
AVERAGE POST REACH

102%
ENGAGEMENT

LAST WEEK:

2,588
VIDEO VIEWS

39
PAGE FOLLOWS

SNAPSHOT OF FACEBOOK VIEWS
MARCH 15

300+ views with additional
175 during the week.

Ⓞ INSTAGRAM

117
PERSON REACH PER POST

145
FOLLOWERS

LOCAL MISISON

FUNDING FOR
**FREEDOM
SCHOOL**
PROGRAMS FOR AT
RISK STUDENTS

**FUNDING FOR
HOUSEHOLDS**
IN CRISIS

**MASK
MAKING**
AND DISTRIBUTION

**FEEDING
SITE**
FOR NEIGHBORHOOD
VIA SCHOOL BOARD
AND USAID

**MEALS
DELIVERED**
TO SHUT-INS

SPIRITUAL FORMATION

🧎 ZOOM GROUPS

🧍 YOUNG DADS GROUP

🙏 WORSHIP STUDY

**CONGREGATIONAL
READS PROJECT**
Summer book coming soon

**NEW STATE & COUNTRY
WIDE AUDIENCE**
Stay tuned for a zoom call to
get to know them better

PASTORAL CARE

**80+
FAMILY UNITS**
In the vulnerable category were
contacted by church leadership
(65 - older, homebound,
comorbidity, etc), In addition

DIGITALLY CONNECTED GROUPS

THOSE NOT IN A GROUP

TOGETHER IN PRAYER
- WEEKLY PHONE GATHERINGS

CAREILNE UPDATED 3X/WEEK

REMOTELY ENGAGED CARE TEAMS

⬇ **THEOLOGY TUESDAY**
We have started a blog by senior pastor called Theology Tuesday.
There has been excellent engagement, 200 downloads each week.

REGENERATION

DISCIPLESHIP | SCRIPTURE | VULNERABILITY | GENEROSITY | MULTIPLICATION

IMPACT REPORT | AUG 2020

ATTENDANCE

85 AVERAGE **IN-PERSON** ATTENDANCE (Early 2020 including kids)

120 AVERAGE **ONLINE** ATTENDANCE

10% Are people who do not usually attend in-person gatherings.

ATTENDANCE BY MONTH

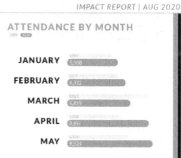

JANUARY	5,508
FEBRUARY	8,112
MARCH	6,855
APRIL	8,891
MAY	9,824

SPIRITUAL GROWTH

SUMMER GROUPS:

- 3 **TASTER HUDDLES**
- 1 **BIBLE STUDY**
- 1 **WOMEN'S PRAYER GROUP**
- 1 **BAND** 6-8 people

30% Early March

40% Mid May

55% CURRENT **GROUP PARTICIPATION**

SMALL GROUP ATTENDANCE

PASTORAL CARE

12 CARE TEAM MEMBERS

 CALLS   **TEXTS**   **PRAYER**

 One member of the Care Team prayed out loud for the first time through this process and in so doing discovered her **spiritual gifts**.

Made in the USA
Middletown, DE
16 August 2024

59198627R00195